Cambridge Studies in International Relations: 3

FORMAL THEORIES IN INTERNATIONAL RELATIONS

CAMBRIDGE STUDIES IN INTERNATIONAL RELATIONS

Cambridge Studies in International Relations is a joint initiative of
Cambridge University Press and the British International Studies
Association (BISA). The series will include a wide range of material,
from undergraduate textbooks and surveys to research-based
monographs and collaborative volumes. The aim of the series is to
publish the best new scholarship in International Studies from
Europe and North America and the rest of the world.

Cambridge Studies in International Relations

FORMAL THEORIES IN INTERNATIONAI RELATIONS

MICHAEL NICHOLSON
University of Salford

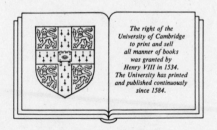

The right of the
University of Cambridge
to print and sell
all manner of books
was granted by
Henry VIII in 1534.
The University has printed
and published continuously
since 1584.

CAMBRIDGE UNIVERSITY PRESS
Cambridge
New York   New Rochelle   Melbourne   Sydney

Published by the Press Syndicate of the University of Cambridge
The Pitt Building, Trumpington Street, Cambridge CB2 1RP
32 East 57th Street, New York, NY 10022, USA
10 Stamford Road, Oakleigh, Melbourne 3166, Australia

First published 1989

Printed in Great Britain at The University Press, Cambridge

British Library cataloguing in publication data

Nicholson, Michael, 1933–
Formal theories in international relations. –
(Cambridge studies in international relations: v. 3).
1. Foreign relations. Theories.
I. Title. II. Series.
327.1′01

Library of Congress cataloguing in publication data

Nicholson, Michael, 1933–
Formal theories in international relations.
(Cambridge studies in international relations: 3).
1. International relations.
2. International relations – Mathematical models.
I. Title. II. Series.
JX1395.N49 1989   327′.01 88-25819

ISBN 0 521 34103 5

CE

FOR CHRISTINE

CONTENTS

PREFACE

In this book I have tried to give a critical account of the present state of formal and mathematical international relations theory, and evaluate its current status and hopes for the future. It is a growing field which, though regarded merely as a passing fashion by some, holds great promise, along with some modest achievement in illuminating some critical problems of international behaviour. While I do not believe that world peace will be achieved by the solution of some appropriate set of differential equations, I do believe that the development of a rigorously developed international theory will help in that direction. This book provides the grounds for my belief.

My primary audience is the international relations specialist who has some interest in international theory. However, I also hope to interest those whose professional concerns are outside the formal discipline of international relations, such as scholars in other branches of the social sciences where the use of formal methods is more widespread. Natural scientists who are interested in the general phenomenon of war and peace might also find this approach congenial. The subject matter of international relations is of obvious crucial importance to us all, involving the survival of the human race. A narrow disciplinary approach would be singularly inappropriate.

The mathematical methods for the most part are not complicated. For example, anyone who can cope with a basic course in economic theory should be able to understand the mathematical aspects of this book. Only in a few sections, is anything beyond a simple knowledge of equations required. Unfortunately those which are the most demanding mathematically are sometimes substantively important – the n- party arms race is a case in point. Whenever possible, I have spelled out an argument with minimum mathematics before considering arguments which require more complex methods. A mathematical appendix outlines some of the methods. L. J. Savage, an eminent probability theorist, once advised that 'Serious reading of mathematics is best done sitting bolt upright on a hard chair at a desk.'

To the temperamentally indolent this is fearful advice, but unhappily correct.

There is the perennial problem of the impersonal pronoun. In the text I use 'he', without wishing to imply any particularly masculine quality to the entities to which it refers. I cite Dora Russell in *The Tamarisk Tree*, whom I hold to have given a general feminist indulgence for this practice. When someone arrives with an acceptable genderless pronoun, I shall happily use it, but in the meantime I shall not torment my language with such hermaphroditic perversions as s/he. In passing, I note with admiration the acuity of Von Neumann and Morgenstern in foreseeing future practice and speaking of the n-person game and not the n-man game, thus saving subsequent generations of games theorists much anguish.

The first glimmerings of the idea for this book came in the early summer of 1984 in various discussions with Bruce Russett and David Singer while we were all fellows of the Netherlands Institute for Advanced Study. In particular David Singer was concerned with the issue of what the social scientists have contributed to our knowledge of the causes of war. I provided a five or six page memorandum on formal methods. That seemed adequate at the time. This book is a delayed but rather fuller response. I am grateful to NIAS and its ever helpful staff for providing a stimulating and happy environment in which such interactions could take place. In the following year, while a Hallsworth Fellow at the University of Manchester's Department of Decision Theory, I kept slipping into working on this without really admitting it to myself. I gained meanwhile enormous stimulus from Doug White, Simon French, Lyn Thomas and Roger Hartley of the Department which now, sadly, no longer exists. The impact of that year shows in many parts of this manuscript.

A number of people have been kind enough to comment on the manuscript. In particular Ken Burrough of the Department of Physics in the University of Sheffield has gone in detail through my mathematical arguments and saved me from many errors. Peter Abell of the University of Surrey, Roderick Ogley, formerly of the University of Sussex, and Keith Webb of the University of Kent have also read the whole manuscript in its entirety and in great detail. Their helpful comments have resulted in substantial revision. Claudio Cioffi-Revilla of the University of Colorado, David Kelsey of Churchill College, Cambridge, Philip Reynolds, formerly of Lancaster University, Phil Schrodt of Northwestern University, and Remi Godal of London have all seen parts of the manuscript and I am grateful also for their help. Much of the actual writing of the manuscript was done while I was a member of the International Studies Unit of Salford University in London. Colin Gordon and Pat Askew were enormously helpful and supportive. I am particularly grateful to Colin Gordon for behaving according to the highest ideals of academic tolerance, for this is most decidedly not his style of international relations. Steve Smith as general editor of the BISA series, has been a constant encouragement, and his initial enthusiasm convinced me that this really would be a worth-while enterprise. Philip Nicholson, formerly of the Physics Department of the Westminster Medical School, gave invaluable help with the detailed reading of the proofs. Christine Nicholson provided support to combat the gloom which afflicts British academia, a gloom not conducive to the academic enterprise. More prosaically, she read the manuscript through its various drafts, and brought many arguments out of their original obscurity. The reader, as well as myself, should be grateful for this.

1 FORMAL THEORY IN AN INTELLECTUAL CONTEXT

1 International relations and formal theory

A common reaction to the view that major developments in the theory of international relations will be achieved through its progressive mathematisation is an expression of bewilderment. That the subtleties of diplomacy, the passions of war, the deceits of leaders can be represented by a collection of mathematical symbols, however skilfully manipulated, seems a foolish conceit and faintly distasteful. Such a reaction is not universal. Others, seeing the unambiguous success of mathematical methods in the natural sciences, and their rather more ambiguous success in the analysis of social relations, from the problems of the scheduling and routing of supertankers to the analysis of economic behaviour, see the development of mathematical theories of international relations as an obvious step, and a prerequisite for their improved operation.

This division amongst people who are gravely concerned about the substantive problems of international relations, and in particular the problems of peace and war, poses the difficulty of how much time to spend in justification of the legitimacy of these approaches. A lengthy justification will bore those for whom it is superfluous. Alternatively, if justification is taken as unnecessary, the sceptic will remain sceptical and some genuine questions will be ignored. Obviously there are some fundamental epistemological issues which are involved in the application of mathematics to the description of theories of any social processes. A crucial one concerns whether the subject matter of international relations is appropriately analysed in terms of theories as normally understood in the social sciences. I have discussed these issues elsewhere (Nicholson 1983) and will not repeat them. Though such issues are important, this book is primarily about ways of analysing some theoretical problems in the field of international relations. I want to retain this emphasis in the core of the book. Thus, I shall largely avoid the epistemological questions on the grounds that

1

the process of description is, in part, a process of justification, which will indicate the use and need of this approach. I analyse what would by common consent be regarded as important and interesting problems in the theory of international relations by formal methods, and, by implication and at times explicitly, ask how such problems could be better analysed by other means. I shall show that there are some problems which can be analysed only by mathematical methods. In particular, many problems which involve large systems reach a level of complexity which can be represented only in mathematical terms. There are also problems whose analysis is facilitated by the use of formal methods, though they can be analysed and understood in natural language. Thus there are areas in which the use of mathematics is a matter of taste.

While it is difficult to define the discipline of international relations precisely, there are a variety of topics which would be generally accepted as falling within its scope. These include arms races, alliances between states, the causes of war and, indeed, most forms of social interaction which involve the interaction of states or which cross state boundaries. States and governments are important, but they are not the only actors in the social systems of concern here, and for some issues may be peripheral. War is the crucial problem which characterises the international system[1] and distinguishes it from most other forms of social interaction. Threats are used in other social systems, such as economic systems, but they are rarely threats of deliberate physical violence designed to achieve goals. Criminal violence, even in violent societies, is viewed with disapprobation and practised by few. Murder is a statistical rarity. However, most states regard the practice of violence to achieve their ends as perfectly legitimate, even if these days, in rhetoric at least, it is denounced as undesirable – particularly in others. International relations is not exclusively concerned with wars and threats of wars, though scholars often spend a lot of time worrying about these, for good reason. Agreements are often made without any threat of violence, such as over many economic issues; societies grow closer to each other both economically and socially as in the European Economic Community (EEC). Other issues such as the conservation of the world ecological environment remain substantially unsolved, though it seems unlikely that anyone will want to fight a war over them.

[1] I use 'international system' to mean 'that which the student of international relations studies' and thus it is no more rigorously defined than international relations itself. I deliberately use it in this loose sense in the text. I discuss a more rigorous concept of system in Chapter 2.

I return to the issue of the definition of international relations and related terms in Chapter 3, Section 3. Though problematic, it is no more difficult than defining 'economics' or 'agriculture' and just as arbitrary. It is perhaps rather easier than defining 'systems analysis'. International relations involves one aspect of human behaviour, and the same general principles can be applied to this as to any other aspect. There are those who deny this, seeing in 'The State' some grandiose mystical entity. I shall eschew such mysticism and concentrate on more prosaic questions.

In a general sense, a lot of the phenomena which occur in the international system are not unique to it. For example, coalitions form in all sorts of social environments. Many of the phenomena of social behaviour can be categorised as either conflict or cooperation, and might be supposed to share at least some generic characteristics, whether they occur between individuals, states, or any other social grouping. This study of conflict in general is often known as 'conflict analysis', and has an important subdivision in its application to international relations. Some of the work I discuss in this book was not originally conceived of in terms of the international system, though I shall show that in some cases it is very directly relevant. The development of conflict analysis, and the recognition of its interpretations in the context of the international system, has gone hand in hand, though it is not identical with, the development of formal approaches.

A great deal of work has been done in developing formal theories of international relations, particularly in the last thirty years or so – rather more than is sometimes recognised by people outside the field. If we add to this that work in conflict analysis which was not originally directed towards the international system, we have a formidable body of theory, such that a comprehensive survey would be vast and well beyond the scope of this book. The constituency to which this work is directed is potentially broad in that the substantive problems in the field, namely war and peace, are of more than specialist interest. While some scholars of international relations, coming from the more traditional backgrounds of history or law, are unaccustomed to such forms of reasoning, this is becoming less and less true. At least, the basic models, such as the prisoners' dilemma, are widely known, and, through such approaches, the essentially scientific habit of building from the simple to the complex. Economists, psychologists, and many natural scientists, who see approaches such as those formulated in this book as a perfectly natural way of going about things, may be only superficially acquainted with the behaviour of the international system, but are properly concerned with both its actual and potential

3

malfunctioning. In this book I hope to expound, synthesise and even add to the body of knowledge in this area, in ways which, I hope, will convince both the methodological sceptic and the methodological sophisticate that this approach has a lot to offer.

2 The origins of formal international relations theory

The development of formal international relations theory has come about as an aspect of the development of the social scientific approach to the study of the discipline. This approach, in which it is argued that we can generalise and discuss the generic aspects of the appropriate phenomena and not just the specific, is itself recent, becoming of importance in the intellectual scene only since about the nineteen fifties. Since then there have been major developments in the statistical analysis of the international system (which, of course, implies the legitimacy of generalisation), and recognition of the significance of the earlier work of Richardson and Quincy Wright. There have been developments in structural theories such as those of Galtung (1971); and developments in the application of psychology to problems of perception and decision making, prominent being the work of Jervis (1976) and Janis (1982).

However, it is misleading to view formal theory solely in the context of the general development of international relations, or even solely in terms of the growth of social scientific approaches to the discipline. It is an aspect of the growth in the application of mathematics to many fields, not only the social sciences where it has been conspicuous, but also to problems in biology, a discipline which has had intermittent if superficially surprising interactions with international relations. In order to put formal international relations into some sort of perspective, I shall relate its development to the general intellectual and political framework from which it has emerged.

Since about the nineteen fifties there has been a great surge in the application of mathematical methods to the social and behavioural sciences. The origins were earlier. *Econometrica* was founded as early as 1933, though the economists were always somewhat ahead of the field in this matter. However, the widespread growth of formal approaches in the social sciences came after the Second World War. Despite its early start, the application of such methods to conflict studies and international relations lagged behind the other social sciences, where, indeed, it still remains. Its development can be seen, nevertheless, in the context of the whole process of the perception of formal methods as a leading tool in the expansion of theoretical

4

knowledge. Taking journal foundation as an indication of the beginning of major intellectual interest, the central journal has been *The Journal of Conflict Resolution* founded in 1957. The journal emphasises the social scientific approach to the analysis of conflict, which includes a lot of formal work, but it is by no means confined to this.

There were two relevant differences between international relations (and political science) and other disciplines such as economics and psychology. These latter disciplines have always been constructed in the social scientific mode. From its earliest days economics used formal methods. As the legitimacy of generalisation was not seriously doubted, so was it not doubted that statistical methods were appropriate forms of testing. These require mathematical manipulation in themselves, and readily encourage the formation of theory in mathematical form. This did not happen in international relations. There were doubts about the legitimacy of generalisation. If this legitimacy were denied, then formal representations in the ways in which they are understood in this book would be irrelevant, while statistical tests and analyses would be similarly misguided. Thus there was a conceptual issue about the nature of the discipline, which made the application of formal methods problematical. This had a secondary social effect. Amongst economists and psychologists there were many scholars who were trained in and very receptive to formal methods. There were very few in international relations. Amongst the earlier postwar scholars who developed formal methods, such as Boulding, Rapoport and Schelling, only a few were themselves political scientists. The political scientists were typically trained in history or some related discipline. Some reacted with interest and enthusiasm, many clearly regarded these new approaches not as a promise but as a threat. The spur to the application of formal methods to international relations came as much from outside the discipline as within it. It should be seen not only as an aspect of the development of international relations as a social science, but also as an aspect of the development of formal methods in the social sciences, the two running together. It is not something which grew up in isolation from the rest of the world of ideas as they were developing at the time.

There are two main strands in the development of formal methods in international relations. One comes from the work of Lewis Fry Richardson, and is explicitly conceived of as an attempt to throw light on aspects of international behaviour. In his best known deductive work, on arms races, he postulates certain plausible relationships between variables and works out the implications. While the work on this was done largely in the interwar period, not much of it was published, and it was not until 1960 that the body of his work finally appeared, having been largely ignored before that. The second strand derives from the work of John Von Neumann and Oskar Morgenstern in *The Theory of Games and Economic Behavior* first published in 1944. This was not initially interpreted in terms of international relations. The book had an enormous impact in almost all parts of the social sciences, notably economics, and in due course it reached international relations. This approach was in the tradition of *decision theory* and more reminiscent of micro-economics.

It is generally conceded that the first person explicitly to apply formal methods to international relations was the English Quaker, Lewis Fry Richardson. He was a meteorologist by profession, and of sufficient eminence and originality in that field to be elected a Fellow of the Royal Society. His major work was published posthumously in 1960 in two volumes, *Arms and Insecurity* and *Statistics of Deadly Quarrels*. In the first of these, he developed a deductive model of an arms race, which we shall discuss later in the book. The model was tested against data, particularly of the period before the First World War. The second volume was primarily devoted to the presentation of a great deal of statistical data which he had collected and with which he tested a large number of *ad hoc* but plausible propositions about violence. These are generally regarded as the pioneering works, but still of current interest, in two important areas of modern social scientific international relations – the development of formal theory, and data collection and analysis. Though the great pioneering significance of Richardson is widely accepted today amongst social scientists interested in international conflict, his work was almost totally neglected during his life-time. Even today his work is ignored by many in the mainstream of international relations scholarship in Britain. It is worth looking at this phenomenon in a little more detail to enquire why it should be.

The initial inspiration for Richardson's work came from his experiences in the First World War during which he served in the Friends' Ambulance Unit (Ashford 1985). This made him determined to devote as much of his time as he could to the development of theories of the causes of war, seeing this as the necessary requirement for them to be stopped. His first paper, called 'The Mathematical Psychology of War', was written during the war itself and privately published immediately afterwards. It had to be privately published as there was in those days no appropriate journal to which, in his words, he 'dared offer so unconventional a work'. He did however dare to offer it to a commercial publisher and Bertrand Russell recommended its publication, calling it 'a remarkable piece of work, which deserves great respect'. This was apparently an inadequate recommendation, though no doubt on commercial grounds the publisher's refusal was correct. The privately published version 'was little noticed. Some of my friends thought it funny'. It finally appeared in the prestigious scientific weekly *Nature* in 1935, where others of his papers appeared. Unfortunately few specialists in international relations in those days were regular readers of *Nature*. In 1939 *Generalized Foreign Politics* was published as a monograph supplement to the *British Journal of Psychology* and was reviewed in *Nature* and the *Mathematical Gazette*, which again indicates its constituency. Richardson's work became known outside only a very narrow circle with the publication of Rapoport's essay on 'Lewis Fry Richardson's Mathematical Theory of War' (1957) in the new *Journal of Conflict Resolution*, and the publication a year before of two extracts from Richardson's work with an introductory essay in James Newman's *The World of Mathematics* (1956). From that point, however, work in this tradition has gone ahead with vigour.

The initial neglect of Richardson's work was not too surprising. In part it stems from the way in which academic life was and is organised with its formal and informal nets of communication. The study of international relations was traditionally viewed as a part of the historical disciplines. Historians, after all, had studied international affairs, so it was not surprising that when, after the First World War, there was an attempt to build up a profession of international relations, it was thought of as a specialisation within the historical disciplines. However, the links between historians and scholars of a mathematical disposition are tenuous, so there is no obvious way in which a historian would have become aware of Richardson's work. Nor did Richardson himself appreciate the problem, or, if he did, he was not disposed to do much about it. He appeared to make little attempt to make his approach accessible to people without mathematical training.

While the initial development of formal international relations theory was done in isolation by Richardson, it is important to realise that the discipline as a whole, which is predominantly a post Second World War product, was part of a wider trend. It was just one aspect of the general move towards the increased use of mathematics in many disciplines. A similar pattern is to be found in other areas of political science. The application of formal methods to the study of the theory of voting goes back two centuries. According to Black (1958), who gives a fascinating account of the history of the mathematical theory of voting, the first formal analysis of voting was made by Jean-Charles de

Borda (1733–99) who was closely followed by the Marquis de Condorcet (1743–94). Condorcet was the first person to demonstrate (or at least publish) that it is possible for a voting relationship to show intransitivities despite all the individuals who vote having transitive preferences. He died in prison, though not because of his mathematical ideas. Various people were interested in the problems in the nineteenth century, conspicuous being C. L. Dodgson (1832–98), better known for writing *Alice in Wonderland* under the name of Lewis Carroll. After that further developments in the formal approach to group and social choice came in the post 1945 boom in the applications of formal methods in the social sciences, Black's own work and that of Arrow being prominent. It is worth commenting that Arrow and Black were both economists, not political scientists. Despite the relatively distant ancestry of the formal theory of voting, interest in the subject was a post 1945 phenomenon. In this it parallels formal international relations. It was the work of one or two scholars, seen by their contemporaries as eccentric, who, by virtue of the barriers of tradition and training, were totally out of touch with the constituency, who traditionally worked on the same or related issues. Later, from being a curiosity, the ideas were recognised as central to a field of study.

There is an interesting and more curious parallelism between the development of formal methods in international relations and in biology. Biologists have shown a similar, though much more muted, diffidence in the application of mathematics to their discipline, as have the specialists in international relations. Statistical methods were obviously accepted, and the concomitant discipline of biometrics developed. There were also less enthusiastically received attempts to develop more general theories in biology in mathematical form. D'Arcy Thompson wrote the impressive *Growth and Form*, published in 1917, describing these processes in mathematical terms – something which was not expected in the biological sciences of the day. Lotka in Chicago wrote *Elements of Mathematical Biology* in 1926. Somewhat later, Rashevsky wrote various books on mathematical biology and edited (and was a prominent contributor to) *The Journal of Mathematical Biophysics* which in its title alone covers three disciplines. Rashevsky hoped to apply his biological methods and findings to social behaviour and wrote a number of papers and books on such extensions, in particular *Mathematical Biology of Social Behavior* (1951). Rashevsky wanted to carry the postulates of social behaviour back into psychophysics – a discipline which lent itself naturally to mathematically expressed theory. This is incredibly ambitious, being far from anything currently achieved in social science. However it is not in

8

principle absurd, and as a long-term goal may be possible. For the moment, though, this research programme lies untended and undisturbed, as I would expect it to lie for some time yet. Such grand ambitions have style. Formal theorists are sometimes accused of triviality, which is hardly a charge which can be sustained here.

The links between the mathematical social sciences and the mathematical development of biology persist. Catastrophe theory, the mathematical analysis of discontinuities in basically continuous systems, has been much popularised recently and applied to a whole variety of different problems (Zeeman 1976), including international relations, as we shall later show. The early applications of the theory were in the area of biology (Thom 1975). More recently the theory of games has been applied to evolutionary theory by Maynard Smith (1982). This is reminiscent of the tradition of economic style models with a large number of actors, such as the perfect competition model. One of the most interesting recent developments in the general area of game theory has been the work of Axelrod (1984) on strategies in the iterated prisoners' dilemma in which the virtues of the strategy of TIT-FOR-TAT are demonstrated. The applications to biology appear to be as important as the applications to the social sciences. The parallelisms between the disciplines are partly accidental but not entirely so. In part, one expects the same mathematical model to describe very different types of empirical systems, as has happened in the past. There are also some direct correspondences between certain sorts of systems. If a biological group is to survive, its members must behave as if they were rationally pursuing the goal of survival. Other groups fail. Consequently, the survivors have the appearance of rationality, and an optimising model should describe their behaviour. The same is true of a human group. In neither case does this imply that either are thinking in any consciously optimising form, though the human group may be. Nevertheless, the same formal structure will describe both the 'unconscious optimiser' and his conscious counterpart. The links between the biological sciences and the social sciences are quite general. There are disagreements in both areas as to the viability of mathematical methods in a way that there are not in, say, physics. The would-be mathematisers are trying to construct general theory in their different disciplines, which means that they look at new approaches optimistically in an urge to apply them to any promising problem. Some scholars, such as Rapoport and Simon, see this as part of a general endeavour, and are explicit in their views that we are in the process of trying to derive general systems with wide applicability. Thus the parallelism is unsurprising, and the similarities to be

9

expected. It is even less surprising that the attempts to apply mathematical methods should have spread from other areas of the social sciences to international relations.

3   The two cultures: the problem of communication

In 1963, C. P. Snow wrote an important essay called *The Two Cultures*. This has had an immense influence on rhetoric, a little on thought, and an almost imperceptible influence on behaviour. Snow argued that, in western countries at least, there was a scientific culture whose members had an accepted basis of shared knowledge and presuppositions, and an arts or literary culture whose members likewise had its basis of shared knowledge and presuppositions. A regrettably small number of people are at home in both cultures, and the separation and at times near hostility between them was deplored by Snow, who argued for the development of some mutual sympathy between them. There are many critical areas which require some contact between them and a pure 'scientific' or pure 'arts' approach by itself is inadequate. Unhappily, Snow's analysis is as applicable to the present situation, at least in Britain, as it was in the early sixties.

The division has its echo in the social sciences and reverberates particularly strongly in the study of international relations. Scholars have come from many different disciplines such as history, law, mathematics and economics, as well as international relations itself. They have very different trainings, and very different underlying assumptions. One might have hoped that this would mean that the social sciences would act as a bridge between the cultures and to a degree this has been the case, but only to a degree. International relations scholars from opposite sides of the cultural divide too often look with suspicion and a well-developed sneer at the work of those outside their tradition.

Some of the issues involved in the intellectual division are practical, while others are more fundamental and concern the way in which intellectual enterprises are conceptualised. At the practical level one of the major issues involved, and one which is of particular relevance to the subject matter of this book, is that people who work in an arts tradition are only rarely familiar with mathematical reasoning. It is not so much an issue of a wide knowledge of mathematics which is crucial, as the habit of following mathematical arguments. This is almost second nature to those with some mathematical background but seems strange and even sinister to those without. The significance of this problem in this present context is that those without the mathematical habit are excluded from those aspects of the development of knowledge which are most conveniently expressed in mathematical terms. In my view this is a most important aspect of the cultural divide, which in part is responsible for its width.

The mathematical habit is not just a question of being able to follow the actual process of the mathematical argument, for there are other aspects concerning the application of mathematical reasoning which seem strange to those not used to them. For example, a common mode of analysis is to build up a complex system from a very simple one. A simple theory is modified (usually complicated) until it reaches some representation of reality. I discuss this further in the next chapter. However, it means that much formal work concerns pictures of an artificial and grossly simplified world which contain (at least in principle) the underlying features of some process but which lack some crucial real world characteristics. A good example of this is the prisoners' dilemma (see Chapter 3) which, at least in its simplified form, represents a situation which almost never would be found in reality. However, its simplified form means that the crucial nature of the dilemma is made starkly clear while also serving as a base for elaborations which correspond more closely to reality. Such procedures are standard in the natural sciences and economics where formal methods are widely used. However, they are not used in disciplines such as history where such methods seem odd to those unaccustomed to them. This often leads to suspicions (sometimes justified) that the mathematical modeller is mistaking the simple models for reality, though in general most modellers are fully aware that their simple models represent a stage in a process, not an end point. Clearly an understanding of such differences in procedure can be readily achieved, but it does emphasise that the cultures differ in many and substantial ways which may not be immediately evident.

The lack of a habit of following mathematical arguments is only one of the impediments to communication. A more fundamental problem is that people trained in different disciplines tend to view the intellectual enterprise in very different ways. Scholars coming from a scientific background tend to look for problems to be solved. In the extreme this is the engineer's approach. Knowledge is not just for abstract contemplation, but for use. Even in the sciences whose purpose is to observe nature rather than to alter it, there is typically a concept of problems which have 'solutions' where solutions are defined unproblematically. A variant of the engineer's approach is found amongst operational research workers. In military operational research, people work on such problems as the optimum size of shipping convoys, or the siting of missiles; in the peaceful uses of operational research, people try to minimise waiting time in telephone net-works or optimise fuel costs in aircraft routing. In both cases, the point of the exercise is to portray a system in such a way that it can be made to improve its performance by some clearly specifiable set of criteria. As with the engineer, these criteria are presumably morally acceptable to the designer – a pacifist would not normally be willing to work on problems of optimum targeting for nuclear missiles – but the criteria for what are regarded as appropriate goals for the system can be separated from the discussion of the workings of the system itself. This representation is extreme. Few scholars in international relations conceive of it as a set of problems which can be solved in the way that a scheduling problem can be solved. Nevertheless there is some under-lying feeling that in the long run this is the purpose of the exercise. The long run may be a long way ahead – Anatol Rapoport puts it at about one hundred years – but there is nevertheless the view that improve-ment of the system is the long-run goal, and the purpose of studying international relations.

Clearly many scholars whose background is in history would share this view. They would argue similarly that they were trying to improve the performance of the international system. However, they see in the simplifications of the formal theorist an excessive naivete. People do not have simple goals which they pursue in systems in which behaviour can be optimised. Life is very complex, and each period of time and each event in the social world is unique, with its own special characteristics. Comparisons can be made, but general theories are suspect. This leads some people to be deeply pessimistic of the possibility of analysing the system at all in a way which would make it amenable to guided change. A good example is found in the work of Martin Wight (Wight 1977 and 1979), a prominent British theorist, strongly of the historical school. He would seem to imply that all the scholar can do is observe and that the possibility of operational theory is fruitless. While Wight's views are probably extreme, related views are not, though I cannot find anyone who states them as unambiguously as Wight states his. Such a view runs as follows:

> The present methods of analysing International Relations are more or less all we can hope for. That is, we can analyse such problems as nuclear deterrence by looking at the facts, and we can improve our knowledge of the phenomenon by a careful examination of what has gone on over the period when it has been in existence. With caution, other cases of non-nuclear

deterrence can be studied to give us insights. However, that there may be a whole new conceptual framework in which to analyse the problems is doubtful.

Later in the book, I discuss some theories of the whole international system in which such concepts as 'systemic hostility' are used in ways which suggest that in principle they might be measurable. Further they can be related to other variables in such a way that, again in principle, it should be possible to say under what circumstances they will increase, oscillate, and so on. This would be regarded as bizarre by many people coming from an arts tradition.

The opposed faults of the scientifically disposed scholar and the arts disposed scholar are respectively the premature application of theory and an excessive diffidence in using theory. The disposition of historically trained scholars is to concentrate on the unique aspects of situations and the scientifically trained to concentrate on the generic. There would be no great harm in this if the two groups had a clear inter-relationship with each other and reasonable mutual communication. This is not always the case, however. In part this may be due to the ways in which from early on people from different backgrounds pose their problems, but also in part it is due to the difficulties of communicating mathematical arguments non-mathematically, while retaining the richness and rigour of the mathematical approach. There is no clear way out of this dilemma, though I shall try at least to clarify the point of the exercise to the non-mathematically trained.

In this book I am adopting the role of advocate, viewing the jury as sympathetic but sceptical. My assertion is that there are whole ranges of legitimate theory in international relations which can be conceived of only if expressed in formal terms. Further, statements about classes of events as distinct from unique ones are often more conveniently stated in formal terms to make them amenable to testing. I hope to justify these propositions. However, this does not mean that one can dismiss the problems of communication lightly. Regrettably the two cultures are a deeply ingrained feature of intellectual life. The study of the international system requires a symbiosis between them if it is ever to become particularly useful even as an interpretative discipline, the more so if it is to act as the base for a policy science.

4 An outline of the book

In this book I discuss some interesting features of the international system in formal terms. Some, such as discussions of verifi-

13

cation problems, come close to policy issues, though most are not as yet developed to anything like that point, while some are fairly abstract. In total I aim to give some general picture of the field as it stands today.

In Chapter 2, I outline some of the presuppositions which lie behind a formal approach to international relations. I do not delve deeply into the philosophy of applied mathematics, however useful this might be at some point. I merely sketch some basic issues. This chapter can be read after the rest of the book by a reader who is willing to take a little on faith.

The rest of the book considers various problems in the analysis of the international system and the chapters can be read independently of each other; only Chapters 4 and 5 form a natural pair. There is nevertheless a certain frail logic to the order in which the chapters appear. Chapter 3 considers a central problem in international relations. When does cooperation take place when there is no government to enforce it? Can an anarchic system exhibit cooperative behaviour? The problem is posed using the prisoners' dilemma model. Some of the most interesting work in this field has been done in the context of a general discussion of anarchism (Taylor 1976, 1987), work I have reinterpreted in terms of international relations. In Chapters 4 and 5 I consider the problem of uncertainty in the international system, another basic issue. The first of these chapters is primarily devoted to the conceptual issues involved in the analysis of uncertainty and is mainly an exposition of the standard issues in the field, though I have not hesitated to take positions on contentious issues. The second considers various problems within the international system such as deterrence where problems of uncertainty are particularly acute. This is currently an active area of research to which I hope this chapter will make some contribution. In Chapter 6 I discuss the issues of bargaining in general terms, though particularly in connection with the termination of conflicts. Bargaining theory has been developed in many contexts other than international relations, and illustrates particularly vividly the need, stressed frequently in the book, for general theories of conflict. We should not imagine that international relations inhabits a private world, living only with theories peculiar to itself. In the chapter on bargaining, I mainly discuss the two-party case. This leads naturally to the case of many actors and the problems associated with coalitions and alliances, the topic of Chapter 7. Chapter 8 moves on to a model of the arms race, normally called the Richardson arms race model. This was originally formulated in international relations and is looked on with some pride by the profession. It is the only clear case of a deductive model originating within this discipline, otherwise mainly characterised by its assiduous borrowing from other areas of the social sciences. In this chapter, I move on from a very simple two-party model, through to more complex models. If anything can be referred to as 'classical' in this field, it is the material of this chapter. Chapter 9 deals with the problems of discontinuities or jumps in normally smooth systems, and is based on catastrophe theory. Chapter 10 is the most speculative. There have been some heroic efforts to formulate very general models of the international system. The insights into the behaviour of the real world have so far been modest, but the potentialities are great. I do not doubt there will be major developments in this area over the years, so I discuss some of these models sympathetically and with some effort to examine the underlying presuppositions which in my view justify optimism. In Chapter 11 I come closer to earth and discuss decision processes. The final chapter is an apologia for the field in the light of the earlier discussions.

There have been many developments in formal modelling in international relations in recent years, many more in neighbouring fields which are directly relevant to our interests. Doubtless there are many more developments to come. This is not a comprehensive survey of the field, which would be vast. I have discussed some of the issues which seem to me to be central, and have drawn attention to some of the neighbouring work which is worth the notice of international relations theorists. I hope I have also shown to scholars outside international relations that there may be some aspects of our discipline which they in their turn might note. I have tried to give appropriate acknowledgment when discussing and describing other people's work. Where I have failed, I hope the original writers will forgive me, and gain solace from the reflection that it means that their ideas have passed into the common well of knowledge.

2 PRESUPPOSITIONS OF A FORMAL APPROACH TO INTERNATIONAL RELATIONS

1 Some underlying assumptions

Formal modelling is commonly predicated on three assumptions. A further two, though not required, often follow. The assumptions are first, that simplified descriptions of processes can often provide powerful insights into basic behaviour and account for the larger part of it. Secondly, that, as we need to complicate analyses when the simple theories prove inadequate, it is easier to do so by explicitly adding to a simple structure which appears to contain the core of the problem than to plunge directly into a complex problem. Thirdly, it is assumed that generalisation is possible, such that in the systems we are examining there are patterns and consistencies and not everything is *sui generis*. The two assumptions which follow (though not as an issue of logic) are that common structures are often found in very disparate phenomena, and that statistical tests are often, though not always, the method of relating the formal theory to the 'real world'.

It is the first two of these assumptions which provide a lot of the attraction of formal modelling. Much of our knowledge of the natural sciences comes from the move from the simple to the complex. Other social sciences such as economics and psychology have used the method with success (though not uncontroversially). It is natural to hope that similar successes will follow from its application in international relations. The method implies the assumption that, within a penumbra of complexity, there is a relatively simple core which it is the scientist's job to isolate. Models such as the prisoner's dilemma (see Chapter 3) are often criticised because of their apparent simplicity and detachment from the world of conflict behaviour (for example, Rangarajan 1985). However, the point of analysing such simple models with just two people with two alternatives is that we can identify a crucial characteristic of conflict structures which is obscured if we try and study the complex structures directly. The

16

complex structures can then be built up from their simpler predecessors. One point needs emphasising. Mathematical methods are useful for the analysis of simple problems but they come into their own in describing complex structures and complex behaviours beyond the scope of natural language. I assert, and use the later parts of this book as evidence, that there are many important propositions about the international system which cannot be said in natural language alone.

This leads on to the next assumption that there are consistent patterns in behaviour and structure in the international system which repeat themselves in essentials. Thus we can examine different situations of bargaining, arms races, coalition formation and so on and perceive some common underlying pattern which can be analysed. It is hard to see how any analysis, by whatever means, would be possible unless some assumption such as this were made, but it is arguable that the formal modeller, in good social science tradition, is prone to stress the consistencies between situations as opposed to their idiosyncracies. It does not mean that in any particular case there are not many unique features which are peculiar to the specific situation. Obviously there normally are. In this way it can be compared with a psychiatric condition. A patient might be diagnosed as manic-depressive. There are some underlying characteristics of his condition which he shares with other manic depressives. If there were not, there would be no reason or even basis for making the categorisation in the first place. This common structure enables some sort of approach to be made to its alleviation or cure. However, any instance of manic depression will be different from every other in important respects. Further, in the perception of the patient the situation will be unique. It is only with difficulty that he will interpret his individual and personal experiences in the particular situation in life that he finds himself as classifiable under some general heading. Effective treatment requires an understanding of the particular and specific situation in the context of the general framework. The same is true of theoretical analyses of actual events in the international system. It is necessary to recognise the underlying structure and make an effective analysis of it. Particular events and particular situations are interpreted in terms of this underlying general structure. Obviously, for this to make sense, there must be an assumption that such an underlying structure exists.

It is clear that many of the crucial phenomena in the international system are not unique to it. Processes such as bargaining, coalition formation or interactive hostility processes are to be found in various widely different social contexts. Thus the social theory which is

17

applicable to many of the events in the international system is not a characteristic of that system alone, even if an international system can be isolated from other social systems, which is doubtful.

Because of the emphasis on common patterns which characterises a lot of formal theory, the testing of hypotheses commonly takes the form of statistical tests, though this is not invariably the case. Nor is it the case that all, or even much, statistical work in international relations involves the testing of formal theories. A lot consists of the testing of plausible *ad hoc* hypotheses. The development of deductive theories to the point of genuine testability, though the goal of theorists and statisticians alike, is still in its relative infancy in this field.

2 Mathematical pictures, models and theories

Until relatively recently, international relations theory was expressed almost entirely in natural language, with such eccentrics as Richardson being neglected by mainstream scholars. The appearance of any symbol or diagram in an argument is still sufficient to identify it as 'mathematical' or 'formal'. Indeed, I have used the terms 'mathematical methods' and 'formal methods' interchangeably, excusable by common practice, but needing justification.

A mathematical system is an abstract deductive system. Starting off from a set of axioms, which are assumed to be true for the purposes of the analysis of the system, and rules for the manipulation of the elements in the system, theorems are deduced. These theorems are logically implied by the axioms, so if the axioms are true, the theorems are necessarily true. In the application of a mathematical system to 'reality', the terms of the mathematical system are identified, or put into correspondence with, the terms in the 'real' or 'empirical' system. Corresponding to the purely formal axioms of the mathematical system are some 'postulates' which are an interpretation of these axioms and are now assertions about the 'real world'. Suppose some points in a mathematical system are put into correspondence with some terms in the empirical system; that is, we write out some empirical assertions in mathematical terms. We can then manipulate these terms according to the rules of the mathematical system and derive some other propositions in mathematical form which follow logically from the original set of mathematical propositions. If these mathematical propositions have been put into correspondence with the empirical propositions, then these empirical propositions will be also necessarily true, providing the correspondence is maintained. As this correspondence is necessarily to some degree inexact, this 'truth' cannot be guaranteed, but this raises some complex issues of the relationship of mathematics to 'reality' which would lead us away from the main purpose of the book (Körner 1960: especially Chapter 8). The point I wish to stress here is that a mathematical system is a deductive system, along which, so to speak, the truth value of the initial axioms flows. A strictly deduced proposition is true if the axioms are true. The same is the case with the empirical propositions which corresponds to mathematical propositions. A deduced proposition has the same degree of truth as the postulates from which it is derived, no more, no less.

Some of the analysis in formal international relations is of this form. A mathematical system which corresponds to some aspect of the international system is set up, and the implications examined. The method of setting up a system in this way, by formulating some initial hypotheses, deducing the consequences of these hypotheses, and testing them, is known as the *hypothetico-deductive* method of analysis, often regarded as the paradigm method of scientific development. There are two significant qualifications to this as a description of the current state of formal international relations theory. First, even those aspects of formal international relations which are in fact genuinely deductive, often involve deductions carried out in an extremely simple system. The 'hypotheses' are not in fact hypotheses about the real system but about some simplified system which has some relationship to the real system but is not the same. Such 'Artificial Worlds' are known as models. An example of this is the Richardson theory of arms races (see Chapter 8). Secondly, a lot of the analysis is not even in a deductive framework. It consists of mathematical pictures in which diagrams and symbols are arranged in order that the significance of relationships can be appreciated better. An example of this is the prisoners' dilemma, discussed in Chapter 3. In the prisoners' dilemma which is played only once, the problem is arranged in such a manner that the essence of the paradox is clearly seen. However, no deductive analysis is carried out. It is simply an arrangement of numbers. Much of the analysis which surrounds the multi-play prisoners' dilemma is genuinely deductive. Further postulates about play and so on are fed into the model so that we have a model in which consequences are deduced from postulates. However, in the basic one-shot model this is not the case.

Thus we can make a three-fold distinction in the area loosely known as formal theory between the mathematical theory, the mathematical model and the mathematical picture. I shall discuss the three in turn (see Snidal 1985 for a related argument).

A mathematical theory is a representation, in mathematical terms, of propositions which purport to describe the actual behaviour within the international system. That is, it is an attempt to describe the real system. Clearly the attempt is subject to test, and a theory is acceptable or not according to how successfully it survives appropriate tests.

Secondly, comes the mathematical model which consists of theory-like propositions arranged in a theory-like manner. That is, there is an initial set of postulates from which are deduced various further propositions. However, the propositions, whether postulated or deduced, are not about the 'real' international system but about a simplified, artificial system which does not exist, but which appears to have some similarities with the real system. The artificial system might be simplified in comparison with the real system in the sense of having fewer variables, fewer actors or more simplified inter-relationships. We develop models as opposed to theories because of the complexity of the real world. In principle one could go straight to the theory; in practice it is often difficult. Thus in the context of the model it is possible to explore the basic nature of the system's behaviour, and perhaps tease out some basic conceptual elements. For example, in dealing with the phenomenon of arms races it is much easier to deal with a race between two independent actors than between an indefinite number, or when actors have allies. One can find out the basic conceptual issues which underly the conflict. This is exactly what is done by Richardson in his theory of the arms race. A simple model of the process with just two independent variables is proposed, related to each other by a simple relationship (namely two linear differential equations) and the discussion is initially in terms of just two countries. This is not more than a very stylised portrait of any real arms race. From the simple picture we find out much more about the general nature of such processes, while not paying any great price in terms of intelligibility. It is much easier to move on from the simple model to more complex ones, for example, a model which includes more countries. The complex model is then simpler to understand with the experience of the simple one, while we already know from the simpler case what sorts of features in the model to look for, such as in this case its stability. The procedure is then to elaborate the model until the artificial system becomes more like the real system, and the model approaches the status of a theory. Though a model is artificial, its function ultimately is to enable us to make propositions about the real world and enable us to move on to theory.

Thirdly, while mathematical theories and mathematical models involve deductive systems, the use of diagrams and symbols does not necessarily mean that a deductive argument has been carried out. I have already cited the prisoners' dilemma as an instance of the mathematical picture where the aim of the exercise is to reveal features of a situation by appropriate presentation. Pictures share with mathematical methods the use of symbols, numbers and the like, and perhaps more significantly the careful and explicit definition of the terms involved. They often lead to the use of deductive methods, as again in the analysis of the repeated game of prisoners' dilemma, so the distinction is more blurred in practice than in the abstract. However, it is important to recognise that the use of symbolic methods is not necessarily the same as a deductive argument. This does not mean that mathematical pictures are trivial. It could be argued that some of the most useful applications so far of formal methods in international relations have been the pictures which have illustrated the paradoxes of choice. I shall draw attention to this issue during the course of subsequent arguments.

From now on, I shall use the term 'formal' to apply to all the forms of analysis in which symbols are used (or indeed which are arranged in an explicit formal format), but restrict 'mathematical' to those arguments involving a deductive line of reasoning.

3   Complexity and the international system

It is a commonplace that the examination of any problem quickly leads to a host of other problems and that the pattern of inter-relationships gets very broad indeed. This is true in the natural world and in the social world it is allegedly more so, or at least it is supposedly less structured than in the physical world. Thus, violence in the Middle East cannot be looked at without considering oil revenues. This leads to considering the structure of international corporations which in turn leads to the domestic politics of numerous states in and out of the area, though perhaps particularly the United States. We need to bring in the factors of religious belief, particularly fundamentalist beliefs, both Jewish and Islamic, while the relationship of the super-powers cannot be ignored. And this is but a glance at some of the possible factors to take into account, no doubt to be dismissed by anyone with a serious knowledge of the situation as trivially naive. However, we do in fact analyse complicated situations (including violence in the Middle East) and as we cannot really analyse everything at once we must have some procedures of simplification to make the problems tractable. One of the many merits of formal statements of problems is that these principles are made clear. In this section I wish to briefly analyse how we go about analysing the complexities of international behaviour. I emphasise again that the problems are not those of formal approaches as such but are the problems inherent in the analysis of any complex and ill-defined structure by whatever means. However, complexity of itself does not necessarily preclude analysis. Indeed the phenomenon of complexity can itself be analysed (Simon 1960, Simon, Ando and Fisher 1961, 1962), though not in this book.

I have used the phrase 'international system' imprecisely so far. In this section I wish to define it more clearly, but in the context of a general discussion of what we mean by a system, which gives us a framework for looking at complexity. Phrases like 'systems analysis' and 'systems theory' are used, rather confusingly, in a variety of ways when applied to international phenomena.[1] Thus, I need to say how I propose to use the word.

First, let us consider the concept of system by using a very simple example which has nothing to do with international relations. Suppose we are interested in the population of foxes and its relation to the population of rabbits. Foxes eat rabbits which themselves feed on grass. If the population of foxes increases they will eat more rabbits and if the fox population increases too much the rabbits will decrease in number. This will mean that the foxes will have greater difficulty in catching rabbits, that the weaker will starve, and the fox population will decrease in number. This will enable the rabbits to live longer and once again their population will increase. Such predator-prey models have been widely discussed (Kemeny and Snell 1962, Lotka 1956). There are three convenient categories in which to place the components of this system. There are the *elements* of the system, namely the foxes and the rabbits which are the things we are interested in. Secondly, there are the *attributes* of the elements, namely the population sizes. Thirdly, there are the *relationships* between the attributes of the different elements, that is, the relationship between the size of one population and the size of the other (which comes in a sophisticated way – that is, it is the size of the fox population which affects the rate of change of the rabbit population). As the attributes are things which vary (possibly on a continuum, or at the other extreme, between one of two binary states), it is often convenient to refer to these as *variables*. We can fit into these three categories the issues of interest in the system.

[1] The divergence of usage is quickly made clear if we look at Kaplan (1957), Burton (1968) and Rapoport (1974). Young (1968) clarifies a number of issues for political science in general.

We can imagine a very similar human social system. Suppose that traffic police on the motorway were to be paid by receiving the fines from speeding motorists. Initially the police would be very assiduous in pursuing miscreants. However, as the probability of being caught while speeding increased, the number of motorists exceeding the speed limit would decrease, and the policemen would make a poor income. This in turn would mean that there were less policemen willing to undertake the job, which would once again lower the probability of being caught. If the policemen were relatively few in number, they could hire an expert on predator-prey models to work out just what percentage of motorists they should catch to provide the best income. In the case of the human systems of this sort it is commoner to refer to the elements as *actors* and attribute to them conscious decision making processes.

Now let us move to the international context. Suppose we are analysing a subset of international relations which I shall call the armaments system. The actors are states, or any political grouping which can control armaments; the attributes of variables are the arms levels, though other features such as the Gross National Product (GNP) are relevant; the relationships are those factors which determine how the values of the arms levels of one state alter in response to a change of another's. This characterisation of a problem emphasises the interdependence within the system. It also shows that the problem rapidly gets very complex. We can go on more or less indefinitely showing that everything is related to everything else, and that we cannot understand the arms race between the USA and the USSR without paying attention to the Peruvian Navy (an admirable force no doubt, but small). There are two rather different responses to this problem; one is a question of analytical tactics and the other comes from an observation of the world. From the point of view of analytical tactics, a two-party model of an arms race alerts us to the problems involved and gives us experience in working them out (see Chapter 8). From the observation of the world, it is clear that some interactions are more important than others. We are usually interested in explaining the predominant features of an interaction and not every detail. Thus there can be pragmatic cut-off points in how far we extend the membership of the system, and which depend on the problems we are interested in.

We defined the system above in terms of an interest. This was an extra-scientific judgement. In this case it was an interest in arms levels and their interactions in the form of arms races and so on. We could define our interest in terms of any of the categories by which we

23

characterise systems. For instance it could be an interest in a form of behaviour (such as armament acquisition), the behaviour being paramount; alternatively the centre of interest might be certain actors in a variety of forms of behaviour. Having announced our interest, the subsequent criteria for inclusion within the system are determined by what is needed in order to explain those issues.

Superficially, an appropriate grouping for international relations would seem to be in terms of the states, regarding them as the prime actors. The attributes of the states which become a part of the system are those which, when they alter in value, affect the attributes of another state. The merit of this definition of an international system is that it is relatively clear cut. Adherents of the 'Realist' school of international relations would argue that this characterisation of the actors was indeed the most appropriate one, and further assert that the attributes of interest in the system were those which related to the power of the states. However, many scholars find this inadequate, arguing that the emphasis on the state as the primary actor leaves out too much, though there are differences as to whether it is mildly inadequate or grossly so (Banks 1986). Even such obvious sets of interactions as economic interactions are poorly explained if too directly related to states. Hence, the international system can be more conveniently defined in terms of its relationships rather than its elements. I would define it as that set of relationships which cross state boundaries. This then defines a domain of interest – though not a particularly eccentric one – and it is shared, I think, by many others. Given this definition, the actors become any whose attributes are affected by something which goes on outside the state. We also include, of course, the states themselves as actors in the system, which brings in the Realist school as a special case.

This makes the international system huge. It includes all relationships which do not take place wholly within a single state. When we take into account variables which are internal to a state, but which influence those which are part of the international system, this encompasses an extremely wide system indeed. This is of course a characteristic of most social systems – it is hard to put a boundary on them. However, to analyse social systems it is necessary to put boundaries on them and form *subsystems* containing merely a subset of the elements of the relationships. Thus we might talk of the economic subsystem or the security subsystem. Clearly there are interactions between the various subsystems, but it is possible to take out of the broader system some categories of behaviour such that fruitful analysis can be carried out internally within that subsystem. The problem is to identify these categories. Subsystems consist of a set of *endogenous* variables; by these I mean a set of mutually interacting variables which are internal to the subsystem. There are also *exogenous* variables which affect the variables in the subsystem, but are not themselves affected by the movements in the subsystem.

The division of the international system into various subsystems such as the security system, international economic system and so on, can be easily represented as saying that there are a number of international systems. While this is a perfectly acceptable convention, it is easier in this context to use 'the international system' to mean the broader system as defined above, recognising that for any particular problem such as an arms race, the relevant elements and variables will in fact be a subsystem of the over-all system. While this means that the term is used in a rather general way, it should not lead to ambiguity, though some purists might feel uneasy (Reynolds 1970).

3 COOPERATION AND CONFLICT AMONGST SELF-INTERESTED STATES

1 International anarchy

It is common to refer to the international system as being one of anarchy. There is nothing equivalent to a domestic government which can enforce general compliance to laws or rules of behaviour on the part of all states. It is now out of fashion to regard World Government as in any way likely to provide an answer, though fashions in these matters could change. However, at least for the foreseeable future, an analysis of the international system must be an analysis of the behaviour of independent units (not all of which are states) each pursuing their own self-interests. Much conventional wisdom holds that this situation is regrettable but inevitable. The perpetual violence and threat of violence which plague the international system is admired by few, but regarded as inevitable by many. In the international system there is not even a parallel to Adam Smith's 'hidden hand' which, purportedly at least, makes an economic market system operate effectively even though its actors all pursue their individual self-interests without any concern for the interest of the system as a whole. Principles such as the 'Balance of Power' which is regarded by many international relations scholars as providing a moderately stable international system, require the actors to deviate from narrow self-interest to having goals for the system as such. There is nothing 'hidden' about the stabilising principles.

The bleakest versions of this view are those painted by the 'realist' school of international relations theorists who hold that states are the primary units in the international system and that their primary aim is to maximise power.[1] This view, once dominant, is now regarded more

---

[1] Classical statements of the realist position are Hans Morgenthau (1974) *Politics Amongst Nations: the Struggle for Power and Peace* (5th edn) New York: Knopf, and E. H. Carr (1939) *The Twenty Year's Crisis*, the latter dealing primarily with the interwar period in terms of a realist perspective which in turn owes a lot to Bertrand Russell's *Power*. Carr has the distinction of

26

sceptically. This is not because it leads to unpleasant conclusions (though this may be a factor) but because it leaves too much unexplained. There are many other actors in the international system besides states, and motivations, even if describable as the pursuit of self-interest, are often complex. However, while acknowledging and welcoming the recognition of broader factors in the analysis of international relations than the realists would allow, self-interest, in an environment which is perceived by the actors to be conflictual, still characterises a lot of behaviour of the international system. The rest of the chapter models such a system where I primarily consider state interactions. In particular we show that self-interested actors can rationally cooperate more than might superficially appear to be the case.

Self-interest is not a self-evident concept. A crucial goal normally and plausibly attributed to the decision makers of states is a desire for security. However, where they see the threat to security as coming from, and the measures they see as appropriate to combatting it, is not some simple observable characteristic of a state such as its population or its land-area. Ultimately security consists of attitudes of mind. Now the people responsible for the actions in the international system tend to have very similar general views about this though they differ about specifics. The capacity to use military force is widely held to be the prime tool of defence, while it is an axiom that one's own state is under some degree of threat. Which are the states who threaten, which the putative victims, and which the peace-loving states whose only goal is world harmony, is a regular issue of dispute.

While it seems that the actors in the international system regard it as highly conflictual, they do not regard their situation as strictly zero sum, in the sense that any gain they achieve must be at the expense of someone else. Adversaries are not strict adversaries as they might be in war, but actors with whom there is the possibility of some agreement at least on certain issues. For example, two states which perceive

writing one of the few books on international relations which, despite its subject matter, one might read for pleasure. A recent critique of realist theory with the development of an alternative is in Richard W. Mansbach and John A. Vasquez (1981) *In Search of Theory: A New Paradigm for Global Politics* New York: Columbia University Press. A survey of the various views on international relations is in James E. Dougherty and Robert L. Pfaltzgraff (1981) *Contending Theories of International Relations: A Comprehensive Survey* New York: Harper and Row. The 'balance of power' is explained in virtually all text books on international relations. Of these, I particularly admire that of K. W. Deutsch (1978) *The Analysis of International Relations* Englewood Cliffs: Prentice Hall which is in sympathy with the approach of this book.

each other as hostile have some mutual interest in restricting the level of arms directed against each other, if only because of the cost. It is generally accepted that there are many conflictual social interactions in which there is some potentiality for collaboration. Commonsense indicates this intuitively; one of the most widely known of mathematical pictures, the prisoners' dilemma, illustrates this more clearly and confirms that our intuitions are not at fault. It is a simplified picture of a widespread social interaction, and one with particular application to the international system.

2 The prisoners' dilemma

I shall describe the prisoners' dilemma briefly but carefully. Care is needed as the various 'solutions' to the initial game[2] come from extending the definition to what is in fact a different situation. The name 'prisoners' dilemma' is used to describe both the one-shot game and the iterated or supergame version. We should be clear where the differences lie as they have considerable significance when the problem is interpreted in social situation. As the original story, excellent though it is, has been frequently told, I shall outline the situation in terms of a laboratory situation, to emphasise the extreme case of the 'pure' prisoners' dilemma.

Two subjects are invited to play a game. Neither knows who the other is, and neither sees or has any direct contact with the other beyond knowing they exist. The game consists of the choice of either pushing a blue button or a red button on a control panel. The two participants will be rewarded according to the table below (known as a 'pay-off matrix'), which is known to both. Thus if A pushes the blue button and B the red, A will get £150 and B nothing. This procedure takes place once only, and at no stage is there any other contact between the two players.

The dilemma is obvious. Look at the game from the point of view of player A; if he plays his blue strategy against the rival's red he will get £150 as opposed to £100 if he plays the red strategy. Similarly the blue

---

[2] I use the term 'game' to mean any conflict situation in which people work out their strategies, whether this is a game in the conventional sense and played for fun, a business competition or a nuclear war. The name may be insensitive, but it is a totally accepted convention. The theory of games is often restricted to the analysis of conflict situations in a direct axiomatic manner in the tradition of Von Neumann and Morgenstern. However, it has also a broader, looser, usage as any analysis of clearly defined conflicts or games will confirm.

28

	B's strategies	
A's strategies		
	Red	Blue
Red	£100, £100	£0, £150
Blue	£150, £0	£50, £50

against the rivals' blue gives him £50 as against nothing which comes from playing the red. Playing blue is obviously the prudent act for any self-interested player and it is hard not to go the extra step and say it is the rational act. As the game is symmetrical, the same is also true for player B. However, by both playing the blue, they both get £50 each as opposed to a possible £100 if they had acted 'imprudently' or 'irrationally'. The achievement of £50 each when £100 was available to both is known as a 'non-Pareto Optimal' solution. For a pair of pay-offs to be Pareto Optimal, it requires that there is no achievable result where both parties could be better off, as distinct from one party being better off at the expense of the other. It seems a modest requirement for 'efficient' social interactions that they should give Pareto Optimal results. Clearly the prisoners' dilemma does not. Those readers who are unfamiliar with this should convince themselves that this is not a sleight of hand, but the straightforward consequence of assuming that people maximise their money gains.

Many people regard this dilemma with interest but without surprise, arguing that they knew all along that the world was a depressing place and that this is merely a little more confirmatory evidence. Others find it shocking and attempt to deny it. This comes because it appears to violate some fairly obvious assumptions we make about the consequences of rational conduct. We assume that if people act rationally they will do better than if they do not. It is of course obvious that, if two rational people are in conflict, one of them could lose with his rationality still intact. However, we also assume that one would win. In the case above we have shown that both people can act with seemingly impeccable rationality and both be losers. This offends many of our deep-seated feelings. It can be avoided by arguing that this is some bizarre possibility of little practical significance in 'real life'. Unfortunately this is not so. There is a genuine and important dilemma, though there are more ways of avoiding it than the pessimists might allow.

I draw attention to some crucial aspects of my description. The experimenter took great precautions that the players did not know each other and had no other social contact with each other. They knew nothing of each other's past and would have no known contact with each other in the future. It was a social interaction which would occur once and once only without a history and without a future. If the experiment were part of a continuing social situation between the two players, then some implicit promise, or even hope of future cooperative behaviour might induce the two to play the cooperative strategy in this particular case. This can be strengthened (or weakened) if there is knowledge of the past, from which each player can observe whether his opponent is in general a cooperative sort of person, or whether he always goes for short-term gain. There may also be some amorphous sense of 'community' which induces cooperation, though this might be interpreted as leaving the prisoners' dilemma format for some other game, as 'community' itself becomes an element in the values (or 'utilities') of the players. However, these arguments all suggest, at least intuitively, that the paradox of the prisoners' dilemma might be due to posing a problem which is isolated from the general social context and that there may be ways of resolving it by putting it back in. This is largely true. Most of the work I shall discuss is in terms of games in which the participants are not so socially isolated as I have described. This is, of course, more realistic. The problem, though, does not completely disappear as I shall demonstrate below.

3   The prisoners' dilemma supergame

If we suppose that a game of prisoners' dilemma is played not just once but a number of times then we place it in a social context. It is the one-off nature of the game that brings out its paradoxical nature. Such a sequence of iterated plays of a prisoners' dilemma is known as a *supergame*.

Suppose that two players are playing a sequence of prisoners' dilemma which has the matrix:

	Player B	
	Cooperate (C)	Defect (D)
Player A		
Cooperate (C)	$(b_1\ b_2)$	$(d_1\ a_2)$
Defect (D)	$(a_1\ d_2)$	$(c_1\ c_2)$

I adopt the convention that the earlier the letter comes in the alphabet, the higher is its value. Thus $a_i > b_i > c_i > d_i$, where $a > b$ denotes 'a is greater than b'. The subscript 1 denotes the player A, and 2 player B. Initially assume that both players use their cooperative strategy. A now wonders whether to defect at the next move and get a_1 instead of b_1. However, he is deterred because he knows that B will respond and the system results in both getting c each period instead of b. Thus, there is a good reason for them both to remain at the cooperative point in that the short period gain of defection will be quickly balanced off by the long period losses of the mutual defect outcome. However, if the gains of the present are much preferred to those of the future, or if the future appears problematic or even non-existent, then this deterrent is weakened. The core of this chapter concerns the conditions for the success or failure in remaining at a cooperative position in the repeated prisoners' dilemma.

There is one immediate problem. Suppose that a prisoners' dilemma supergame is proposed which consists of twenty iterations. In the early stages it would seem that it would be rational to play the cooperative strategy as any defection would be punished in later plays. However, a player can reason as follows: after nineteen plays there will be just one more to go. But this last play then becomes an instance of the one-shot prisoners' dilemma. Hence, I, and my rival, will certainly defect. Now imagine we have just finished the eighteenth play, planning the nineteenth. As on the twentieth, the defect strategy will be played regardless, because the last game is determined and there is no punishment for defect play. Hence, defect again becomes the rational strategy. The same argument applies to the eighteenth play. The last two games are already determined, so once again no punishments are possible in the sense of conditional acts. Again it becomes rational to defect. It is clear that this argument can be taken by backwards induction to the first play. That is, if the supergame consists of a known number of plays then we are back in the original paradox and the defect strategy is played throughout. This emphasises the curious nature of the problem. It is not just the one-shot prisoner's dilemma to which it applies; it applies to any finite sequence where the number of plays is known. Twenty was clearly an arbitrary number. The same formal argument would apply if it had been a million. Happily there is considerable experimental evidence to suggest that people do not always lapse into rationality (Rapoport and Chammah 1965).

Another feature of real-life behaviour helps us to avoid this potential paradox. If we assume that the future is regarded as less important than the present – in other words the future is 'discounted' – then providing the end is not too near at hand there is no need to bother about definite ending points. Suppose that, in every successive period, the future is discounted by some percentage, say 10%. Thus, each term in the series is valued at 90% of its predecessor. If the two players use their cooperative strategies in a game which goes on

31

indefinitely, they get b_1 and b_2 respectively in each period, but looked at from the present perspective each successive payment appears less important. As we look sufficiently far into the future, 0.9 becomes raised to sufficiently high power for it to become almost zero. For example $0.9^{20} = 0.122$, meaning that at the twenty first iteration the value of the pay-offs are less than an eighth of the current value, while after forty-one iterations this has been reduced to 0.0148 of its current value – that is, about $1\frac{1}{2}\%$ which for most purposes is negligible. This does not happen abruptly at some specific point. The pay-offs just gradually fade away. Further, if we were to imagine ourselves at some distant point in the future with the perceptions of what it would look like, then the future from there would look much like the future does from here. That is, the discount rate would be moved up in time. This gets us out of our problem. The sum of this sequence of pay-offs to A up to period t will be

$$b_1 + (.9)b_1 + (.9)^2 b_1 + \ldots + (.9)^t b_1 = [(1 - (.9)^{t+1})/(1 - .9)]b_1$$
$$\rightarrow 10 b_1 \text{ as } t \rightarrow \infty \qquad (3.3.1)$$

Now suppose that a player is contemplating defection at step 1 in the game. His gain will be $(a_1 - b_1)$ for one period. Assuming an immediate response by the rival, his loss will be $(b_1 - c_1)$ for all the subsequent periods, which as we have seen will become less and less significant as time goes on. Now suppose more generally that the discount rate reduces each successive value by a fraction w of its predecessor, which was 0.9 in the previous example. This is called the 'discount parameter'.[3] When it is high (that is, close to unity) it means the future is highly regarded and when low the future is disregarded. The loss is now represented as

$$w(b_1 - c_1) + w^2(b_1 - c_1) + \ldots = (b_1 - c_1) . w/(1 - w) \qquad (3.3.2)$$

Rearranged, this means that A will abandon the cooperative strategy if

$$(a_1 - b_1)/(b_1 - c_1) > w / (1 - w) \qquad (3.3.3)$$

Unsurprisingly the higher the ratio of loss to gain, the more likely is a cooperative strategy to be played. Importantly, the higher the value of

---

[3] Notice that the discount parameter relates directly to the discount rate as $w = (1 - d)$ where d is the discount rate represented as a proportion (it is more commonly expressed as a percentage). Thus a ten percent discount rate equals a 0.9 discount parameter. There is a source of possible confusion in that a high discount parameter is a low discount rate and vice versa.

w, that is the more the future is regarded, the smaller is the right hand side of the inequality and the more likely is this condition for a cooperative solution to hold. This confirms the suggestion made earlier that the more an instance of the prisoners' dilemma is placed in a wider context of social activity, the greater is the pressure for cooperative play. The same effect could be maintained if we abandoned the assumption that the various games were played in sequence. If a large number of games were to be played in the near future, some of them simultaneously, then the size of the discount parameter would be of less importance as, on most interpretations, it is related to time as measured by clocks and not as measured by the number of iterations of the game. The more games played with significant pay-offs which take into account the rival's cooperation or non-cooperation in a specific game, the more are cooperative strategies likely to be used in that game. The significance of a high discount parameter is that it broadens the number of games whose pay-offs are regarded as relevant to the current situation.

4 Technological arms races

An extension of this analysis can be used to analyse a problem of technology in the arms race. A major characteristic of the present arms race between the USSR and the USA is the development of military technology. While each side perceives the quantity and growth in the quantity of arms owned by the rival to be a threat (to an exaggerated degree in the opinion of the author), the possibility of major technological change in the rival's arms is perhaps seen as more serious. Technological changes in armaments, as elsewhere, often take the form of a series of relatively minor innovations which cumulatively are important. However, there are also major changes which could seriously disrupt the strategic balance which would be seen by the loser, whichever of the superpowers it was, as destabilising and a threat to security. An example would be a significant development in the tracking of submarines, as they carry some of the missiles regarded as crucial to strategic nuclear deterrence by the nuclear powers. A characteristic of many such innovations is that if one party alone had it, it would be at a strategic advantage, but if both did then the original strategic balance would exist but it would be costing more. They would both be better off if they could not introduce this 'innovation'. This situation is modelled by a basic prisoners' dilemma matrix:

	Country B	
	Not introduce weapon	Introduce weapon
Country A		
Not introduce weapon	$(b_1\ b_2)$	$(d_1\ a_2)$
Introduce weapon	$(a_1\ d_2)$	$(c_1\ c_2)$

At some initial point in time neither party has introduced the innovations and both can be said to be playing the cooperative strategy. The supergame can be thought of as a sequence of basic games which are packed very densely in time. That is, either party can change its mind about what strategy to play whenever it wants. The pay-offs are now interpreted as the rate of benefit. Suppose we think of political life as moving on a day to day basis. The new technology is introduced on some specific day and the pay-offs are regarded as the daily benefit of this occurring. There are two evident restrictions in applying the standard prisoners' dilemma supergame to the technological arms race. First, while it is possible to move from the cooperate to the defect strategy the reverse is harder, so a move is effectively irreversible. Secondly, a major technical innovation cannot be introduced overnight. It takes a long time from the point of deciding about things to actually achieving operational weaponry. In the case of new aircraft it is about ten years. In the case of the nuclear weapons it was six years for the United States and about the same for the Soviet Union (Meyer 1983, Holloway 1984). Let us look at A, who is contemplating some possible major weapons development. We assume also that A believes that his rival B will introduce the innovation only as a reaction to A but would not initiate it. Suppose it takes T periods from deciding on the weapons to introducing them for both sides. Thus there are three stages.

Stage 1
Time 0: Decision by A to introduce innovation.
      Pay-offs: to A b_1
            : to B b_2
Stage 2
Time T: Introduction of weapons by A.
      Decision by B to introduce weapons.
      Pay-offs: to A a_1
            : to B d_2
Stage 3
Time $2T$: Introduction of weapons by B.
      Pay-offs: to A c_1
            : to B c_2

34

The over-all pay-offs in the supergame are therefore

to A:

$$b_1 (1 - w^T)/(1 - w) + a_1 w^T (1 - w^T)/(1 - w) + c_1 w^{2T}/(1 - w)$$
$$(3.4.1)$$

and to B:

$$b_2 (1 - w^T)/(1 - w) + d_2 w^T (1 - w^T)/(1 - w) + c_2 w^{2T} (1 + w)$$
$$(3.4.2)$$

If the innovation is not introduced then the pay-offs will be

$$b_1/(1 - w) \text{ and } b_2/(1 - w) \text{ respectively} \qquad (3.4.3a \text{ and b})$$

Thus, A will introduce the innovation if (3.4.1) is greater than (3.4.3a). With rearrangement this condition is

$$(a_1 - b_1)/(a_1 - c_1) > w^T \qquad (3.4.4)$$

This assumes the discount factor is the same for both. The modifications if not are obvious and make no difference to the general analysis. Inequality (3.4.4) is related to inequality (3.3.3) and the same general considerations apply though with the added factor of T. The larger is T then the smaller will the right hand side of the inequality be and the more likely is the non-cooperative strategy to be played. T is the number of periods which it takes B to respond to the introduction of the new weapons, and also the number of periods which it will be at the serious disadvantage of having to put up with the 'sucker's outcome' of d. The value of T can be regarded as an indicator of the rigidity of the system. The lower it is the more quickly can the system adjust whereas the higher it is the slower the response.

This assumes either rather passive behaviour on the part of B or ignorance either of the nature of the technical innovation or of the fact that A was about to introduce it. Suppose, that B was more alert than assumed. B knows that (3.4.4) holds for A. Thus, if he is simply reactive and plays along with this, he will spend time at the 'sucker's outcome'. To avoid this, he will immediately take steps to introduce the weapons and eliminate or at least minimise stage 2 of the above course of events. The pay-off to A will therefore be

$$b_1 (1 - w^T)/(1 - w) + c_1 w^T/(1 - w) \qquad (3.4.5)$$

This is clearly not merely less than (3.4.3a) but also than (3.4.1) and everyone is worse off as a result. Both parties would be better off without the innovation, but are forced into it for fear that the other will gain an advantage.

For given values of the discount parameter, clearly T is the crucial factor. The lower it is, the less likely is (3.4.5) or its equivalent for B to hold and produce the defect outcome. The quicker one party can respond to the defect strategy of the other, then the less will the defector gain and the less will the slower party lose. Hence the more flexible the system is, the more likely are players to use the cooperative strategy. Conversely, the slower actors can respond to the aggressive acts of their rivals, the more are those strategies likely to be played.

These results can now be summarised in a pay-off matrix for the supergame. Let us consider two strategies in the supergame, passive and aggressive. The passive strategy is 'Do not initiate the defect strategy in the basic prisoners' dilemma, but if the rival defects, respond as soon as possible. The aggressive strategy is 'defect in the basic prisoners' dilemma as soon as possible'. If we denote the pay-offs to A as α_{ij} and to B as β_{ij} then we get the following matrix:

	Country B	
	Passive	Aggressive
Country A		
Passive	$(\alpha_{11}\ \beta_{11})$	$(\alpha_{12}\ \beta_{12})$
Aggressive	$(\alpha_{21}\ \beta_{21})$	$(\alpha_{22}\ \beta_{22})$

The values are derived from the principles above. Thus α_{11} is given by expression (3.4.3a) and α_{21} is given by expression (3.4.1). If the condition indicates remaining at the cooperate strategy, namely if inequality (3.4.4) is reversed along with the analogue for B, then the ordering of the terms in the matrix is

$$\alpha_{11} > \alpha_{21} > \alpha_{22} > \alpha_{12}$$
$$\beta_{11} > \beta_{12} > \beta_{22} > \beta_{21}$$

In this case the point $(\alpha_{11}\ \beta_{11})$ dominates the others and the passive strategy would appear to dominate in the supergame.

However, if the condition for aggression holds, the ordering of the terms in the matrix is

$$\alpha_{21} > \alpha_{11} > \alpha_{22} > \alpha_{12}$$
$$\beta_{12} > \beta_{11} > \beta_{22} > \beta_{21}$$

This last produces a prisoners' dilemma in the supergame also. However, in this case it is not possible to have a prisoners' dilemma iterated through time and it becomes a one-shot prisoners' dilemma which cannot be avoided. In the one-shot game the aggressive strategy has a lot of appeal and the arguments of Section 2 appear to apply.

Even here there is still a way of keeping the game from being totally isolated from a social context. If a state has interactions with another state on lots of different issues all of which are of similar importance, then plays across the issues in the individual games of the set of prisoners' dilemmas should be interdependent. That is, cooperative play in one area (say trade) is 'rewarded' by cooperative play in another (say military agreements) even though the supergames of each are of prisoners' dilemma form. How relevant this can be depends on the relative significance the decision makers attribute to the different games. If security is held to be of over-riding importance, then any benefits which might be derived from cooperative play in other games may still be inadequate to compensate for any risks in the security game.

In general it is assumed that the more cooperatively powers play in the international system the better it is for everyone, including the onlookers. I shall continue with this assumption. If gains and losses are given then this cooperation is fostered by influencing the discount parameter or T. Here I shall concentrate on T.

Complex technical weaponry takes a long time to evolve. Research and development takes time and the results are not guaranteed. This is particularly evident in the middle nineteen eighties with the much publicised technical problems of 'Star Wars' (the Strategic Defence Initiative to its admirers) where a lot of the underlying scientific theory has still to be worked out. Even when designed, complex equipment takes time to build and make operational. While intense perceptions of threat can speed this process up as in the Second World War, there is a limit to how far it can go. There is some minimum development time which it is impossible to curtail. In itself this is a factor increasing the rigidity in the international system and the likelihood of defect behaviour. However, what is crucial is the lead one side has over the other and, hence the period during which it can force the sucker's outcome on the rival. Even if the development period is long, providing a rival realises a programme has been started, then it can also initiate a programme and minimise T. If this in turn were known by the initiator, it would mean the programme would not be started in the first place as it would be self-defeating. Thus the technical rigidity need not spill over into systemic rigidity. For this argument to apply it requires that all the parties in the international system have a high degree of confidence that they will be able to detect quickly when a rival has undertaken a major programme. If they are not confident that detection is possible, then pre-emptive defect strategies will be played even in the knowledge that this might result in a generally worse situation for both parties. A system is more stable, the more information both parties have about each other. According to this argument not only is information about one's rival a benefit – military intelligence is generally accepted as useful – but also it is in one's own long-term interest for one's rival to know a lot about oneself. The spy, in international relations theory as well as in fiction, becomes the true hero.

5 Discounting and uncertainty

The discount parameter has played a crucial role in much of the preceding analysis. It is undoubtedly a convenient device, but given its significance it is appropriate to consider how it should be interpreted in international politics as distinct from economics where it is well known and, at least in some contexts, unproblematic. The scientific question is whether in fact decision makers discount the future in the way suggested, or at least whether their actions can be described in this way whether they explicitly consider a discount factor or not. A relevant moral question is whether they ought to discount the future. Decisions are made by decision makers on behalf of a populace whose influence is often negligible. More significantly, for our present purposes, they are also taking them on behalf of future generations whose influence is non-existent. A comment then on the moral issues is therefore appropriate.

In its simplest form the discount rate simply reflects the often observed fact that people do not regard the future as being as important as the present. Benefits which come about in the future are not as highly valued as current benefits. Thus, to induce people to give up present benefits, they need the prospect of rather larger benefits in the future. No doubt the degree of discounting varies from individual to individual. This is not a moral evaluation; it is simply a comment. As long as an individual chooses for himself, this is a matter of personal choice. If a decision maker is making decisions on behalf of a group, he might similarly argue that, while each member of the group will have a different discount rate, the phenomenon is sufficiently widespread to assume that the members of the group all share it to a greater or lesser degree. Therefore it is quite proper to use a discount rate as a factor in his decision. However, decisions in social affairs affect future generations also. Decision maker A might decide of individual X on whose behalf he is making a decision that X, like himself, prefers present benefits to future. However, has he any right to give a benefit to X now instead of to Y in the future, merely because Y has not been born yet? This seems to me hard to justify (Ramsey 1928).

However, there is a similarity between the discount rate and risk (I blur the distinction between risk and uncertainty for reasons discussed in Chapter 4). A discounted sum of payments of k per period which extends indefinitely into the future looks as follows

$$S = k + wk + w^2k + \ldots + w^tk + \ldots = k/(1 - w) \qquad (3.5.1)$$

S can be interpreted as the current market price of this stream of payments. Now consider a gamble where £12 is offered providing a throw of a dice does not result in a six. There is an obvious sense in which such a gamble is worth 12.5/6 = £10 which would be the most a rational gambler would wager – that is, the highest price for which he would 'buy' the gamble. More generally, if a payment k is conditional on the occurrence of some chance event with probability p, then its *expected value* is $p.k.$ which can be regarded as the market price of the gamble. Suppose now the gamble is extended such that, if successful on the first go, a second turn is allowed under the same conditions. Now, before the first throw has taken place, the probability of the second gamble being successful is p, for it has to jump through two hoops. Consequently the market value of this double gamble is

$$V = pk + p^2 k$$

It is easy to see that a gamble which will go on indefinitely until the chance event occurs which stops it, will have an expected value of

$$V = pk + p^2 k + \ldots + p^n k + \ldots = kp/(1 - p)$$

or if there is an initial certain outcome, then it will be

$$V = k + pk + p^2 k + \ldots + p^n k + \ldots = k/(1 + p) \qquad (3.5.2)$$

There is an obvious straightforward mathematical parallelism. However, the parallelism goes further. Let us suppose that there is a prisoners' dilemma supergame with the rule that before every play a card is selected from a pack and the game goes ahead if the selected card is not the ace of spades. If it is chosen, the series stops. The expected values of the various elements in the pay-off matrix over time take on exactly the same form as the discounted elements of a pay-off matrix, and the two games are formally identical. In particular, there is no 'ending point' which leads to the paradox discussed earlier in which any finite game of prisoners' dilemma played by self-seeking rational players would always result in defect strategies being played.

Though discounting and risk give identical patterns of play in the prisoners' dilemma and many other situations also, it does not follow from this that they are the same thing or indeed that there is any relationship between them. However, in this case the parallelism is more than a mathematical pun. Decisions in social affairs are always taken under situations of uncertainty. Thus, the strategy which might now appear the best for some future circumstances, might turn out in fact to be quite inappropriate when the time comes. A decision maker knows this. He quite properly weights highly the relatively likely consequences of his acts in the near future against the more problematic values of the distant future when in some reasonable sense the current game might be said to have ended. Weaponry might be built up today with the present perceptions of threat which will be totally irrelevant at some future point in time due to different perceptions of threat. Hadrian's Wall was built across Northern England to keep out the Scots. Being of sturdy construction it was a long lived investment. However, its later value as a defensive measure was negligible as technology advanced, and anyway no-one minded if the Scots came in or not. Thus, the discount parameter can stand in for a general uncertainty factor. This is completely justifiable even when the parameter applies to benefits to be enjoyed by as yet unborn generations, providing we make the normally reasonable assumption that the further into the future we go the greater is the degree of uncertainty. This does not justify the use of a 'true' discount factor. It is an assertion that the interpretation of the model in terms of probabilities is really closer to the point than a model interpreted narrowly in terms of discount parameters.

One significant result for the international system follows from this. It was shown in Section 2 that, the lower the discount parameter, the more likely it was that a defect strategy would be played. This followed from inequality (3.4.4). It follows directly that, in a formal game, the lower is the probability per play that the iteration will in fact take place, the more likely is a defect strategy to be played. This is readily extended to asserting that, in a conflict system of this sort, the higher the level of uncertainty, the more likely are defect strategies to be played, and conversely the greater the predictability in the system the more likely is cooperative play. Unfortunately predictability in the international system is clearly very low. One would expect defect strategies to be played commonly, simply because the effect of doing so on the long-run outcomes is so unclear that they might as well be disregarded, and a strategy aimed at maximising short-run gains would appear to be the most appropriate. This is not just short-sightedness, it is perfectly rational under the circumstances. Increasing the predictability of the system is partly a policy matter; actors could deliberately behave in more predictable ways and take care not to introduce uncertainty wantonly into the system. The development of congenial norms is a device for reducing uncertainty. However, it could be equally well claimed that the uncertainty in the international system is due to our ignorance of its behaviour as much as it is a characteristic of the system as such. That is, its behaviour is knowable but not so far known. It is not self-evident that the international system (or indeed any other social system) is inherently prone to great uncertainty. A greater knowledge of the system might mean that observers and actors within it can predict its behaviour better. The more one knows about the system, the lower is the degree of uncertainty.

6 Modes of play

The analysis above gives an account of the conditions under which self-interested actors are likely to use cooperative strategies. It was done by restating the game such that the dilemma disappears. In other words, we have not 'solved' the prisoners' dilemma but shown that some situations which have characteristics similar to the prisoners' dilemma (i.e. its supergame) do not always suffer from its difficulties. There remains the issue of how to induce cooperative play in a prisoners' dilemma when condition (3.3.3) holds and the crux of the dilemma remains.

The use of the cooperative option in a particular instance of an indefinite sequence of iterations of prisoners' dilemma is brought about by some notion of threat of future defection if the opponent does not also cooperate. Strategies are thus conditional, and what is actually chosen after the early iterations depends on the pattern of play of the rival. What sort of threats are likely to be effective?

The question appears conceptually innocuous, but in fact it is rather difficult. It is possible to attempt the sort of analysis which was undertaken in the last section and see how a self-interested player would play by assuming certain rules. We could also look empirically at how people threaten and see which type of threat is most success-ful. An ingenious alternative approach to the question was carried out by Axelrod (1984). He devised a set of computer tournaments using different rules for strategy selection and playing the rules against each other. The rules were suggested by various scholars who have been interested in the prisoners' dilemma. The decision rule which was most successful was benevolent TIT-FOR-TAT which is the rule of 'Start with the cooperate choice and thereafter use the strategy which the rival used on the previous move.' It was the most successful in the

41

sense of getting the maximum pay-off for the players against any other strategy. It further appears to have been a very robust strategy. The tournament was played a second time with suggestions from a broader group of people. In the second round, the players (in the sense of the suggesters of strategies) knew the results of the previous tournament and hence that TIT-FOR-TAT had won. Even with the knowledge that any strategy would be competing against TIT-FOR-TAT, it still came out ahead. What is perhaps more surprising is that the simple TIT-FOR-TAT, which only takes into account play in the previous iteration and punishes or rewards for one iteration only, wins against more sophisticated versions of the strategy. It is not difficult to devise 'improved' versions of TIT-FOR-TAT, such as making the cost of defection more severe for the rival the more often it is done. An example would be to defect for one move after the first of the rival's defections, for two moves after the second defection and so on. Surprisingly, and against at least this writer's intuition, the more sophisticated versions do not do as well as the simple version.

The TIT-FOR-TAT strategy is a relatively benign strategy. It is a forgiving strategy in that it returns to cooperative play whenever it can. Its success is therefore encouraging, in a modest way, for anyone who believes in social harmony. Of the other strategies which Axelrod tested the benign ones tended to do better than the harsh ones, which offers further encouragement.

The methodology of Axelrod's investigation is interesting as well as its conclusions. The computer tournament is not a piece of deductive mathematical reasoning. Nor is it a psychological experiment with individuals to see how they choose in specific situations. It is a simulation in which the consequences of operating a specified set of interacting rules are observed, but the results are not proved as they would be in a standard mathematical argument. In this section (and indeed chapter) I have restricted myself to the analysis of the two-party game. The extensions to larger groups are significant, but this will be deferred until the chapter on alliances.

7 Metagames

A 'strategy' in a two option game is a rule which prescribes whether to play the cooperate or the defect alternative in any particular move of the game. In effect it consists of a list of the options to be played. A more general rule of play, called a *meta-strategy*, is to posit a rule for the selection of a strategy in the face of a rule by the opponent. From the meta-strategies the specific choice in a particular game can be determined. An example of a meta-strategy is 'simple' TIT-FOR-TAT. This is a rule which states 'Select the same alternative as the rival'. (I call it 'simple' as it does not prescribe a rule for starting as in 'benevolent' TIT-FOR-TAT). In a sequential game, this can be interpreted as the selection of the alternative chosen in the previous play by the rival. In the case of the one-shot game its meaning is more obscure, but this is a problem which will be looked at later. For exposition it is simpler to describe the principles in terms of iterated games of prisoners' dilemma.

The concept of meta-strategies and the resulting theory of meta-games is due to Nigel Howard (Howard 1971). The principles are as follows.

Consider a basic prisoners' dilemma:

	Player B	
	C	D
Player A		
C	(3,3)	(1,4)
D	(4,1)	(2,2)

The *DD* strategy choice is commonly regarded as the equilibrium, in that for any other point in the matrix one or both of the parties could gain by making a unilateral move to another option. An equilibrium point is where neither can make such a unilateral move profitably. Now suppose that player B considers the following conditional strategies:

I Play C regardless of A's choice
II Play D regardless of A's choice
III TIT-FOR-TAT
IV TIT-FOR-TAT (i.e. the opposite of player A)

Against the simple strategy choices of A this will give a matrix:

	Player B			
	I	II	III	IV
	C Regardless	D Regardless	TIT-FOR-TAT	TAT-FOR-TIT
Player A				
C	(3,3)	(1,4)	(3,3)	(1,4)
D	(4,1)	(2,2)	(2,2)	(4,1)

This is known as the *b*-metagame, so called because B plays strategies which are conditional on A's choices. This does not alter the situation very much, as the equilibrium choice will still result in a mutual defect strategy being played.

However, we can now go on to a further level of meta-strategy,

Table 3.1. *The* ab-*metagame derived from prisoners' dilemma*

	I	II	III	IV
B's meta-strategy	C	D		
A's meta-strategy	Regardless	Regardless	TIT-FOR-TAT	TIT-FOR-TAT
1 C/C/C/C	3,3	1,4	3,3	1,4
2 C/C/C/D	3,3	1,4	3,3	4,1
3 C/C/D/C	3,3	1,4	2,2	1,4
4 C/D/C/C	3,3	2,2	3,3	1,4
5 D/C/C/C	4,1	1,4	3,3	1,4
6 C/C/D/D	3,3	1,4	2,2	4,1
7 C/D/C/D	3,3	2,2	3,3	4,1
8 D/C/C/D	4,1	1,4	3,3	4,1
9 C/D/D/C	3,3	2,2	2,2	1,4
10 D/C/D/C	4,1	1,4	2,2	1,4
11 D/D/C/C	4,1	2,2	3,3	1,4
12 C/D/D/D	3,3	2,2	2,2	4,1
13 D/C/D/D	4,1	1,4	2,2	4,1
14 D/D/C/D	4,1	2,2	3,3	4,1
15 D/D/D/C	4,1	2,2	2,2	1,4
16 D/D/D/D	4,1	2,2	2,2	4,1

whose rationale I shall give after its exposition. Consider a meta-strategy for *A* which reads:

        Against I play *C*
        Against II play *D*
        Against III play *C*
        Against IV play *D*

If we denote the strategy by *C/D/C/D* the pay-offs will appear as:

	I	II	III	IV
C/D/C/D	(3,3)	(2,2)	(3,3)	(4,1)

C/D/C/D is just one of the sixteen possible strategies which can be made up of the various permutations of *C* and *D*. This will result in a table of strategies and pay-offs (see Table 3.1).

This yet further expanded game is known as the *ab*-metagame, a notation which indicates that A plays conditionally to B's conditional strategies. Three entries are boxed. These are equilibria in the sense defined above. Once at an equilibrium outcome, neither A nor B can get a unilateral advantage from moving away from it. Thus, A cannot get a better outcome by moving up and down the column, while B cannot do better by moving along the row. This is a standard definition of equilibrium used in the theory of games known as the Nash equilibrium condition.[4] It has the added advantage of making good intuitive sense. What is interesting about these is that two of the candidates are the consequences of playing the CC strategy in the basic game. We now come to a significant formal result for metagames. If the metagame is extended to the *bab*-metagame, which would give $16 \times 4 = 64$ strategies for B to relate to the 16 strategies of A in the above matrix, then this will still result in the same three equilibrium points already found in this second level metagame. The same applies to any further levels of the metagame. This is crucial as far as a metagame analysis of prisoners' dilemma is concerned. If it were not the case and every new level of the metagame produced new sets of equilibria, then we would not know which should be regarded as the solution.

However, how do we find which of the three equilibria is the solution? There are two courses of action in a situation like this. One is to accept that the theory only gives us a set within which the solution must lie but is not able to give us a unique solution. The second is to introduce a new principle which reduces the set of possibilities, ideally to a unique result. The principle introduced here is that of *dominance*. Consider the two sets of numbers (4,2,3,4,) and (3,2,3,4) which are the pay-offs to A in strategies 14 and 7 respectively. Such sets of numbers arranged in order are known as *vectors*. The first vector is said to *dominate* the second because each number in all the numbers in the first is at least as large as their equivalents in the second (i.e. the first number in the first vector, 4, is larger than the first in the second, 3, while all the other numbers are the same as their equivalents). Thus if A were making a choice between these two vectors, it would seem fairly obvious that the first (that of meta-strategy 14) would be preferred to the second (that of meta-strategy 7). By using this same principle, we find that 14 also dominates 16, making 14 the single best meta-strategy for A. As far as B is concerned neither of the two relevant strategies, II and III, dominate each other. However, on the full information assumption B knows that A will play 14 and hence plays the optimum response, namely III. Thus, we can select the strategy pair (14, III) as the solution to the metagame.

Meta-strategy 14 is clearly a relative of TIT-FOR-TAT, though sterner than genuine TIT-FOR-TAT against the unconditional cooperate

---

[4] After J. F. Nash, a major contributor to the theory of games. See Nash (1951).

strategy of B. Meta-strategy 7 can be fairly directly interpreted as true TIT-FOR-TAT.

What stands out about this analysis is that the basic strategies in the prisoners' dilemma which are played as a consequence of meta-strategies 7 and 14 (and in particular 14) are the cooperative ones. This has led one or two commentators (notably Anatol Rapoport) to refer to metagames as providing 'The' solution to the prisoners' dilemma, though it does not solve the chicken game as satisfactorily (Rapoport 1967). For reasons discussed throughout this chapter, this seems extravagant, though it is not to deny the interest and fruitfulness of this theoretical approach.

The core of the metagame analysis is that the choice in a play of the prisoners' dilemma is conditional on the choice of the rival. This involves having some expectation (a deliberately vague phrase) about what the choice of the rival is going to be. In the case of the supergame this is not conceptually problematic. A player deduces the meta-strategy from past play. TIT-FOR-TAT, or any other strategy, can be an observed feature of play in a sequence of individual plays of the game. However, there has been a lot of controversy about the meaning of this analysis as far as the one-shot prisoners' dilemma is concerned. Howard argues that the principles apply to the one-shot game (Howard 1969, 1970), though others are sceptical (Harris 1969a and b, 1970). The issue fundamentally concerns what is meant by a conditional strategy in a one-shot game. If I do something which is conditional on some other event, then either the event must have taken place or I must have reliable evidence that it will take place. There must be a credible commitment, or at least some reason for belief. If the two players both commit themselves to a meta-strategy, then this combined commitment will generate a solution in the case of the one-shot game. Thus, if the game is such that both players submit their rules to a referee then one can reasonably assume that the solution would be as indicated in the metagame analysis. Further this is more secure than submitting a commitment to a simple strategy. If two parties submit a simple strategy in the prisoners' dilemma then the dilemma still remains, as it is rational for both parties to submit the defect strategy. For this to be a solution to the prisoners' dilemma, however, it does need some procedure for both players to know that the rival has made a commitment. The intriguing thing is that each does not need to know the actual commitment made. The obvious interpretation of the way of making such commitments is to assume a referee, but there may be others.

A weakness at the conceptual level is the asymmetry in the meta-strategies. The metagame illustrated above is the *ab*-metagame. In this the equilibria and indeed solutions come out quite reasonably, but it is not at all clear why it should be this rather than the *ba*-metagame. The basic prisoners' dilemma from which this starts is symmetrical and either there must be some assumption at some stage of asymmetry or alternatively the participants must agree, explicitly or tacitly, to act asymmetrically. No principle of asymmetry is produced despite its significance in the theory. The asymmetry is a necessary feature of the analysis in the case of the one-shot prisoners' dilemma as otherwise the principles of choice such as TIT-FOR-TAT are left *in vacuo* without being tied down to either a *C* or a *D* strategy option. One can argue that, while symmetry has an appeal in mathematical analysis, 'real life' is not particularly symmetrical. In many actual situations an asymmetry will be more relevant than symmetry. While it may be inelegant to arbitarily introduce an asymmetry into the analysis, it does not thereby mean that the solution might not be just as interpretable as the symmetrical case.

In the case of the supergame these problems do not exist. It is possible to give meaning to the strategy of TIT-FOR-TAT without any problem providing one is willing to assert a starting point for play ('benevolent' TIT-FOR-TAT starts with *C* and 'malevolent' TIT-FOR-TAT starts with *D*). However, in this case both parties can use TIT-FOR-TAT and the distinctive feature of the metagame analysis disappears.

While metagame analysis is not without its problems, it is clearly very insightful. The whole idea of introducing meta-strategies is of great significance, a significance which is also emphasised by the work of Axelrod which can be interpreted in meta-strategy terms (though I suspect neither Howard nor Axelrod would particularly like this interpretation). The two analyses approach the problems from very different points of view, which gives added significance to the crucial role that TIT-FOR-TAT plays in both of them.

8   The analysis of options: the Suez crisis

A convenient way of representing situations with a large number of outcomes has been developed in the context of metagame theory and is known as the analysis of options (Fraser and Hipel 1984). As it stands it is merely a method of arranging problems and as such is a mathematical picture. It is a convenient way of arranging things not only for metagame analysis but for any other sort of analysis in the game theoretic tradition, which is useful even if one is sceptical of the merits of metagame analysis as such.

It is convenient to explain the technique in terms of an example. I shall give a simplified version of the Suez crisis of 1956. I do not pretend that this is an analysis which will confound all previous analyses and from now on will prove definitive. It is a simplified account to explain a technique, but in a manner which should illustrate its much richer potentialities for the analysis of this and other conflict situations.

Let us simplify this by supposing that the Egyptian government had two classes of options available, the nationalisation of the Suez Canal and the act of military confrontation with Israel. For the sake of the example, and not because they are seen as the only logical or practical possibilities, suppose these two classes are themselves divided up in a binary manner. Thus the Suez Canal could either have been nationalised or not nationalised, with no intermediate possibility, and similarly the military options could have either been taken or not taken. If we denote by 0 the option of not carrying out the policy and by 1 the option of carrying out the policy then there are four options available to the Egyptian Government represented by:

Nationalise the canal	0	1	0	1
Military confrontation	0	0	1	1

Similarly the British and French governments (which for convenience I shall assume operated as a single unit) also have two classes of options, using economic pressures or sanctions or military attack. These can likewise be represented as:

Military attack	0	1	0	1
Economic pressures	0	0	1	1

In this simplified case these represent sixteen combinations of acts and are represented below. The reason for naming the bottom row, 'decimal equivalent' is explained later.

Egyptian options

Nationalise canal	0	1	0	1	0	1	0	1	0	1	0	1	0	1	0	1
Military confrontation	0	0	1	1	0	0	1	1	0	0	1	1	0	0	1	1

British/French options

Attack	0	0	0	0	1	1	1	1	0	0	0	0	1	1	1	1
Economic measures	0	0	0	0	0	0	0	0	1	1	1	1	1	1	1	1
Decimal equivalent	0	1	2	3	4	5	6	7	8	9	10	11	12	13	14	15

Clearly any strategy pair can be listed as a vector of zeros and ones, and its consequences likewise. Thus, taking column 9 as an example and starting from the bottom we can write an outcome as (1,0,0,1). A more convenient way of representing this consequence is to consider the column of zeros and ones not as a vector but as a number written in binary form, that is as (1001). It will be remembered that a binary number system is one in which any place can be occupied by one of only two symbols, 0 and 1, unlike the decimal system in which any of ten symbols can fill any particular slot. To translate a binary system into the conventional decimal system we proceed as follows. The right hand digit in a binary number is either 0 or 1, the next to the right hand number is 2×0 or 2×1, the third number is $2^2 \times 0$ or $2^2 \times 1$ and so on. To express the left hand number of a binary number of n digits into its equivalent decimal number we simply raise 2 to the power $n - 1$. Thus the number which in binary form is written as 1001 appears in decimal form as $(2^3 \times 1) + (2^2 \times 0) + (2^1 \times 0) + (2^0 \times 1) = 9$. This is the number in the row which I have called the decimal equivalent and which also stands in as the number of the column. Thus the outcome denoted by (1001) in binary numbers can be equally well be denoted by (9) in decimals. It would be disingenuous to pretend that I have not arranged the measures such that they come out neatly, though this is for clarity and not a requirement for the procedure to work.

Now the decimal equivalents (or indeed the binary forms) are only methods of labelling the columns and are in effect names. There is no way in which a number such as 1 has any sort of precedence over a number such as 5. In principle, we could carry out the procedure by labelling the columns in any way we wished, such as with the names of colours. This would be logically impeccable but practically perverse as it would make things more complicated, whereas the aim of this procedure is to provide a way of making some very complex situations more tractable.

The next stage is to examine the outcomes to see whether any of them can be excluded on the grounds of logical inconsistency or manifest implausibility. 'Manifest implausibility' should always be regarded with great care as it may well be that the more imaginative resolution of conflicts will involve attention to the superficially implausible. However, in the analysis of past conflicts in particular, some possibilities can be excluded as very unlikely. While the British government in particular was quite anxious to get rid of the Egyptian regime under Nasser, it seems unlikely that it would have actually carried out a military attack if the Egyptian government had made no positive move whatever. Hence, I shall exclude outcomes (4) and (12) from the analysis. While some of the rest might appear a little unlikely, it gets risky to exclude much else. Having done this we now wish to

49

examine the preference orderings of the two parties (still assumed to be monolithic unitary decision makers) over the set of alternatives. Using the notation as before of > to indicate preference, I suggest the following are plausible though not, of course, incontestable.

For Egypt:

$$(1) > (3) > (9) > (11) > (2) > (10) > (0) > (7) > (6)$$
$$> (5) > (8) > (15) > (14) > (13)$$

For Britain/France:

$$(8) > (0) > (13) > (14) > (15) > (5) > (6) > (7)$$
$$> (9) > (10) > (11) > (1) > (2) > (3)$$

Next we carry out a *stability analysis*. At this point we move beyond merely laying out the problem and introduce an assumption about behaviour. The main interest of this approach is nevertheless in the method of laying it out. In analysis in the theory of games tradition, a point is regarded as stable by one of the parties, if it is impossible for it to improve its position, on the assumption that its rival holds to its current strategy. A point is an equilibrium if, in a two party game, a point is stable by both parties. There is nothing in the definition of a non-zero sum game which requires an equilibrium to exist, nor a requirement that there should only be one if it does exist. Clearly it is important to search for such equilibria. Table 3.2 is a way of laying out the problem which makes the search relatively easy to carry out.

Arrange the alternatives in order of the actor's preference with the most preferred on the left. Beneath each alternative is listed the other alternatives which are preferred to the one at the head of the column and which the actor could achieve providing the rival did not alter his strategy. For convenience, I remove the brackets from around the names of the outcomes.

Table 3.2. *The stability analysis*

For Egypt:

1	3	9	11	2	10	0	7	6	5	8	15	14	13
	1		9	1	9	1		7	7	9		15	15
			3	11	3			6	11				14
					2					10			

For Britain/France:

8	0	13	14	15	5	6	7	9	10	11	1	2	3
	8				13	14	15	13	14	15	13	14	1
					5	6	7	4	6	7			
								9	10	11			

It is obvious that an outcome which is alone in its column is stable by the relevant party.

The stability analysis procedes as follows. Let us start with Egypt's most preferred outcome, 1. Now look for 1 in the preference ordering for Britain and France and find that it is unstable with respect to 13, 4, and 9 of which 13 is the most preferred. This in its turn is unstable by the points 15 and 14 in Egypt's ordering of which 15 is the most preferred. Further, by looking at the column which is headed by 15 we find there is nothing preferred to that outcome so it is stable for Egypt. Going back to the Britain/France table we find that 15 is alone there also and hence is stable for Britain and France as well. Thus, being stable by both parties, the point 15 is an equilibrium. An examination of the two tables shows that in fact it is the only equilibrium, though this is fortuitous. There has been nothing in the analysis which entails this uniqueness. It is also reassurring that this point is the one which actually occurred which is a modest confirmation of this interpretation.

As portrayed, the analysis of options and its attendant stability analysis is a clarificatory scheme which highlights some of the characteristics of the situation which would not be evident otherwise. It would be argued that the additional clarity is bought at the price of a great deal of effort, particularly as we admit that this portrayal of the Suez crisis is an excessively simple one. However, one of the big merits of this particular schema is that it can be complicated by the addition of additional strategies almost indefinitely and still be soluble, if necessary by computer. A complication of this problem means introducing more of the same, and is thus a computational problem not a conceptual one.

4 THE PROBLEM OF UNCERTAINTY: THE CONCEPTUAL ISSUES

1 Uncertainty in the international system

A glaring feature of the international system is that both actors and observers are all in considerable ignorance about what is going to happen next and in even greater ignorance about what might happen in the more distant future. In this it does not differ greatly from most other social systems where uncertainty is ubiquitous. However, decisions have to be made which have consequences in the future, but these consequences will be different or have different significances depending on other, as yet unknown, aspects of the future. Accordingly any theory of decision making has to consider the issue of uncertainty as crucial. This is not a point that decision theorists neglect. It is well-mined territory, and though the philosopher's stone has so far still eluded us, there is still some good quality ore which is worthy of attention. Of the large literature on risk and uncertainty, some has been applied, and much more is applicable, to the analysis of the international system. Because of the complexity of some of the significant issues which have been raised, I shall use this chapter primarily to describe some of the major conceptual aspects of the field as a preliminary to their application to the international system in Chapter 5. One issue to bear in mind in this, as in theories of other aspects of decision making, is the need for being clear between theories which *describe* conduct and those which *prescribe* conduct. In the description of the basics of the theory, these two aspects can be conflated, but it is important to distinguish between them when we come to make applications.

Whilst I shall deal with some issues of systemic uncertainty in Section 7, the core of this analysis concerns decision making. The central concepts are those of *probability* and *expected utility*. These are described in outline in the next section and in more detail in subsequent sections. Despite the apparent clarity of the mathematical formulations in this area, many of the conceptual problems of interpretation and application are both subtle and controversial. A crude application of the concepts can create far more confusion than clarification. The aim of this chapter is to develop the conceptual tool box, warning of dangers and controversies, such that the applications of the next chapter can be made with a clearer methological conscience.

2 An outline of the theory

I shall discuss the twin concepts of 'probability' and 'utility' which are central to the theory of decision making under risk and uncertainty, showing their intimate inter-relationship.

Probability is the basic concept which is used to express the degree of risk and uncertainty. At least in a loose sense this is a familiar notion in our culture in such forms as the 'odds' in a horse race or the 'chances' of getting two aces in a deal of cards. It is the measure of the likelihood of something happening. In some cases we can attribute a particular numerical value to it. Thus, if a die is thrown, the chance (or probability) of the three appearing on top is 1/6. One interpretation of this is to say that if a large number of die are thrown, that 'about' 1/6 of the throws will result in threes. Another interpretation is that it represents a degree of 'rational belief' that a three will be thrown on a particular occasion. These views are not incompatible. It is sometimes argued that probability, at least as defined here, is not applicable to single events and that the first of these interpretations is misconceived. I shall discuss this objection shortly. There is a significant way in which the odds of a particular horse winning a race differ from the chances of a particular result occurring with a die. With the die we have precise rules which generate the probability. In fact we have two. We can argue from the symmetry of the die or we can observe a large series of trials. We would hope that the two procedures would give the same result. In the case of a particular horse winning a race there are no such rules which give precise results. Different people might put different odds on a particular horse winning a race. This raises the issue of subjective probabilities which is the concern of Section 5.

The second central concept is utility. By explicitly focussing on the issue of uncertainty, the fact that a number of different outcomes might be the consequence of an act is emphasised. In choosing between acts, each of which has a range of possibilities with different probabilities, it becomes necessary to have some sort of valuation of the consequences of the acts. In a simple case there may be a choice between a highly valued outcome which is nevertheless unlikely to happen and a less valued outcome which is nevertheless highly probable. There is a trade-off between the desirability of an outcome to an actor and the likelihood of its eventuation. Utility, as discussed here, is a measure which can be used, at least in principle, to determine the strengths of these preferences.

For the sake of argument, suppose we have a unitary decision maker who is taking a decision under uncertainty in a non-strategic environment, that is, an environment in which the uncertainty is not due to the actions of specific individuals but to 'nature'. There are certain events and situations in the world that the decision maker prefers to others. It is clear that this is a characteristic of the individual, not the situations in question. Thus, a statement that 'Venice is preferable to Vienna' is meaningless unless we say in whose view this is true. This is unsurprising, but the similarity with subjective probability, where the issue is more often overlooked, is clearly close. Suppose we have an individual K and three states of the world, A, B, and C. K prefers A to B to C, relationships that we shall denote by $A > B > C$. The symbol '$>$' here stands for 'is preferred to'. Let us now use the notation $u(A)$ to indicate the utility of A which is in some sense the strength of preference. Thus $u(A) > u(B) > u(C)$ where the symbol '$>$' is now used to mean 'is greater than'. Any set of numbers which obey these rules will do as measures and such relationships are known as *ordinal measures*. Clearly we have so far added nothing, merely translating the information from one terminology to another. There have been no deductive arguments which have revealed anything novel. If we are to conceptualise the process of decision making more clearly, it is necessary to find some stronger measure than this purely ordinal one. The following procedure was suggested by Von Neumann and Morgenstern (1944) in one of the major classics of the social sciences, *The Theory of Games and Economic Behavior*. I initially present this utility measurement procedure in a simplified form where it is described in the form of a hypothetical experiment. It is not suggested that this experiment is a practical possibility except in rare and artificial circumstances. However, this is not the point. The problem before us is to define a measure in principle to show that such a measure is feasible and does not involve contradictions. It is primarily a procedure for clarifying our language and only rarely a device for producing data.

Suppose we start at point C, the least preferred of the positions. There are two choices before K. The first is to move to point B which he knows he can do without doubt. The second is to move to point A which he can only do with a probability p. If he fails then he will have to remain at C, an alternative with probability $(1 - p)$. Suppose now that the decision maker is unsure which choice to make, or, in the language of decision theory, he is _indifferent_ between the two. It seems appropriate to describe this as a situation where the utility of the outcomes is equal. The greater utility of A over B is damped down by the lower chance of success. If this is accepted then we can write

$$[u(B) - u(C)] = p.[u(A) - u(C)] \qquad (4.2.1)$$

This can be simply rearranged to read

$$p = [u(B) - u(C)]/[u(A) - u(C)] \qquad (4.2.2)$$

This gives us a measure for the relative size of the _intervals_.

There is still a lot which is arbitrary about this but we shall show that it has tightened up the measurement procedure more than might be thought at first. Let us suppose that in the choice situation $p = 0.5$. This is not an arbitrary figure but one which is determined by the situation (or, in most real cases, the observer's perception of the situation). Now let us _arbitrarily_ ascribe utilities of 1 and 0 to $u(B)$ and $u(C)$ respectively. We could attribute any number we wished providing only that the first was greater than the second. The numbers given make the interval $[u(B) - u(C)] = 1$. However, given this arbitrary ascription to $u(B)$ and $u(C)$ we are compelled by our procedure to give $u(A) = 2$. This is now no longer arbitrary but is a consequence of our rules. Suppose now that we had made $u(B) = 10$ and $u(C) = 5$, by the same argument $u(A) = 15$. However, the ratio of the interval $[u(A) - u(C)] : [u(B) - u(C)]$ would remain as $2:1$ as is clear from equation (4.2.2). This procedure has then determined the ratio of the two intervals to each other. For it to work it required that the decision maker was indifferent between the two possibilities. If he had not been indifferent then we could have only set up an inequality relationship between the two intervals. However, if this is transferred into the context of an idealised experiment, we can envision revising the probabilities and offering the new gambles until we found the probability for which the individual was indifferent between the two options.

In principle we can carry on deriving utility points in this way until we have sufficient observations for us to ascribe a _utility function_ to the individual, which enables us to predict his choices in situations of risk. The principles of choice which a decision maker must adopt for this sort of scheme to work are not unrealistic as I shall illustrate in Section 5.

3 Probability

While the interpretation of probability is controversial, the _calculus of probabilities_ is not. I shall explain the set of rules which a measure must follow if it is to be called a probability, and demonstrate the not always self-evident implications concerning the inter-relationships of probabilities. The lack of controversy persists only if the interpretations remain bland, for the calculus in itself involves simply the manipulation and rearrangement of various symbols.

First I shall pose the formal rules of the theory of probability. In this context it is convenient to regard a probability as a numerical value relating to the truth of some sentence. Thus $P(A) = 1/2$ is interpreted as 'the probability that the sentence A is true is $1/2$'. When there is no ambiguity, it is sometimes less ponderous to refer to 'the event A'. The sentence A must be one which can be true or false and might be, for example, 'The horse, "Red Rover" is the winner of the 2 o'clock race', a statement which will in due course become either true or false. Prior to this it can be said to be true with some degree of probability. The rules which follow are widely accepted and are not issues of controversy. I use the following notation. $P(A)$ is the probability of A; $P(\sim A)$ is the probability of 'not-A'. $P(A \cap B)$ denotes the probability of 'both A and B' and $P(A \cup B)$ denotes the probability of 'either A or B'. Rule 1. A probability is defined as a number between 0 and 1, where 1 is interpreted as indicating the relevant sentence is certainly true, and 0 is interpreted as being that the relevant sentence is certainly false. Suppose there are two events, denoted by A and B, the probabilities of their being true are thus

$$0 \leqslant P(A) \leqslant 1, \text{ and } 0 \leqslant P(B) \leqslant 1 \tag{4.3.1}$$

To take the interval $(0,1)$ is of course a pure convention, but it is convenient and nearly universal in mathematical work. In everyday speech it is also common to express probabilities as percentages where 'a 75% chance' can be interpreted as a probability of 0.75. An expression such as 'odds of 9 to 1 against' means that there are 9 possibilities of losing to 1 of winning which hence means that the probability of winning is 0.1 or 1/10 (not 1/9).
Rule 2. Suppose that A and B denote independent events in the sense that the probability of A is not affected by the occurrence or non-occurrence of B and vice versa. The probability of *both* A and B occurring is the probability of A multiplied by the probability of B. Thus

$$P(A \cap B) = P(A) \cdot P(B). \tag{4.3.2}$$

For example, suppose we toss a coin twice in succession. On 1/2 the number of occasions a head appears on the first throw. On a half of these occasions a head will also appear on the second throw, meaning that the number of occasions on which there will be two heads will be $1/2 \times 1/2 = 1/4$.

Rule 3. Again assuming independence (so the events are not exclusive), the probability of either A or B is the sum of their individual probabilities minus the probability of them both occurring together.

$$P(A \cup B) = P(A) + P(B) - P(A \cap B)$$

or, from Rule 2

$$P(A \cup B) = P(A) + P(B) - P(A).P(B) \qquad (4.3.3)$$

Taking away the last term is necessary as it is contained in both $P(A)$ and $P(B)$ and would be otherwise double counted. An example of this is when a gamble is offered in which the prize is paid if a head comes up in either of two separate throws of a coin. The probability of winning is thus $1/2 + 1/2 - 1/2.1/2 = 3/4$, which is the probability of each of the heads coming up separately minus the probability of them both coming up, in which case one of them is redundant as far as contributing towards success.

Now, while independence is an important concept, it is often the systematic relationship between events which is under analysis. We are commonly looking for patterns which involve dependence not independence. A lot of statistical testing takes the form of comparing data amongst which some interrelationships are suspected with some idealised 'random' (i.e. unsystematic) data. This is to check whether the data has genuine patterns in it, or whether the supposed patterns could be due to chance. If we are interested in the truth of some proposition we must look for information which alters the probability of it being true – that is information which is *not* independent of the final result. Here a crucial concept is *conditional probability*, which is the probability that something is the case given that some specific information is known to be true. The conditional probability that A will be the case if B is known to be the case is denoted by $P(A \mid B)$. If A is more likely to be the case if B is the case, that is, they are positively related, then $P(A \mid B) > P(A)$, and conversely if they are negatively related. The relationship between the conditional probability and the over-all probability is given by

$$P(A) = P(A \mid B).P(B) + P(A \mid \sim B).P(\sim B) \qquad (4.3.4)$$

That is, the probability of A is the probability that A is the case if B were to be the case, multiplied by the probability of B in fact being the case, plus the probability that A will be the case if $\sim B$ were to be the case (that is, B were *not* the case) multiplied by the probability of $\sim B$. We then investigate whether B is in fact the case or not, that is whether $P(B) = 1$ or 0. Formally speaking, all this does is break down the various components which go to making up the probability of A. It can be broken down further if more than the event A is deemed to be relevant to determining the probability of B. Clearly it is a tautology (as arguably are all mathematical statements), but it also provides a healthy procedure for analysing practical problems to ensure the internal consistency of beliefs. For example, suppose that the sentence whose truth is of interest is 'Country X will develop nuclear weapons at time T'. There are obviously many factors which could be taken into account. One of them, which would be generally regarded as relevant, would be the number of physics and engineering graduates working in the economy. Suppose that N is some threshold number such that if there are less than this number of graduates there is no possibility of building nuclear weapons. A crucial statement which we denote as B would be 'The number of physics and engineering graduates in X at time t (prior to T) is greater than N'. Let this have probability $P(B)$ of being true. According to these assumptions it follows that

$$P(A \mid \sim B) = 0$$

and hence

$$P(A) = P(A \mid B) . P(B) \tag{4.3.5}$$

Obviously the question is posed in a very over-simplified manner as there are many other factors affecting the probability of a state acquiring nuclear weapons. This complexity is not introduced by the mathematics but by the nature of the problem and is hence an argument for more, not less, systematic analysis.

The question of conditional probability, the question of how information effects probabilities, is clearly a crucial one. A brief elaboration of some of the issues involved is therefore worthwhile.

In the Diagrams 4.1A, 4.1B and 4.1C, the rectangles represent the set of possible events in the universe we are concerned with. The area A represents the probability of event A, and the area B represents the probability of event B. The area in which they overlap, the probability of A and B happening together, is denoted by $A \cap B$. The area comprising both A and B, that is the probability of either A or B is denoted by $A \cup B$. The final area of neither A or B is noted by $\sim (A \cup B)$.

In diagram 4.1A, the two areas are completely separate meaning that A and B cannot happen together. Hence, the knowledge that A is the case gives us complete knowledge that B is not the case. Thus

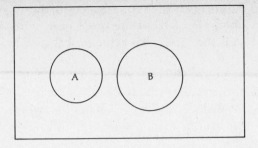

Diagram 4.1A

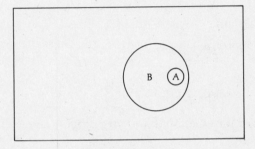

Diagram 4.1B

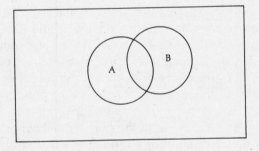

Diagram 4.1C

$P(A \mid B) = 0$ and $P(B \mid A) = 0$

In Diagram 4.1B, A is completely contained within B. Hence from a knowledge that A is the case we can say for certain that B is necessarily the case. Thus $P(B \mid A) = 1$. Naturally we cannot say the reverse, and without further information we can merely say that $0 < P(A \mid B) < 1$. If A and B completely coincide then the knowledge that one is the case gives us certain knowledge that the other is also the case.

The really interesting problems come when we consider Diagram 4.1C where the two sets overlap. The greater the degree of

59

overlap then the greater is the support of one of the hypotheses for the truth of the other. First look at the problem in purely visual terms. Suppose that A is the case, what is the probability that B will also be the case? Suppose that a quarter of A overlaps B then it would suggest that there was a probability of a quarter that B would also be true. Put more formally, the ratio of the over-lap to the total size of A is the conditional probability of B given A, or in other words

$$P(B \mid A) = P(A \cap B)/P(A)$$

or

$$P(B \mid A) \cdot P(A) = P(A \cap B) \tag{4.3.6}$$

By a similar argument we see that

$$P(A \mid B) \cdot P(B) = P(A \cap B) \tag{4.3.7}$$

and thus

$$P(A \mid B) \cdot P(B) = P(B \mid A) \cdot P(A) \tag{4.3.8}$$

This particular formulation is known as *Bayes Theorem*. Let us re-write it as

$$P(A \mid B) = P(B \mid A) \cdot P(A)/P(B) \tag{4.3.9}$$

In this form it emphasises that our rational belief about A on the evidence that B is the case is directly related to our belief about B on the evidence that A is the case. These beliefs are proportional, the proportion being dependent on the relative prior probabilities. It relates the prior probability of A, that is the probability without the evidence, to the posterior probability, the probability after the evidence has been gathered. To give an example: suppose that $P(A)$ is the probability of any individual in the population having a heart attack, and $P(B)$ is the probability of a randomly selected individual being over sixty. $P(A \mid B)$ is the probability of an individual having a heart attack given that they are over sixty, which is larger than the probability for the whole group $P(A)$. From this we can deduce $P(B \mid A)$ which is the probability that if we know that someone has had a heart attack he will be over sixty.

The crucial thing about Bayes Theorem is that is shows how the evidence for a proposition modifies our *prior beliefs* about an event and is not something absolute. Suppose that B is associated with A. Thus $P(B \mid A)$ is high, but $P(A \mid B)$ could still consistently be very low (depending, of course, on the other factors in the expression) if $P(A)$ were very low. Thus, even if very strong evidence, B, of a nuclear attack from Britain were received by the United States, it would still be regarded as very improbable in that it would only have increased a very low prior probability, $P(A)$.

Clearly there are numerous ways in which we can rearrange the relationships between the conditional probabilities of various sets. One further one is worth of comment. Take the particular case when the prior and the posterior probabilities of A with respect to B are equal, meaning that the two events are independent. From Bayes Theorem we can write

$$P(A \mid B) = P(A) . P(B \mid A)/P(B) \tag{4.3.10}$$

and hence, if $P(A \mid B) = P(A)$, then $P(B \mid A) = P(B)$ or in other words, if B is not evidence which alters the likelihood of A then neither is A evidence which alters the likelihood of B. Similarly, if B is evidence which increases (decreases) the probability of A, then A is evidence that increases (decreases) the probability of B. So, if $P(A \mid B) > P(A)$ then, $P(B \mid A) > P(B)$ which follows again directly from equation (4.3.10).

4 The interpretation of probability: subjective probability

While the calculus of probabilities may not be controversial, the interpretation of probability is deeply problematic. Much of the controversy revolves around the issue of whether probabilities can appropriately be regarded as degrees of belief in some sense. I shall consider three basic issues. The first is the vexed question of whether there is meaning to the concept of the probability of a single event. I shall argue this only briefly. Secondly, I consider the issues of objective and subjective measures of probability (the latter called by Savage *personalistic probability*) and in particular what we mean by subjective probability. Finally, there is the critical issue of how we evaluate new information relating to some issue. The rules which concern the inter-relations of different degrees of probability in response to the alteration of one of them are clear. What is less clear is whether some event should or should not affect our degree of belief in the truth of some statement; that is, whether it should be counted as evidence for or against. The issue of relevance depends on prior theories of the relevant processes and is not a problem within probability theory as such, though it is crucial for its application.

It is not in dispute that the probability of some event such as the occurrence of a head in the tossing of a coin can be interpreted as the relative frequency with which heads occurs in a long (in principle, infinite) series of throws of a coin. This is very helpful when talking about classes of events as in the case of most statistical analysis. Much of the statistical analysis of the international system consists of observed frequencies. Thus, if we want to know whether alliances tend to promote war or inhibit it, we compare the amount of war in situations when there were many alliances with the amount of war when there were few alliances (Singer 1968 has done a lot of work on alliances and the incidence of war). Clearly concepts such as 'alliances' and 'amounts of war' are more complex and more open to ambiguity than those of 'heads' and 'tails', but the principle is the same.

However, there is controversy over the relationship between a probability derived as a measure of relative frequency and a probability as a measurable degree of belief about particular single events. Thus, there is an argument that 'the probability of a single event' is a meaningless phrase, particularly if the single event is 'crucial' in the sense of being very important (Shackle 1952 and 1955). Thus, statistics about mortality in aircraft accidents rarely console the traveller who trembles on the end of the runway, concerned only with his own apparently imminent demise. The question is whether the nervous but rational traveller should be consoled by such statistics. I argue that he should.

This issue is of importance for many of the problems we must consider in that some measure of degree of belief about uncertain events, however obtained, is central to an analysis of decision making. I do not wish to add to the debate here, but merely offer the following example in favour of the view that there is meaning to the concept of a probability of a single event relevant to decision making. Suppose that we have a method of generating 'objective probabilities' such as blindly selecting a playing card from a pack.[1] If an individual is offered a choice between two gambles where gamble 1 consists of a prize £100 if the selected card is any club (that is, a probability of 1/4) and gamble 2 has the identical prize of £100 if the selected card is the ace of spades (probability 1/52). I assert that as a matter of fact it would be normal for gamble 1 to be chosen, and that in any case it should be recommended to anyone in doubt about his choice. Thus, I regard it as a principle of rational conduct as well as a description of actual behaviour. Even if the stakes were high and negative, I would still assert that the probability would be relevant. Thus, if the victim were to be shot according to which card were selected, but had a choice of

[1] I use 'objective' here to mean that there are a generally accepted set of rules which, when applied, produce the measure. I imply nothing more basic than this.

which principle to adopt, he would be well advised to choose that which had the lower probability, and in most cases would. From this I assert that at least in some situations a probability can stand in for a measurable degree of belief.

We should now look more closely at the measurement of probability. In relatively structured situations there are two different approaches to the measurement and hence to the definition of probabilities. First, are cases where a consideration of symmetry gives us reason for categorising the relative likelihood of various possibilities. Thus, in the case of a die, symmetry suggests that there is an equal chance of it falling on any of the six sides. The second approach is to throw a die a large number of times and observe the frequency with which the various possibilities appear. We use the second procedure when there is no principle of symmetry to appeal to. For example suppose we have a large class of observations, such as a population of human beings, some of whom have an attribute such as suffering from diabetes, and some who do not. The proportion of people who have diabetes can be defined as the probability of the next person I meet having diabetes. However we could not have deduced this from any principle of symmetry.

In the cases where it is possible to apply both procedures of measurement of probability one would hope that they would agree, but this is not guaranteed. Thus we must say which of these measures has precedence in the case of a disagreement. In the case of a sufficiently long run, the frequency criterion would take precedence in that one is less confident of symmetry than of deviations from the expected proportions. Thus one might be readier to accept that one had a biased coin than to consider that one had a proportion of heads to tails which would only occur once in a million sets of throws.

This perhaps makes clear the point that in describing how we will measure probability we are asserting a set of rules which both generate a number and which also *define* a concept of probability. The definition of the concept is inherent in the procedures of measurement. I am not suggesting that this is the only concept of probability, as will become clear in a moment, but this version of probability, which I shall call 'objective probability' is defined in this way. This notion of the definition of a measurable concept being implicit in the procedures of its measurement applies elsewhere. There are several definitions of 'power' depending on what devices are used to measure it. This point will be emphasised again when we come to talk of utility.

Probabilities determined by at least something approximating to the procedures defined above are relevant to some problems in international relations. In particular, probabilities concerning technical issues, such as the probability of detecting an underground nuclear test can be calculated by appeals to both frequency and symmetry. However, even if the argument concerning the interpretation of probability in the case of at least some singular events is accepted, we still run into the problem that the rules outlined above for deriving an 'objective' probability number are inapplicable to some important issues we come across in the study of the international system. Consider the following sentence: 'There will be a single common currency in the countries of the EEC by January 1 2010' which I shall call sentence S. I believe most observers would think that this is a possibility, which means that they would not attribute to the truth of the statement a probability of 0; conversely few people would regard it as certain and hence give it a probability of being true of 1. Any probability value would go somewhere in between. However, there is no obvious way in which either of the above rules could be applied to determining a probability value for the truth of this statement, though one would be loth to say that there was no possibility of giving some meaning to the probability of its truth. The problem then becomes: what is the meaning of a probability value attributed to the above statement, and how would it be determined? I suggest the following analysis which is essentially due to the classic work by L. J. Savage (1972, 2nd edn), though similar analyses are common. In such cases we cannot talk of the probability of the statement being true in isolation. The probability of the truth of the statement is an observation about the state of mind of the observer, not about the sentence S as such. Thus, any meaningful statement about the probability of the truth of the statement must contain reference to the observer and be of the form 'Jim Bloggs believes the statement S to be true with probability p.' This probability can be discovered by asking Jim Bloggs, but if we doubt his veracity or skill at introspection we can offer him a choice between two gambles. A prize is offered which is the same in two gambles. In gamble 1 the prize will be given if a coin falls heads for which we can say that the probability of winning is 0.5. In gamble 2 the same prize is offered if statement S turns out to be true (the prize to be paid on January 1, 2010 in both cases). If the decision taker chooses the gamble which is determined by the coin it implies that he believes that the conditions described by the statement S are likely to occur with a probability of less than 0.5. In principle we can offer gambles with different probabilities until we arrive with whatever precision we wish at his personal probability. This procedure depends on all interested parties agreeing that there is at least one event which gives an agreed or 'public' probability which can be used as a basis for comparison.

One obvious point is that individuals will normally differ in the personal probability they attribute to the truth of statements such as S. Because there is no external principle of measurement, there is no way of getting them to agree. One figure is not rational and another irrational. How significant differences of opinion are is an empirical matter. The decision taker will obey the rules of the probability calculus in relation to conditional probabilities as discussed above and elaborated below (though, if course, the actual decision maker may not be rational). However, the initial assessment of the probabilities will be a-rational in situations such as the above where there is no principle of either symmetry or relative frequency to appeal to. Two decision makers in identical situations and with the same evidence available may therefore differ in their views as to the likelihood of different events without either evaluating evidence irrationally.

I have made a distinction between objective and personal probabilities. It is related to a distinction which is sometimes made between 'risk' and 'uncertainty'. Risk is the situation where the probabilities are objective and the outcomes have probabilities associated with them determined by some agreed procedure. Uncertainty is where the probabilities are unknown or, as I would prefer to put it, personalistic or subjective. I prefer my characterisation of the problem in that it stresses the relationship of the observer to the problem. A more useful distinction is between those situations where the exclusive set of relevant distinguishable events is known to the observers and those where it is not. Events keep occurring in the international system which are surprising not because they have low probabilities attached to them but because no one has ever thought of them. The significance of the distinction between risk and uncertainty can easily be exaggerated. Decision making in the face of 'objective' probability distributions is a great rarity in most situations in social systems.

Even though there is no particular reason why two given individuals should have the same personal probability concerning some event, one would like to think that if new relevant information became available to both of them that they would adjust their probabilities in the same direction. Unfortunately this need not be the case.

The problem can be posed formally as follows. Denote the personal probability of individual A concerning the truth of S on evidence E as $P_a(S \mid E)$ and on evidence G in addition to E as $P_a(S \mid E, G)$. Is there a 'normal supposition' that, if $P_a(S \mid E, G) > P_a(S \mid E)$, then $P_b(S \mid E, G) > P_b(S \mid E)$? A simple example illustrates the case. Suppose we assert that a programme to build fall-out shelters (which, when it becomes known, is a piece of information to the observer) is a defensive act merely indicating a prudent desire not to be blown to bits should certain unfortunate events occur. If A holds this view and $P(S)$ is his probability of nuclear war, then such an act would certainly not increase it and might be held to decrease it. However, B may regard it as an offensive act, increasing a state's readiness for war and hence willingness to undertake it. In this case, such a piece of information will increase the subjective probability of the observer concerning the probability of nuclear war. Thus, the same piece of information can quite rationally move the beliefs of the observers concerning the probability of nuclear war in opposite directions. This is because they hold different theories concerning international behaviour and if they were to agree on the directions of the moves in probabilities they would have to first reach agreement on the more basic theories. I shall refer to the views of the world which determine the effect of given information on probabilities – including whether it is relevant information – as *schemas*. A schema is a set of presuppositions about how the world behaves. In some context these may be scientific theories in their full sense, and in others may be simply a set of prejudices. In this terminology, the view that the EEC is a Popish plot is a schema, though with little scientific standing. However, it would define the sort of evidence which would be deemed relevant to the probability of my earlier statement 'There will be a single common currency in the countries of the EEC by January 1, 2010. The election of a Pope with a Ph.D. in economics would mean that an adherent of the Popish plot schema would increase his personal probability of the truth of the statement, and, given his schema, would rationally do so. Most other observers, with their different schemes, would equally rationally regard the information as irrelevant and not alter their subjective probabilities.

This is a somewhat disappointing conclusion as subjectivity appears to reign supreme and we seem to be able to make few general 'objective' propositions. It confirms that simply an appeal to the 'facts of the case' even when these facts are not in dispute, is not sufficient when the underlying theories are different, for the same facts can have opposite implications.

5   The concept of utility

The definition of a utility function over some set of alternatives enables us to predict (in principle) or put in a conceptual framework (in practice) the choice of a decision maker between risky alternatives. In Section 2 we dealt with the simple case of three alternatives. In

66

principle we can extend this argument further and consider not just three but a whole range of alternatives which it becomes more convenient to represent by $x_1, x_2 \ldots x_n$. We can do repeated experiments and determine any utility interval in terms of any other. Having defined one interval we derive the rest. This is identical to saying that if we can define two points (subject to the ordering conditions) and derive the rest. It is therefore much more restrictive and hence more powerful than a purely ordinal relationship though it is weaker than some cardinal measures. This was illustrated in the example given at the very beginning. In the first example with the three alternatives A, B and C, I multiplied the initial interval by 5 and this left the measure unaffected. This is not a great restriction and is widespread. Length can be measured in metres, kilometres, miles or whatever. However, I also shifted the measure of $u(C) = 0$ to $u(C) = 5$ which is not something which would be possible in a measure of length where 0 is the same irrespectives of whether it is in miles or millimetres. In the measure of utility, the zero point is arbitrary. Such measures are referred to as *unique up to a linear transformation*, meaning that if $u(x)$ is a measure of utility over some set, then $a . u(x) + b$ is also a measure for any $a > 0$ and for any b whatever. Measures of temperature are of this form. Neither the units nor the zero points in centigrade and fahrenheit measures of temperature are the same. To derive fahrenheit measures (y) from centigrade readings (x) one uses the linear transformation $y = 180x/100 + 32$.

Consider a decision maker A, whose current situation is x_o which, following the above argument, we are entitled to define as $u(x_0) = 0$. He contemplates an act A with possible consequences x_1 and x_2 with associated probabilities of p_1 and p_2 respectively. I shall refer to this as a *lottery*. Using '&' to denote 'and' in a sentence such as, 'there are two exclusive alternatives, P and Q', the lottery will be denoted by

$$\{u[x_1] \ \& \ (1 - p)[x_2] \text{ and named } L(A_1) \tag{4.5.1}$$

The *mathematical expectation* of this is

$$p . u(x_1) + (1 - p) . u(x_2) \tag{4.5.2}$$

That is, the mathematical expectation is the sum of the utility values of the possible outcomes, each multiplied by their respective probability. This is also referred to as the *expected value* of the lottery. We pose the following rule. If the expected value of the lottery is greater than the utility of the existing position, then the lottery will be accepted and vice versa. That is

$$p . u(x_1) + (1 - p) . u(x_2) > u(x_0) = 0 \tag{4.5.3}$$

is the condition for accepting the lottery.

Now suppose A considers a second lottery named $L(A_2)$

$$\{q[x_1'] \;\&\; (1 - q)[x_2']\} \tag{4.5.4}$$

This is likewise chosen in favour of the status quo position if its expected value is greater than that of the status quo position. By a fairly obvious extension, $L(A_1)$ will be chosen in preference to $L(A_2)$ if its mathematical expectation is greater. That is, if

$$p \cdot (x_1) + (1 - p) \cdot u(x_2) > q \cdot u(x_1') + (1 - q) \cdot u(x_2') \tag{4.5.5}$$

This can readily be extended to lotteries containing any number of possible outcomes and to any number of possible lotteries. The decision maker chooses that lottery (which may be the null lottery of the status quo) which has the highest mathematical expectation.

The above is plausible, but we still need to establish the conditions under which it applies. The power of the Von Neumann and Morgenstern approach was that it provided a set of axioms, which can be interpreted as postulates of choice, from which it could be proved that a utility measure of the sort described above existed. I give an informal outline of these axioms below expressed informally as principles of choice. Three underlying postulates or rules of behaviour are assumed.

The first rule states that there must be a consistent ordinal ranking of preferences over the set of possible alternatives for there to be a cardinal measure. This is not a very surprising requirement.

Rule 1. Given a set of alternatives, $(x_1 \, x_2 \ldots x_n)$ a decision maker must have a transitive preference ordering over them. Remembering that $>$ stood for 'is preferred to and introducing $=$ to stand for 'is indifferent to' this means that if

$$x_i > x_j \text{ and } x_j > x_k \text{ then } x_i > x_k \text{ for all } i, j \text{ and } k.$$

Similarly if $x_j = x_k$ then x_k can be substituted for x_j in any ordering relationship without affecting any other orderings. That is

$$\text{if } x_i > x_j \text{ and } x_j = x_k \text{ then } x_i > x_k$$

The second rule states that lotteries can be formed. In practice this is a parallel to the first requirement that the decision maker must have a clear idea of preferences, now extended to saying that the decision maker must have a clear idea of probabilities.

Rule 2. Suppose we take three alternatives $x_i \, x_j$ and x_k ranked $x_i > x_j > x_k$. A probability p must exist, which is unique, for which

$$\{p.[x_i] \, \& \, (1-p)[x_k]\} = \{1.(x_j)\} \qquad (4.5.6)$$

The final rule effectively states that decision makers do not have any probability preference; they do not over-weight certain probabilities such as 0.5, giving them more than proportional significance as against small probabilities.

Rule 3. Suppose a lottery with fixed prizes is offered to a decision maker. One of the prizes in the initial lottery is then replaced with the entry ticket to a new lottery. For example, the money outcome paid for a successful bet in a horse race is replaced with a bet on another horse race. If the decision maker has already determind that he is indifferent between betting and not betting in the second lottery, this replacement should make no difference to his preference ordering. Formally this reads

Suppose that
$$\{p.[x_i] \, \& \, (1-p)[x_j]\} = M \text{ and } \{q.[M] \, \& \, (1-q)[x_k]\} = N$$
then
$$\{q.p.[x_i] \, \& \, q.(1-p).[x_j] \, \& \, (1-q).(1-p).[x_k]\} = N \quad (4.5.7)$$

Note that in this combined gamble $q.p + q.(1-p) + (1-p)(1+q) = 1$ meaning that one of the outcomes has to happen.

It is widely agreed that this last assumption is the most restrictive of the three in that if it were violated it would be the least offensive to our intuitive feelings of what should be appropriate rules for decision making. Indeed there is some experimental evidence which suggests that it is frequently violated. The first two seem more obvious and certainly the transitivity rule does seem a fairly reasonable requirement for even minimally rational decision making.

However, even if we suppose that the requirements for the cardinal utility function are met in experimental situations, what possible use is this in the analysis of decision taking in the international system or in any other social system? The answer is that it legitimises the use of the concept of utility in analysis. Utility has been slipped into a number of arguments surreptitiously already in this book. This is legitimate only because it is possible to show that a utility function can be derived in principle even if its measurement in practice is not feasible. If decision takers systematically violate the Von Neumann-Morgenstern axioms then the use of a utility function, at least of the sort described here, is illegitimate in that an analysis based upon it must involve contradictions. If behaviour does conform to the Von Neumann-Morgenstern axioms sufficiently closely for the expected utility analysis to be a legitimate tool, then at least two useful procedures are opened up.

First, on the basis of much weaker evidence than that which would give a direct measure, we are entitled to speculate about the shape of the utility function. Thus we might argue that over a particular region the utility function of an individual with respect to money is concave (that is, 'bends upwards') meaning that he would accept bets at unfair odds. While the observation about betting habits can obviously be done without the utility analysis, and doubtless has been throughout history, the interpretation of it in utility terms depends on us accepting the analysis, and in particular the postulates, as described. If we deny the postulates of utility theory while using the language, then we are involved in contradictions, unless we are prepared to posit a further set of postulates about behaviour in which such statements could meaningfully be made. Secondly, and perhaps more significantly, if we accept the legitimacy of utility measures in principle, then we are entitled to use indicators of utility in analyses even though direct measures are not practicable. Indicators are widely used in statistical work in that frequently there is a variable which is difficult or expensive to observe directly. However, if we have a secondary theory which suggests that this variable is closely correlated to some other more readily observable variable then we can use this indicator as a stand-in for the underlying variable. Thus, in his study of war initiation, Bueno de Mesquita (1981) uses an expected utility model. As he cannot get direct measures of either probability or utility, he uses indicators. Regarding utility as relative utility between two actors, the indicator of this relative utility is the similarity of alliance patterns between the two. If state A has alliances with exactly the same states as B, then the utility to A is defined as 1, whereas if they are all different the utility is defined as -1, with numbers in between for varying degrees of agreement. Probability, meaning the probability of winning a war, is indicated by an adjusted relative power index. The use of indicators in such a context is legitimised by the above arguments, given the tacit assumption that the decision makers analysed by Bueno de Mesquita follow the above rules of behaviour with respect to these indicators.

These procedures may seem to legitimise what the uncharitable might regard as Bare-Faced Benthamism. Numbers measure utilities, apparently in the full spirit of the felicific calculus. This is not so, however. The choice of the word 'utility' is misleading for this rather narrowly defined concept which is used to conceptualise behaviour under conditions of risk. However, it has no necessary interpretation beyond that and should not be understood as a successful measure of a Benthamite utility in the sense of 'that property in any object, whereby it tends to produce benefit, advantage, pleasure, good or happiness' (Bentham 1823). Because of the first assumption from which the Von Neumann-Morgenstern utility was derived, namely that there has to be a consistent transitive preference ordering, it is to be supposed that the two different concepts of utility are ordinally related to each other, but not that a Benthamite utility is measured in a cardinal sense by these procedures.

6 Experts' probability judgements

Governmental decision makers confront a vast array of problems on which they cannot hope to be personally particularly knowledgeable. In consequence they have experts to advise them. The problem of uncertainty does not disappear with the appointment of an expert. All the expert can do is give his probability judgement to the decision maker, and let him evaluate it as he wishes. The problem is how to evaluate the advisor, on the assumption that the advisor is not omniscient.

In the case of a single advisor there are no acute conceptual problems. The decision maker can simply adopt the expert's own probability judgements. If the expert has systematic biases in his judgements, then his estimates can be *reliable* even if they are not *accurate*. Thus, if an advisor is of an obsequious disposition and constantly over-estimates the probability (determined, somehow, 'objectively') of the outcome most preferred by the decision maker by 20%, then the decision maker can easily adjust the advisor's probability appropriately. Notice that a description such as 'An advisor is 50% reliable' is extremely ambiguous. It could mean that, if an advisor asserts confidently that something will happen, it will in fact do so on half the number of occasions. This would be the commonsense interpretation of this. Another interpretation is applicable to a situation where there are long sequences of events of two categories, one with a 0.9 probability of success (unambiguously defined) and one with a 0.1 probability of success. The advisor is giving judgements concerning into which of the two categories an event will fall. In this case the concept of a 50% reliability is meaningful. This might be applicable to an advisor on horse races or football scores where there are long sequences of relevant events. Indeed it could be refined, and another concept, the costs of error, brought in. However, it is only appropriate where there is some objective check on the reliability of the advisor, this being rare in international relations. Where the pure personalistic probability interpretation is appropriate, such assertions about an observer's reliability are meaningless, or at best a figure of speech.

The problems arise when there are several advisors who give different probability assessments (French 1984). If we assume that the decision maker is going to take notice of all the advisors then some principle of averaging has to be adopted. The two commonest forms of average are the arithmetic mean and the geometric mean. If there are n advisors the first is

$$P = \alpha_1 p_1 + \alpha_2 p_2 + \ldots \alpha_n p_n \qquad (4.6.1)$$

$$\sum_1^n \alpha_i = 1$$

The α are the weights which are given to the different observers by the decision maker. No point of principle is involved in making them equal, so it is simpler to use

$$P = \sum_1^n p_i/n \qquad (4.6.2)$$

This is known as a *linear opinion pool*. The geometric mean, with equal weighting for all experts is

$$\pi = \sqrt[n]{p_1 \cdot p_2 \ldots p_n} \qquad (4.6.3)$$

This is known as a *logarithmic opinion pool*. I shall deal in detail with the problems involved in the first, but comment in less detail about the problems of the second.

For exposition I shall take a gambling illustration. Two horses, Alpha and Omega are running in two separate races on different days. Two racing tipsters are called in to advise on the probabilities of the two horses winning. Both tipsters are agreed that the events are totally independent, so that knowledge that one of the horses had in fact won (or lost) its race would leave their assessments of the probability of the other winning unaffected. However, they disagree on the probabilities involved. These are illustrated in Table 4.1.

Table 4.1.

	Tipster 1	Tipster 2
Probability Alpha winning	0.8	0.1
Probability Omega winning	0.75	0.5

Table 4.2A. *Tipster 1*

	Omega wins	Omega loses	
Alpha wins	0.6	0.2	0.8
Alpha loses	0.15	0.05	0.2
	0.75	0.25	

Table 4.2B. *Tipster 2*

	Omega wins	Omega loses	
Alpha wins	0.05	0.05	0.1
Alpha loses	0.45	0.45	0.9
	0.50	0.50	

Table 4.3. *Arithmetic mean of the Tipsters' joint probabilities*

	Omega wins	Omega loses	
Alpha wins	0.325	0.125	0.45
Alpha loses	0.3	0.25	0.55
	0.625	0.375	

Given that both tipsters assert that these events are independent and, being successful gambling men, they understand about the calculus of probabilities, they will then accept the legitimacy of the probabilities of joint events (see Tables 4.2A and 4.2B).

The top left hand box of Tipster 1's table is derived by multiplying his probability of Alpha winning, 0.8, by his probability that Omega will win, 0.75. This gives the probability that both will win. The other entries are obtained analogously. Now take the arithmetic mean of these joint probabilities and put them in a joint table (4.3), deriving from these the marginals (i.e. the sums of the joint events to give the probabilities of one or other horse winning or losing).

A most unwelcome conclusion stands out. The probabilities of the various joint events no longer indicate independence. From Table 4.3 it is glaringly clear that Alpha is much more likely to win if Omega wins than if it loses, which is directly against our assumption that the events are independent.

A more abstract presentation, though more relevant to international relations, gives no more cheer. Experts on the international system are likely to be experts on particular aspects where the events are unlikely to be independent. For apparently independent events there will be separate experts. Let us assume we have two experts A and B in the Star Wars programme, and two experts on European Monetary Integration, C and D. A statement is proposed: 'By the year 2010 a 'Star Wars' umbrella of the sort currently conceived will be in place over the United States.' Strategic expert A gives this a probability of being true of p and expert B gives it a probability of q. Another statement is proposed namely: 'A central bank will be in existence in Europe by the year 2010'. All the experts agree that these statements refer to independent events in the sense that the truth or otherwise of one does not affect the truth of the other. Experts C and D give this a probability of r and s respectively. The experts are now teamed up, to form the AC team and the BD team, who might be from rival 'think tanks'. (The teams, in fact, need not be explicitly formed. It is a way of considering the various probabilities). The joint probability table of the AC team is as shown in Table 4.4 and that of the BD team is as in Table 4.5.

Table 4.4. *Expert team AC: predictions for 2010*

	European Central Bank	No European Central Bank	
SDI works	pr	$p(1-r)$	p
SDI does not work	$(1-p)r$	$(1-p)(1-r)$	$(1-p)$
	r	$(1-r)$	

Table 4.5. *Expert team BD: predictions for 2010*

	European Central Bank	No European Central Bank	
SDI works	qs	$q(1-s)$	q
SDI does not work	$(1-q)s$	$(1-q)(1-s)$	$(1-q)$
	s	$(1-s)$	

Table 4.6.

	European Central Bank	No European Central Bank	
SDI works	qs	$q(1 - s)$	q
SDI does not work	$(1 - q)s$	$(1 - q)(1 - s)$	$(1 - q)$
	s	$(1 - s)$	

Calculating the arithmetic mean of these joint probabilities and then adding to get the marginals we have Table 4.6.

For the joint probabilities to retain independence, it requires that the ratio of each of the terms in the three columns are the same. Compare the final column of the marginals and the second column under 'No European Central Bank'. This can be arranged as

$$[(p + q)]/[(1 - p) + (1 - q)] \text{ in relation to}$$
$$[(p + q) - (rp + qs)]/[(1 + p) + (1 - q) - (1 - p)r - (1 - q)s]$$

These ratios will be the same if they also equal

$$[(pr + qs)]/[(1 - p)r + (1 - q)s]$$

which will be the case only if $r = s$. By an equivalent argument the ratio of the two entries in the first column will also be consistent if $p = q$. These conditions would make the problem trivial. If the probability judgements of the experts are different, then the linear pool means that the independence assumption has to be abandoned, which is absurd. This is a severe conclusion, as the simple arithmetic average would seem to be intuitively the most natural of amalgamation methods. It is clearly grossly inadequate.

The logarithmic pool looks rather more hopeful as an amalgamation device. I will not demonstrate it here but, by an analogous form of analysis, it can be shown not to suffer from the false dependence which mars the linear pool (French 1984). Unfortunately it has another severe drawback. It has been proved that, if the pool is to involve more than four independent events, then it is dictatorial. That is, the views of just one of the experts become those of the pool. This is perhaps not so damning as the problem with the linear pool, though it makes the point of having a pool in the first place somewhat redundant.

These objections are rather disturbing. The question of how to take into account the differing probability views of experts is an issue in any decision problem, from investing in the stock market on the basis of the newspaper pundits to international relations, where it is crucial. Unfortunately I cannot produce any solution that surmounts these problems, and to date I am not aware of anyone who has. It is an active field of research and hopefully some more satisfactory method will be discovered shortly.

7 Systemic uncertainty

While the emphasis in this book is on uncertainty as an aspect of decision making, it is useful to consider briefly whether we can measure the degree of uncertainty in a system. Intuitively there appears to be some meaning in affirming such statements as, 'There is more uncertainty in a system at time t than at time T'. The problem is whether this can be put into a more rigorous framework. The literature on this mainly comes from information theory, and has been eagerly seized on in other disciplines such as psychology. The concepts have been applied in the study of international relations, though perhaps less than one might have imagined.

Uncertainty can be looked at as the opposite of information. The

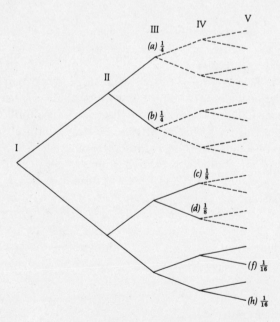

Diagram 4.2

more information we have the less uncertainty there is. This suggests that a measure of the degree of uncertainty is the amount of information we would need to get certainty. On this view, if we can measure one we can measure the other. A widespread measure is as follows. Suppose we have a decision tree where each decision path involves four nodes, and there are two alternatives at each node. There are thus 16 possible ending points, as illustrated in the Diagram 4.2 in which we consider both the continuous and the broken lines. If we know nothing else about the system, then they are all equally likely. If at the first node we receive the information that the choice was the left path, L, then we have reduced the number of possibilities to 8, that is by a half. There is a clear sense in which this is a reduction in uncertainty by a half. I do not claim that this is the only concept of uncertainty, but it is a definition which conforms with one's intuitive understanding. A piece of information which reduces the level of options by a half is regarded as the basic unit of information and is known as a *bit*. If we return to the tree, at the second step the information that the R alternative was taken reduces the possible outcomes to 4 and once more provides a further 'bit' (in the technical sense) of information. By going further we see that we require the answers to four questions to decide uniquely on the ending point, or in other words, four 'bits' of information. This can be used as the measure of the degree of uncertainty, that is

$$U = \log_2 16 = 4 \qquad (4.7.1)$$

In general, if there are k possible ending points which are equally probable, the measure of uncertainty is

$$U = \log_2 k \qquad (4.7.2)$$

While there is a convenience in using a logarithmic measure, there is no particular reason for it to be to the base 2, other than that doubling and halving seem in some sense 'natural' operations. More importantly, this has become the standard convention, so the 2 will be omitted from now on.

This can easily be reinterpreted in probability terms. The probability of a particular outcome being the case is $p = 1/k$. Hence

$$U = \log (1/p) = -\log p \qquad (4.7.3)$$

The 'bit' is defined in terms of equally probable alternatives. This is very restrictive as far as international systems are concerned, but fortunately we can expand the concept. Suppose we take the part of the Diagram 4.2 which is represented by the continuous lines. Assuming there is an equal probability of taking L or R at each fork, the probability that it will arrive at point (a) at stage III is 1/4, as it is with point (b). Points (c) and (d) at stage IV have probabilities of 1/8 each and the remaining four points at stage V have probabilities of 1/16 each. It requires only two 'bits' of information to determine the outcome if the system is in fact at one of the top two points, but four 'bits' to get to one at the bottom. To get a measure of the uncertainty of the system as a whole we need a concept of *average uncertainty*. For this we consider each of the outcomes, taking its uncertainty measure $-\log p$. This is then weighted by the uncertainty, p, of its occurring giving $-p \cdot \log p$. These are then averaged, which, as $\Sigma p_i = 1$, appears as a summation, namely

$$U = - \sum_{1}^{n} p_i \cdot \log p_i \qquad (4.7.4)$$

In the case of the example given above this comes to 2.75 'bits'.

This analysis relates to reasonably well structured systems with an exclusive list of the possible states of the system, such that there is some reasonable basis of attributing probabilities to each of the possible states. While a clearly defined system as described above is as unlikely as the precise model of an international situation, there is no reason why it may not be an approximation to various subsystems over limited periods of time. For example, McLelland (1968) has used this methodology to analyse the intermittent crisis over the access to Berlin between 1948 and 1963. Instead of states of the system, actions such as 'protest', 'reject', 'accuse', were taken as the phenomena to be analysed. Actions were divided into eighteen different categories (equivalent to system states). The frequency with which they occurred was taken as the probability, p, and the average uncertainty was computed on an annual and monthly basis. This statistic, as would be expected, shows systematic variation between crisis and non-crisis periods, though rather less so than the actual volume of interactions. It is obvious that to interpret the theoretical concepts in practical terms, approximation is necessary. Even the categorisation into eighteen possibilities is an arbitrary process. However, this is a general issue in all applied mathematics. The interpretation of a concept in the external world does not correspond exactly to the mathematical concept (Körner 1960). The problem is whether the approximation is sufficiently close. The assumption of an ongoing subsystem would seem quite proper in this particular case.

There are two comments about the use of this methodology. First, I have referred to 'uncertainty' as is conventional in this field. However, in other discussions of risk and uncertainty, the concept discussed here would more often be regarded as risk. The probabilities are intended to be 'objective' in the sense of being generated by explicit procedures and known to all observers, though of course the appropriateness of the procedures could be queried. The uncertainty measure is thus different from the subjective or personalistic probabilities which are the main subject of this chapter. Secondly, this is an analysis of systemic properties. While one would expect the uncertainty within the system as defined here to be related to the perceived uncertainty of the actors, it is not necessarily the same. It is a useful technique for looking at systemic behaviour, and, as a remote approximation, as a tool for looking at individual behaviour. However it does not provide objective measures of uncertainty which can be used in the decision models which are central to the rest of the discussion in this and the next chapter.

5 UNCERTAINTY IN THE INTERNATIONAL SYSTEM: APPLICATIONS

1 The probability of nuclear war

The most frightening question facing the world is whether there will be a nuclear war. Despite the capacity for mutual annihilation which has existed between the super-powers since about the nineteen sixties, along with the capacity and general belief that this would involve the annihilation of everyone else, this has not so far happened. The non-appearance of a nuclear war has caused some people to be sanguine and argue that, though the situation is distasteful, it works, and because it has worked for so long it can be expected to carry on working. (Garden 1985, Howard 1983). A less sanguine argument is as follows. Conceding that the probability of nuclear war is low in any given year, the deterrent system appears to be a more or less permanent feature of the international system and may still be in place as an institution, if not with the same techniques, in a century or more. By the cumulation of probabilities argument a very low probability per trial (in this case a period of time) can become a large probability over a long period of time. Hence, unless the probability of war is actually zero in each year, the presumption of near permanency to the nuclear situation means that over a sufficiently long period this probability becomes very high – perhaps approaching certainty – a point originally made by Quincy Wright (1942) and Deutsch (1978). I shall discuss this argument in the light of the previous discussions of probability.

Clearly the probability of nuclear war is an inherently subjective probability. There is no procedure for working out what it is, and no amount of research will reveal such a procedure. Thus, there are as many different probabilities of nuclear war as there are people who care to think about it. As stressed in the last chapter, the heading of this section is meaningful in a strict sense only if we say whose probability we are talking about. However, that probabilities are subjective does not mean that they are completely arbitrary. To assume this would be to assert that there was no such thing as relevant evidence and that probabilities were indicative only of our emotional state. Given that one has a theory of some process – in this case the outbreak of nuclear war – then there is evidence which will make an observer either increase or decrease his probability of its occurrence. For example, if it were found that the operational rules of a nuclear state prescribed nuclear response for relatively minor military set-backs, then this would be held by most people to increase the probability of a nuclear war.

In an early paper on the probability of nuclear war, I. J. Good (1966) argued that the probability of a war could be derived from considering a distribution of those points when the international system had approached close to nuclear war, and extrapolating this distribution to the points beyond which nuclear war would have occurred. The information for this would probably only be available in the secret files of the nuclear powers and it is unlikely that the whole of it would be known to any individual. Good accepts that the extremities of a distribution often behave 'improperly', in that factors which are negligible in the main distribution are significant at its extremities. This is simply stating what is obvious from this technique, that it would be an extrapolation of an empirical distribution. It also assumes that we accept that whatever criterion of 'nearness' is adopted it is the appropriate one. In its turn this means accepting a common theory of possible war causation. However, it is a method of systematising thought, surely a commendable goal.

We can also go and ask the 'experts'. Unfortunately, in a case such as nuclear war, the experts will not agree. Press's analysis (1984) of the views of 185 'experts' or 'neo-experts' concerning the probability of nuclear war gave results which varied considerably from each other, and were justified by appealing to a wide variety of different consider-ations. This suggests that their implicit (and sometimes explicit) theories about the causation of war were very different. The prob-abilities of many were also disconcertingly high for the decade 1980–90 for which they were asked their opinions. As suggested earlier, in such situations we should regard these expert views, amalgamated by whatever procedure, as data which are relevant but not decisive, in much the same way as we may regard the views of the critics before going to an art exhibition.

Now the probability of a nuclear war is an extreme case of the probability of a single crucial event. Let us consider the problem in terms of the probability of a nuclear war sometime during the next century starting from now. I take a century as this is a long period but

81

not too long to understand imaginatively as distinct from purely intellectually. Amongst the richer nations, the children of a baby born today might reasonably hope to be still alive at the end if all goes well. During the next hundred years a nuclear war will either happen or not happen, and if it happens it will happen only once. Unlike earthquakes, where we can have repeats, there is no question of it happening in $x\%$ of the years. Hence there is no possible frequency interpretation of probability. Likewise there is no appeal to symmetry which will enable us to derive a probability. If the earlier arguments about degree of belief are accepted, this should leave us unperturbed. However, the argument that a degree of belief in a single crucial event behaves like a probability is put to its most extreme test in this case. Let us shorten the time span to two years. Suppose that I believe that it is possible but unlikely that a nuclear war will occur in year 1 and similarly in year 2. From this it seems to me obvious that I believe that it is more likely that it will occur in either year 1 or 2 than in 1 on its own. If this is accepted, and I find it difficult to see how it can be doubted, then we are already a long way to accepting the applicability of something like a probability as a degree of belief, which we notice is independent of the unpleasantness of the event. If r were to be the probability of war in year 1, and s the probability in year 2, then, if degrees of belief were to follow the probability calculus, the probability of the war in either year 1 or year 2 would be $r + (1 - r)s$. Thus the probability of there not being a war in either year is

$$1 - [r + (1 - r).s] = (1 - r)(1 - s) \tag{5.1.1}$$

Whether in fact the psychological probability does follow this rule, particularly if it is over a large number of years, I hesitate to say, but I reaffirm the position asserted in the last chapter that it ought to do so as a principle of rational belief. This paragraph is a reiteration of some of the arguments made earlier, but now in its toughest context.

It is easy to extend the argument above to a large number of independent events. If there are two events with probabilities q_1 and q_2 then the probability of both occurring is $q_1 . q_2$. In the last paragraph, the event which 'occurred' was the non-occurrence of nuclear war. By extension the probability of a large number, n, of independent events all occurring is $p_1 p_2 p_3 \ldots p_n$. This is often denoted by

$$\prod_1^n p_i \tag{5.1.2}$$

This has an obvious interpretation in terms of nuclear deterrence. Given that the nuclear deterrent system shows no sign of withering away, we must face the fact that, even if the reliability or stability of the system is very high over periods of, say, one year, such that no events have more than a small probability of triggering off a nuclear war, over a long period there will be a very large number of these low probability events and the cumulative probability becomes very high when looked at over a period such as a century.[1]

To give a numerical feel for the problem, if the probability of war in any year is 0.1, then the probability of a war not starting is 0.9 for any given year. However, the probability that it does not start over a period of ten years is $0.9^{10} = 0.35$ which is a lot lower. A probability of nuclear war of 0.1 per year might seem unduly pessimistic. Smaller probabilities of war such as 0.001 per year (that is, one chance in a thousand) would be felt more appropriate by many people. Two interesting cases are that $0.999^{10} = 0.99$ and $0.999^{100} = 0.9048$. That is, if the probability of war is one in a thousand in one year, then the probability of war at some point in ten years is about one in a hundred. Extending this to a century, then the probability of war is about one in ten. There are some points to stress. First, while it is easier to give examples on the assumption that the probabilities for each year are all the same, there is of course no requirement that this should be so. It does draw attention, though, to the fact that the probability of a system failing is greater than the probability of its weakest necessary part failing, for the system has to survive that hurdle and all the others as well. The parts (in our case, years) have to be of high reliability without exception. The second point to stress is to check a possible error. If we assume that there is an equal probability of nuclear war of 0.001 each year giving the cumulative probability over a century of 0.095, it does not mean that the probability at the end of a hundred years has become 0.095. It simply means that the probability of war sometime *within* that period is a little under 0.1.

The gloomy conclusions so far can be slightly alleviated if we abandon the assumption that the probability, though low is either constant or at least varies unsystematically over the years. Suppose, however, that the international system is a learning system in which the probability of nuclear war declines steadily over the years by a factor of k where $0 < k < 1$. That is, if the probability in year 1 is p, in year 2 it is kp, year three k^2p and of war in year n, $k^{n-1}p$. Thus, the probability of there not being a war during the first n periods is

$$(1 - p)(1 - kp)(1 - k^2p) \ldots (1 - k^{n-1}p) = \prod_0^{n-1} (1 - k^r p) \quad (5.1.3)$$

---

[1] Notice that these probabilities need not be independent. One probability could be a function of its predecessor without this effecting the argument.

Let us call this probability, π_n. In the appendix we show that this probability is greater than zero, or to be specific, we demonstrate that

$$\pi_\infty > (1 - p)^{1/1-k} \qquad (5.1.4)$$

As $\pi_\infty > \pi_n$ for any finite n it follows that this result holds for any finite period we care to consider. Thus the pessimistic conclusion which followed from our basic model where we showed that as the period of time considered lengthened, the probability of war sometime within it tended towards certainty, with this learning model it does not, which is consoling.

I have argued that the probability of a nuclear war is necessarily a subjective probability. Hence, as an issue of principle, we cannot calculate it except as a characteristic of an individual. What we can say, however, is that any probability per period, no matter what its value, will cumulate as the length of time goes up. Given that we are talking about long periods – and it would seem imprudent not to think of anything less than a century – then even very small probabilities cumulate to disconcertingly large numbers. This applies even if the probabilities decline over time, unless they do so very rapidly, and so the result above should be regarded with only restrained delight. It rescues us from the worst aspects of the problem that the probabilities cumulate to unity but no more. That war can happen, no matter by how bizarre and improbable a process, gives it some positive probability. When viewed over a century, any positive probability is still too much.

The analysis of the problem does not end here. First, it is generally agreed that there are periods of crisis in the international system where the probability of war goes up. Most people believe that in the Cuba Missiles Crisis the probability of nuclear war increased. This statement means that at the time the degree of belief that a war might happen increased, and most people in retrospect think that they were correct in that judgement. This suggests that we should look at the probability of a crisis in a particular year and the conditional probability of a war if there is a crisis separately. Denoting the probability of a crisis as $P(C)$ and the probability of war as $P(W)$ then, using the earlier notation, the probability of war as a consequence of a crisis in a given year is $P(W) = P(W \mid C).P(C)$. To this must be added the probability of a nuclear war occurring which is not preceded by a crisis. The whole expression becomes

$$P(W) = P(W \mid C) + P(W \mid \sim C).P(\sim C) \qquad (5.1.5)$$

The first of the terms on the right hand side is generally assumed to be the dominant one, though it should be remembered that as the

84

point of the argument is that we are cumulating over a long period nothing can be ignored.

It has been argued that the nature of the Command and Control system for nuclear weapons (called C^3I for Command, Control, Communication and Intelligence) as presently constituted for the United States could break down in a severe crisis (Bracken 1983). The system in the Soviet Union is almost certainly subject to at least as much potential error. Hence the expression $P(W \mid C)$ might have increased since the nineteen sixties. This assertion is itself based on the possibilities that there are more opportunities for error in the more complex technical equipment. This is not a suggestion that the super-powers have become more bellicose but that once the system starts going there are far too many opportunities for it to become irreversible. However, this point is accepted by the Political/Military authorities and it has been suggested that the fear of this means that there is a deliberate effort to keep $P(C)$ as low as possible – that is to avoid super-power confrontations. According to this argument $P(W)$ is kept as low as in the sixties despite the increase in $P(W \mid C)$ because of compensating decreases in $P(C)$. Notice, however, that the arguments are that it is kept low; it is not zero and hence the above arguments about cumulation still stand. The point of disaggregation in this manner is to consider the processes involved in the problem and consider the probability judgements with more care.

Finally we should consider the problem of other nuclear powers. In 1988 there are five overtly nuclear powers, a further one which has exploded a nuclear device but no weapons (India), two probables (Israel and South Africa), and one ambiguous (Pakistan). There are many other powers which could quickly become nuclear if they wished and may do so in the future (Meyer 1983). Thus it is quite possible that a nuclear war will be fought between states other than the super-powers. This may or may not draw the super-powers in but in view of the worries about C^3I it is possible that this would happen by accident. Thus I am asserting that there is a non-zero probability that there will be a nuclear war between two states other than the super-powers, and I would suggest that the more states get nuclear weapons the greater is this probability, though Brito and Intriligator (1981) argue a more complex case. Now at one level this is merely an assertion of my own subjective probability which may or may not interest anyone else. However, even if my judgement is disregarded, this point does not decrease the probability of a nuclear war between the super-powers. That still remains the same, unaffected by this. The only way in which this could reduce the over-all probability of a nuclear war would be if one held the view that a direct super-power confrontation is less likely if there is nuclear proliferation, because the knowledge of it will induce super-power caution to compensate for the increased danger caused by the proliferation. This is the same sort of argument as was made about the probability of international crises reducing to compensate for their increasing danger.

However we mull around the problem, I find the conclusion inescapable. Unless the probability per year or per other time period is zero the cumulation problem is inescapable, though the probability only tends to unity on certain assumptions (not unhappily implausible ones though). This is not an argument for any other specific policy as such, but it is an argument against the tacit assumption that because a system has a low short-term probability of breaking down that we should be sanguine about its long-term prospects.

An interesting related application of this form of argument was made by Cioffi-Revilla (1983). He argues that current weapons systems are of great complexity and require a large number of necessary conditions to be fulfilled if they are to work. These all have some small but non-zero probability of failure. Hence a complex deterrence system might lack credibility simply because the deteree thinks that the probability of it working is low enough to take the risk. This arguably becomes the same sort of probabilistic deterrent discussed below – that is, the nuclear button is a decision to enter a lottery not a certain outcome.

This problem is a somewhat different one from the analysis of nuclear war, in that we are now looking at a deterrent system which can be designed. Now one way to reduce the weaknesses of the cumulation problem is to design things in parallel as much as possible, that is to make it possible to achieve the goals of the system by several different means so that, if one fails, another will function. There are two ways in which deterrent systems are designed in parallel. The first is to have different methods of nuclear retaliation such as land-based missiles, sea-based missiles and the like. The second is to have independently operating units within those systems, that is, if the instructions to one rocket crew fail, then the instructions to another will still get through.

The use of different types of deterrent systems is justified (or rationalised) by the need to guard against the development of defences against any particular one of them. Both the Soviet Union and the United States have what is called the Triad System of manned bombers, missiles launched by submarine, and missiles launched on land. This defends them against the possibility of new technological developments which might make one sort of system very vulnerable.

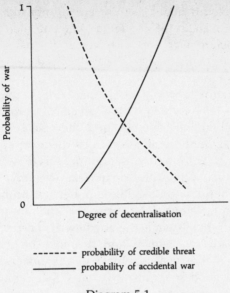

Diagram 5.1

Currently, for example, nuclear powered submarines in which missiles for nuclear retaliation are located are difficult to detect. However, methods of detection may well improve and submarines would become highly vulnerable. By having the alternative systems, the probability of maintaining a deterrent in the face of unforeseen technical developments is increased.

The more alarming analysis is the following. It is accepted that, the more systems there are in parallel which can be operated independently of each other, the greater the probability that, if a war did occur, the deterrent would in fact operate. For example, if everything depended on one person such as a President not being killed then the probability of retaliation would be low. This probability is that as perceived by the deteree. According to deterrence theory, the higher the probability of retaliation, the lower the probability of initiation, that is, of there being a war at all. However, the greater the degree of parallelism in a system (which is roughly the same as decentralisation), the greater is the possibility that it would be activated without the initial attack, either through technical fault, or through some break-down in the human system. Thus, in order to increase the probability that the deterrent system looks credible in the sense of having a high probability of really retaliating, the higher the probability of the other sort of error of it 'retaliating' when there is nothing for it to retaliate to. This is illustrated in the Diagram 5.1.

On the surface this might seem to be an unbearable paradox. By lowering the probability of accidental war one increases the probability of deliberate war and vice versa. If one was sufficiently cold-blooded, one could analyse the system and derive the optimum point which minimises the over-all probability. Without wishing to dismiss the paradox, I would assert that, even if the probability of retaliation were perceived to be low, even low probabilities would deter against all-out nuclear war, and the goal of minimising the accidental probabilities would seem to be the most appropriate one. What should be clear from this last argument, is that it is implicit that there will be some probability of nuclear war, and by my earlier arguments, though low probabilities are better than high, any probability is unacceptable over long periods. In the personal view of the writer, the deterrent system is thereby flawed. The analysis does not suggest any ready alternatives and this may be the best way of running the international system that we can think of. It suggests that it is not a very good way, however, and that sanguine observers should stop being sanguine.

2 An analysis of deterrence

Deterrence is one of the most widely used concepts in the study of the international system. In the form of nuclear deterrence, more than anything, it dominates our thoughts about the future of the world. Any set of theoretical constructs which could not address the problem would be limited, to say the least, as a tool for the analysis of the system.

The concept of deterrence has much broader application than might be thought by reading the nuclear deterrence literature. It is essentially a conditional threat of the form 'if you do act X, I shall punish you by carrying out act Y'. Such conditional threats are widespread from the nursery to the chancellories, going through virtually every form of social interaction in the middle. Another form of it is blackmail, which is a conditional threat of the form 'If you do not do X (such as pay me some money) then I will do Y'. Conceptually, if not morally, it is the same principle.

Now, while such deterrent threats are often posed deterministically, this is often not how they are perceived by the deterree. In the middle there is the problem of detection. Thus, while a motorist might be punished with a fine if he exceeds the speed limit and while the law might be deterministic in the sense that all motorists who are caught are fined, the deterrent is still probabilistic as far as the motorist is concerned in that there is only a probability that on any given occasion he will be caught. Thus, in deciding whether to exceed the limit, the motorist will weigh up the advantages of speeding, the level of the fine and the probability of being caught. This is a clear candidate for a utility analysis. If we denote the utility of speeding as $u(S)$, the utility of the legal speed as $u(L)$ and the utility of the fine as $u(F)$, and the probability of being caught as p, then the motorist will speed if

$$(1 - p).u(S) + p.u(F) > u(L) \tag{5.2.1}$$

Even a casual observation of driving in most countries would indicate that this inequality holds in the direction suggested for most drivers. Any disutility (or for some people the utility) which attaches to disobeying the law as such, as distinct from the value of the outcome on its own, is allowed for in the utility terms.

Now if one wants to improve compliance with the law it is clear from the above inequality that the variables which can be adjusted are the level of the fine or the probability of detection. (To be fair it was also clear to Jeremy Bentham who was able to work this out without the benefit of expected utility theory – see his *Introduction to the Principles of Morals and Legislation*, 1823). What we have done by expressing it in this way is to pose the problem clearly and unambiguously, but without adding anything which could not be reasonably expressed in words.

The above example depicts an asymmetrical situation where one party deters the other, who either complies or not. In the case of the international system, situations of mutual deterrence are more common, and the relationship between the two super-powers is usually depicted as such. Both parties seek to restrain the other, while themselves being restrained by the other's conditional threats. Put in its deterministic form, nuclear deterrence is commonly represented as a game of 'chicken' which is represented below, where, as before, the letters represent the ordinal rankings of the pay-offs; the earlier the letter appears in the alphabet, the higher is the value of the pay-off.

		Country B	
		C	D
Country A			
C		$(b_1\ b_2)$	$(c_1\ a_2)$
D		$(a_1\ c_2)$	$(d_1\ d_2)$

A mutual deterrent threat can exist when both parties are using the cooperate strategy. It consists of threatening to defect if the other side defects. It scarcely needs to be pointed out that the game is a repeated game as long as the parties stay at the cooperate strategy but thereafter is a very complete form of one-shot game.

Chicken is similar to prisoners' dilemma in many respects, the major difference being that the mutual defect strategy is the lowest possible outcome for both parties. Deterrence as operated in the prisoners' dilemma game means that, if the rival defects, the victim applies the deterrent and moves up from the worst outcome to the next worst. Thus it seems very credible that the deterrent will be applied. However, in the game of chicken, the application of the deterrent involves the victim in actually making his own situation worse. In a strict sense this violates a principle of rationality and raises doubts about the credibility of the deterrent. Would a victim in fact respond? There is some irony in a principle, represented as being a rational theory of international behaviour, depending on each side convincing the rival that in certain situations they might act irrationally.

Consider the problem from the point of view of A wondering whether to defect. If he could be certain that B were rational in the narrow sense, and would not apply the deterrent, then he would certainly defect. Conversely, if he were sure that B would apply the deterrent, then he would certainly not defect. The problem then comes in the middle when he thinks that B might apply the deterrent if he defects, but cannot be sure. Suppose this probability is p. Remember that this is the probability that A thinks that B will use the deterrent and is thus something which goes on in A's mind (some problems of when A is a collectivity are considered in Chapter 11). This means that the expected value to A of the defect strategy is

$$(1 - p) . u(a) + p . u(d) > u(b) \tag{5.2.2}$$

If this inequality is to mean anything we must put numerical values to the utilities of the outcomes. Simple ordering relationships are all that is necessary in the straight-forward chicken game, but, once we bring in probabilities, this is inadequate. Clearly what B must do to maximise the deterrent threat is to convince the opponent that the probability of defection is as high as possible. This is generally perceived as being the crucial problem in deterrence. However, as Brams (1985) has pointed out, there may be difficulties in this. I shall now give a modified version of Brams' argument which I shall initially make in terms of a game in its mundane sense.

A is considering B's conditional threat to defect if A initiates defection. B can make his deterrent threat with any probability including 1, a probability which is of course communicated to A. For convenience we assume that this probability is determined by some

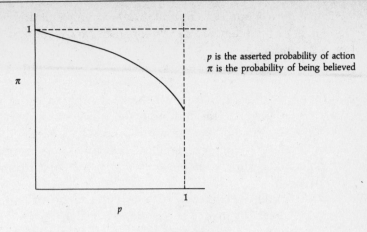

p is the asserted probability of action
π is the probability of being believed

Diagram 5.2A

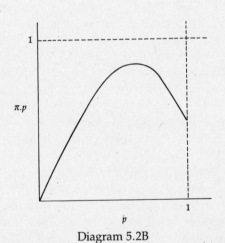

Diagram 5.2B

chance device that B will operate if the occasion arises. The cost to B is $u(c) - u(d)$ and hence the expected cost is $p \cdot [u(c) - u(d)]$. Knowing the costs to B, A may be very sceptical if they are high. In many deterrent situations, the outcomes are given and not readily adjustable. However, the probability can be varied, and this makes the expected cost adjustable. If the probability is high, then the expected cost is high and the deterree might feel sceptical about whether the deterrer really intends it. However, if the probability is low, A might accept it at face value. Hence, the over-all probability is the asserted probability multiplied by the probability that it is believed. Call the first of these p and the probability of being believed π, then A's subjective probability

91

that B will in fact carry out the deterrent threat is $\pi . p$. The relationship of p to π, and of p to $p . \pi$ denoted by $f(p)$, for given c and d are shown in Diagram 5.2A and 5.2B.

$\pi . p$ peaks before $p = 1$ occurs if π is decreased sufficiently, but a maximum of this sort prior to $p = 1$, as illustrated in Diagram 5.2B, clearly does not necessarily happen if the dampening effect of π is insufficient to compensate for the increasing value of p operating through $\pi . p$. The formal condition for a peak existing is that $d(\pi . p)/dp = 0$. By applying the standard rule for differentiating a product, this condition holds if $df(p)/dp = - f(p)/p$ (see the mathematical appendix).

What is clear from this is that a high value of p is not necessarily the best deterrent threat. Even if it is, and the function on the right continues to go up until $p = 1$, the full deterrent effect will not be experienced. There is also the factor of how it appears to B. In a world in which he had to tell the truth to A, he might well not make the defect threat with probability 1 because of the high cost in utility this would involve. If a lower cost threat is not possible in the situation, the high cost threat can be reduced to a lower cost threat by making it probabilistic. Thus, the severe chicken game is transformed into chicken with more moderate expected costs ('expected' being used in its technical sense).

This sort of analysis seems to apply to the present structure of the nuclear threat between the super-powers. It is not supposed that either side is going to throw a die in order to decide whether or not it will activate its deterrent threat. However, the prior situation is not dissimilar. Most commentators from both East and West appear not to expect a 'bolt from the blue' attack. In the horrific event of a war starting, it is presumed that it would come from some more limited conflict escalating to a potential nuclear war. For example, suppose that there is a war in Europe which one side is losing. This would be a serious set back for the loser (and the Europeans in any case). However, would anyone be prepared to go as far as initiating a full scale nuclear attack involving the response which would totally destroy human society in order to stop the loss of the small war? If this was a world of cool decision makers it would seem improbable. However, the deterrence against a limited war (which might be fought with tactical nuclear weapons) is the threat of a nuclear war. But is this credible? The argument from the above analysis is that it is the *doubt* about the threat which gives it its credibility. If A threatens B with a threat which will also impose horrific costs on A itself (namely nuclear war) then B will simply disbelieve the threat. However, if A indicates that it *might* activate the deterrent then the threat becomes much more credible. Even this however, must be put in a context that is socially credible. No-one really supposes that the Queen or the President of the United States would be asked to throw a die to decide whether or not to have a nuclear war (apart from anything else, the problems of protocol would be too severe). However, we can (and in fact have) available a set of procedures which would come into play and whose consequences we cannot predict. Thus, it is perfectly credible (indeed not seriously doubted) that if either side made a major incursion into the other's territory in Europe, such as a military occupation of West Berlin by the Soviet Union, this would be responded to militarily by the other side. This would, by any standards, be a major crisis. There is now abundant evidence (for example, Janis 1982) that people do not always act very rationally in times of crisis. It is possible that the combatants will fight for a little and, realising the dangers, come to an agreement. This is the official doctrine. It is also possible that the whole situation will get totally out of hand. Military escalation could follow escalation and the whole business end in a total nuclear war. No one can predict with certainty what would happen. Further, with varying degrees of sophistication, decision makers are aware of this (or so we must hope). Thus we have what in effect is a random device. No-one is called upon to throw a coin or operate any similar chance mechanism, and to suppose they would is implausible. However, it is very plausible that the procedures dictated by the military structure would be put into operation if the events were to occur. As we cannot predict what would be the result of this, the actual consequences of the structure we live in is that we have a probabilistic deterrent, though without objective probabilities.

3   The verification of arms agreements

While the moralist might deplore it, the analyst must accept that governments are constantly trying to deceive each other. Thus governments are frequently faced with the problem of verifying whether another government is in fact carrying out the requirements of some treaty or agreement. This problem is most often discussed in terms of arms control and disarmament agreements, though it applies to many forms of joint behaviour between governments, particularly in the military and strategic field. There is of course a related problem of how to convince some rival that one is telling the truth and keeping an agreement, when he has reason for doubting it. I shall explore

93

some aspects of this in this section, again using an analysis akin to Brams (1985).

The problem is trivial if the activity in question is very visible and can readily be observed. However, in many practical situations, tests do not exist (independently of the assurance of the putative defector), which demonstrate without doubt that some event has or has not taken place. It is still hard with present detection techniques to distinguish between a small earthquake and a small nuclear detonation. Some of the difficulties are imposed by the states involved, but some are inherent.

Difficulties arise from three sources. First, even if the putative defector apparently cooperates with the observer, such things as the size of a country can mean that a lot of things can be hidden. Even a geographically small country like the Netherlands could hide a number of nuclear weapons such that they would not be discovered no matter how rigorously outside inspection teams investigated. A more worrying issue for the future (for I trust the Dutch) is that if there were major disarmament it would be difficult to be absolutely sure that a country, particularly a geographically large one such as the US or USSR did not have 'a few' missiles, even if one could be fairly confident that they did not have many. Thus, verification problems would become harder at lower levels of arms. We have the paradox that, however anxious a state is to demonstrate that it has in fact no weapons, in the last analysis it would be hard for an outsider to be totally convinced that it was telling the truth.

The second source of difficulty is when the putative defector is not willing to cooperate beyond a certain point – a much publicised issue has been the earlier refusal of the USSR to allow on-site inspections. This might be due to bad faith. However, it might also be due to the fear of the inspectee that other information will also be acquired which will harm it. For this reason, few countries would allow a rival power to look round their military laboratories, even if to do so would provide convincing information that some treaty was being abided by.

The third and most difficult problem is to verify intentions. If a state is generating energy in nuclear power stations, it is virtually impossible to demonstrate that it is not also designing a bomb which could be made quickly. Intentions are unobservable, and can even alter in all good faith.

Let us consider the more tractable problems first. Suppose that one state is concerned as to whether another is building up some new sort of weapon. The decision makers of the state (for simplicity assumed to be unitary) have some subjective probability of it being the case.

Verification is the application of some tests giving further information which modifies this probability, and hopefully brings it closer to 1 or 0. In any sort of test there are two types of error and two relevant independent probabilities. If we apply the test and it indicates positive, we denote this by T_D and if negative, then by T_C. We are testing to see whether D (to be understood as defect) is the case or not.

The problem of testing is a general one which applies to non-strategic as well as strategic situations. Tests in medicine are not strategic in the sense that the body is not trying to either help or mislead the observer (though a patient may at times mislead). However, in the case of states in conflict, one state might gain an advantage if its rival were misled. Let us pose the problem asymmetrically and suppose we have an 'actor' who either collaborates (C) or defects (D) and a 'detector' who acts either as if he believes C or believes D. Notice that 'believes' means a decision to act in a certain way and is not descriptive of a state of mind.

Let us suppose that the problem in question is characterised by the statement 'The actor has carried out some nuclear tests', which is the defect or D strategy whereas C is the cooperative activity of not carrying out tests.

First we shall put some utilities to the various outcomes. Supposing that the actor chooses rows and the detector chooses columns, the following sets of utilities seem plausible where I adopt the earlier convention that the earlier a letter appears in the alphabet, the higher is the utility value.

	Actor	
	Choose C	Choose D
Detector		
Believe C	$a_1\,b_2$	$d_1\,a_2$
Believe D	$c_1\,d_2$	$b_1\,c_2$

If this were a simultaneous, one-shot game, the solution would be obvious. The second column dominates the first as far as the actor is concerned, therefore D would be chosen. Detector, knowing this, would believe D. This result would not be Pareto Optimal. However, we should be careful about the interpretation of the context of this application. If there is a perfect detection technique such that detector knows for sure whether actor is playing C or D, detector can choose his strategy accordingly. Thus it is a game where actor chooses first and detector chooses in the knowledge of this. In this case, if actor chooses D then detector chooses believe D and the pay-offs are ($b_1\,c_2$) whereas if actor chooses C, detector believes C and the joint pay-offs are ($a_1\,b_2$).

Thus, with perfect detection techniques, the joint cooperative strategy is played.

The converse is the case if there is no detection technique and detector is not aware of what has happened until the damage is done. It becomes like the one-shot game, on the assumption at least that any future discounted benefits of cooperation are already embodied in the pay-offs.

As detection techniques are rarely perfect, the problem lies somewhere in the middle. Suppose that detector has a testing mechanism which reads T_C for 'no explosion' and T_D for 'explosion', though neither totally reliably. If the test reads T_C there is a probability p that this is correct. We denote this as $P(C \mid T_C)$. There is also a probability $(1 - p)$ that the test misses the explosion and gives a false reading, denoted by $P(D \mid T_C) = (1 - p)$. These probabilities are objective, being determined by technical factors, and we shall assume known to both sides. Similarly if the testing mechanism reads T_D we have $P(D \mid T_D) = q$, and the probability that it incorrectly 'detects' an explosion is $(1 - q)$. Both forms of unreliability are common in many tests. In nuclear explosions, an explosion can be missed, or an earthquake falsely recorded as an explosion. A common problem is to ensure that the improvement in reducing one form of error is not bought at the cost of worsening the other. We wish to see the conditions under which the cooperative strategy is played.

First consider detector. Suppose that the test reads T_C so he has probability p that actor is in fact not testing. The expected value of believe C is thus $pa_1 + (1 - p)d_1$. Similarly the expected value of believe D is $pc_1 + (1 - p)b_1$. Thus he will choose believe C if

$$p a_1 + (1-p).d_1 > p.c_1 + (1-p) b_1 \qquad (5.3.1)$$

This holds if

$$p > (b_1 - d_1) (a_1 + b_1 - c_1 - d_1) \qquad (5.3.2)$$

Hence, if the probability of the test giving the correct result when the C strategy is played is as given in the inequality, then the 'believe' act will be followed if

$$(1 - q).c_1 + q.b_1 > (1 - q).a_1 + q.d_1 \qquad (5.3.3)$$

which likewise holds if

$$q > (a_1 - c_1)/(a_1 + b_1 - c_1 - d_1) \qquad (5.3.4)$$

If these probabilities do not meet the relevant inequalities then the tests would be redundant. If the 'not believe' policy were followed irrespective of the result of the test, there would have been no point in carrying it out in the first place. Similarly if the detector plays believe despite the test turning out negative, the test would be a non-test. These two inequalities define the conditions for which the tests are useful. What should be noticed is that the criteria for useful tests are not just dependent on the probabilities themselves, but also on the various utilities.

Next consider when actor chooses the C strategy. He knows detector's strategy is determined by whether the test comes out positive or negative. This is not a probabilistic matter. If we assume the tests obey the conditions of (5.3.2) and (5.3.4) then the act detector adopts is completely determined by how the test turns out, but how it turns out as far as actor is concerned is a probabilistic matter. Suppose that $P(T_C \mid C) = \pi$, which is the probability that the test T_C will indicate correctly that actor plays C. Define $P(T_D \mid D) = \varrho$ similarly. The expected value of playing the C strategy is therefore

$$\pi \, b_2 + (1 - \pi) \, d_2 \tag{5.3.5}$$

Similarly the expected value of playing the D strategy is

$$(1 - \varrho) \, a_2 + \varrho \cdot c_2 \tag{5.3.6}$$

Hence the C strategy will be played if the first of these expressions is larger than the second and vice versa.

The analysis demonstrates that the achievement of a Pareto Optimal solution depends on the reliability of the detection mechanisms, as well as the relative values and costs of being right and of making different sorts of mistakes. This is not inherently very surprising. However, what is clarified is that, to achieve the Pareto Optimal point, it is in the interests of *both* sides that the detector has good detection mechanisms. Actor needs it as much as detector. Further, the analysis shows it must be possible to avoid (or reduce the probability of) *both* thinking defection has taken place when it has not, *and* thinking defection has not taken place when it has. In the relevant inequalities which must be satisfied for the Pareto Optimal solution to be achieved, the probabilities of all the forms of error appear. The ability to conceal is a short-term gain on the assumptions made here. Deceit is rational only under certain assumptions about the discount rate in the sort of framework discussed in Chapter 3.

I have expressed the analysis in terms of detection used in a relatively technical sense. In the case of the detection of nuclear detonations, this is reasonable and the relevant probabilities can be regarded as objective. If the analysis is applied to general rearmament, such tests would be more complex and subject to different interpretations. As far as the actor is concerned, the probabilities such as π can be more readily interpreted as the probability of being believed, and not just the probability of a particular set of tests yielding a particular conclusion.

This means that there are cases where a general reputation for being believed on the part of the actor can increase the probability held by the detector that the truth is being told on some specific occasion. If an actor had a reputation for total probity, then the only test which the detector would need to apply would be to ask a question. This would be an unusual assumption and procedure in the relations between states. However, a reputation for truth telling is useful even in the international arena, and might be pursued occasionally. Even if it is against one's own direct short-term interests, it might be in the longer term interests of policy as a whole. Suppose that the actor did put some positive value on telling the truth, either because of valued reputation or even out of moral principle. The pay-off matrix might then be expressed as:

	Actor	
	Choose C	Choose D
Detector		
Believe C	$a_1\, a_2$	$d_1\, b_2$
Believe D	$c_1\, d_2$	$b_1\, c_2$

In this case the choose C/believe C option is clearly the dominant one, being not only Pareto Optimal, but also the highest value in the matrix for both parties.

4 Arms control with hawks and doves

In the analyses so far, a high degree of knowledge has been assumed about each partys' knowledge of their rival. While this assumption gives us considerable insight into a number of problems, it is unrealistic and misleading for others. In this case I discuss a simple model where each party has doubts about its rival's goals due to uncertainty as to which of two internal groups has dominance in the decision making process.

A major problem in deciding strategy concerns the actual goals of the rival. To give an important class of example. It is often recognised that a rival's government is not a unitary actor. There may be hawks and doves, conflicting internal economic interests, or separate political parties who have different utilities for various issues. Thus, there may be doubt not just over what a rival may actually do, but what it even wants. The assumption of clear-cut pay-offs is often a gross, even grotesque, simplification. However, we can still analyse the conceptual points in terms of a simple model.

Consider two countries endeavouring to come to an arms control agreement. Suppose that the doves are dominant in both countries. This then gives the joint pay-off matrix with rankings of:

	B	
	Arms control (C)	No agreement (D)
A		
Arms control (C)	(4,4)	(1,3)
No agreement (D)	(3,1)	(2,2)

If the hawks are dominant in the two countries, the rankings will be:

	B	
	Arms control (C)	No agreement (D)
A		
Arms control (C)	(2,2)	(1,4)
No agreement (D)	(4,1)	(3,3)

With these pay-offs, agreement will be reached in the first case but not in the second. The problem arises if neither side is sure whether the hawks or the doves are dominant in the other side. To look at this, it is more convenient to pose the pay-off matrices more abstractly as:

	B	
	Arms control (C)	No agreement (D)
A		
Arms control (C)	$(\alpha_{11} \ \beta_{11})$	$(\alpha_{12} \ \beta_{12})$
No agreement (D)	$(\alpha_{21} \ \beta_{21})$	$(\alpha_{22} \ \beta_{22})$

Suppose both parties in fact are dominated by doves. The ranking of the utilities will therefore be

$$\alpha_{11} > \alpha_{21} > \alpha_{22} > \alpha_{12}$$

and

$$\beta_{11} > \beta_{12} > \beta_{22} > \beta_{21}$$

If both sides know this, then there is a presumption that CC will be the equilibrium point. This game is sometimes known as 'Assurance' in that if one party is assured that the other will play the cooperate strategy then it will likewise cooperate. Suppose, however, that both sides are dominated by Hawks, the ranking of the utilities will be as follows

$$\alpha'_{21} > \alpha'_{22} > \alpha'_{11} > \alpha'_{12}$$

and

$$\beta'_{12} > \beta'_{22} > \beta'_{11} > \beta'_{21}$$

In this DD will clearly be the equilibrium point.

Let us now assume that the doves of A know that for themselves α is the case but only with probability p that the doves have won in B and that β is the case (and hence with probability $(1 - p)$ that β' is the case). Assume that in fact that β is the case but B is unable to convince A, though he knows that p is the probability with which A believes it. Clearly A might play the D strategy out of fear that B will play D, due to their erroneous fear that the hawks dominate. Similarly B might also play D out of fear that A will have played out of fear. What are the conditions under which this will happen?

The expected value to A of playing C and D assuming that B will not defect out of fear but only because he is in a prisoners' dilemma are

$$E_A(C) = p(\alpha_{11}) + (1 - p)(\alpha_{12})$$
$$E_A(D) = p(\alpha_{21}) + (1 - p)(\alpha_{22})$$

Thus he will play the C strategy if $E_A(C) > E_A(D)$ and vice versa. Defining $V_A(D)$ as the net expected value of playing the D strategy we get

$$E_A(D) - E_A(C) = V_A(D) = -V_A(C)$$

where

$$V_A(D) = p(\alpha_{12} + \alpha_{21} - \alpha_{11} - \alpha_{22}) + (\alpha_{22} - \alpha_{12}) \qquad (5.4.1)$$

A will play the C strategy if $V_A(D) < 0$ and the D strategy if $V_A(D) > 0$. B has all this information about A and hence can work out whether A will play the C strategy, or at least would if he were not afraid of B acting out of fear. A knows that B knows whether $V_A(D)$ is positive or negative. Hence, if it is negative, the possible cycle of fear becoming self-fulfilling is aborted. If $V_A(D)$ is positive, then A will play D, B will know this and likewise play D.

The assumption that it was only B who was in doubt was for expository convenience only and can ready be extended. If, in addition to the above, B believes that α' is the case with probability q, then he will play D even if he is in fact on an assurance matrix if

$$V_B(D) = q \cdot (\beta_{12} + \beta_{21} - \beta_{11} - \beta_{22}) + (\beta_{22} - \beta_{21}) > 0 \qquad (5.4.2)$$

Thus, a game which in fact has the assurance pay-offs, but where the players are in some doubt about the rival's pay-offs, will have DD as its equilibrium point if either or both of (5.4.1) or (5.4.2) are

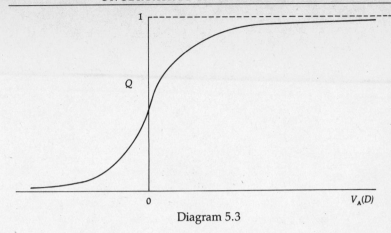

Diagram 5.3

positive. However, there are clearly values of the variables for which they would not hold, and uncertainty as such does not necessarily cumulate and produce aggressive play.

This model still involves enormous assumptions about the level of knowledge of both parties about their opponents. However, a modest extension of the model greatly extends its applicability while retaining its essential features.

In the above model, if $V_A(D) > 0$, B would know it with certainty and himself play the D strategy whether or not he was himself on the assurance type of matrix. Suppose now that B believes that $V_A(D) > 0$ holds with probability Q. B's over-all subjective probability that A will use the D strategy is now governed by two factors. The first is q which is the probability that A will play D out of simple self-interest; the second is Q which is the probability that A will act out of fear of B. Thus, the aggregate probability is $(q + Q - qQ)$. The net expected value of playing D to player B must therefore be redefined to read

$$V_A^*(D) = (q + Q - qQ)(\beta_{12} + \beta_{21} - \beta_{11} - \beta_{22}) + (\beta_{22} - \beta_{21})$$
$$(5.4.3)$$

The parallel expression for A is

$$V_A^*(D) = (p + P - pP)(\alpha_{12} + \alpha_{21} - \alpha_{11} - \alpha_{22}) + (\alpha_{22} - \alpha_{12})$$
$$(5.4.4)$$

As with expressions (5.4.1) and (5.4.2), if either or both of $V_A^*(D) > 0$ or $V_B^*(D) > 0$, the DD strategy pair will result. Both these expressions are conditions of play which either hold or do not hold. They are not in themselves probabilistic statements.

We should briefly look at the relationship between the starred and

101

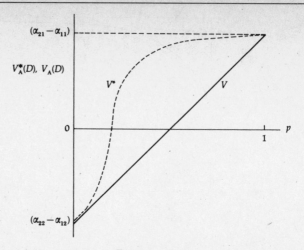

Diagram 5.4

unstarred versions of V. In general we would assume that P and Q were close to either unity or zero when $V_A(D)$ and $V_B(D)$ were clearly either negative or positive. It is when they are close to the zero point themselves that the probabilities might indicate a significant degree of uncertainty. A likely pattern is indicated in Diagram 5.3.

This would lead to the following relationship between $V_A(D)$ and $V_A^*(D)$. First, it follows from the fact that $P + p - pP \geqslant p$ that $V_A^*(D) \geqslant V_A(D)$. From this we can see that the new model is more likely to give a defect result than the original. Clearly $V_A(D)$ is linear with respect to variations in p as indicated above by the continuous line in Diagram 5.4. As argued $V_A^*(D)$ will always lie above this. Let us assume that the alphas are such that when p is small $V_A(D)$ is clearly negative. Hence P is also very small and $V_A(D)$ is close to $(\alpha_{21} - \alpha_{12})$. Thus $V_A^*(D) \simeq V_A(D)$. When p approaches unity we again find that both $V_A(D)$ and $V_A^*(D)$ approach $(\alpha_{21} - \alpha_{11})$. In the middle there can be a considerable divergence, illustrated by the broken line in Diagram 5.4.

It seems that this model captures some of the essential properties of a very common situation. The attitudes of the USA to the USSR, and vice versa, constantly involve concerns about which groups dominate the decision making process at any given time. This leads to worries about how to interpret moves in the arms control and disarmament fields. This model shows that the fear of hawks on the other side need not always bring about the DD result. More pessimistically it is possible, though it is not necessary, that the mutual defect strategy might result even when the hawks do not in fact have dominance.

102

6 BARGAINING AND CONFLICT TERMINATION

1 The termination of wars

Bargaining is the process whereby a 'solution' is reached between two or more actors with partially conflicting aims. A solution is simply the way in which they divide up the benefits. This definition is by intention extremely general and could apply to almost any non-zero sum situation. Indeed, as defined, bargaining could be a synonym for 'conflict'. Like many other aspects of conflict behaviour in the international system, bargaining is a widespread activity which operates at all social levels. I shall narrow this definition as we procede by discussing bargains between 'rational' actors. I shall argue that, to a degree, war itself can be looked on as a bargaining process, and the distinction between the bargaining and the non-bargaining aspects of warfare is crucial to its understanding.[1]

Let us suppose that war is 'Clausewitzian', initiated rationally in order to achieve certain goals. It may be initiated in order to disturb the status quo or to defend a country from demands which would be harmful to the initiator. I assume that violence is perceived as a cost, and that the various economic consequences such as the diversion of resources to warlike pursuits and the interruption of trade are also seen as costs. Clearly this assumption is not always true, but for the moment I shall retain it. In these circumstances, war has certainly the general characteristics of a bargaining process such as described later in Section 2. Assuming two parties, both want to achieve a position which would be harmful to the other. They are both willing to undertake costs in order to get to their favoured position, or at least a better position than the rival is willing to concede, which makes the situation non-zero sum. If in fact the motives are rational (in the sense of explicit and consistent), then each party must have gone into war supposing that it would get a better outcome by fighting the war than

[1] There is a large literature on formal approaches to bargaining which is largely covered in Young (1975). In this chapter I select a few of the issues which seem to me to be of relevance to international relations.

it could have done without, even allowing for the costs involved. We shown in Section 3 that one, if not both, must be mistaken in this belief. Thus, a war will go on until one party realises that the anticipated costs of continuing the war will exceed any benefits from possible negotiations and may then be prepared to terminate it on certain conditions. I use the term *negotiation* to mean the process of explicitly communicating to try to arrange a solution to the bargain. A *bargaining situation* is the over-all picture of the problem.

However, there are some special characteristics of war which mean that we must modify this picture. Initially, I shall deal with the 'rational' elements. There are two characteristics of warfare which make it particularly difficult to terminate as a bargaining situation. First, in war it is common for communication between the parties to be poor, and indeed it is often regarded as treasonable. Thus, unlike in a strike where there is often almost continuous communication between the parties, and hence almost continuous negotiation, between warring parties communication comes as something of a special event. Pillar (1983) finds that relatively few wars end as a consequence of overt negotiations prior to hostilities ending, whereas in most bargains such an ending is the norm. Pillar speculates that in future this method of ending armed conflict will increase, which I find an unconvincing though attractive notion. This does not mean that there is no tacit or indirect negotiation, but there is a general presumption that the easier and more open is communication, the more likely is a solution to be reached quickly providing such a point exists within the bargaining set at a given time. Secondly, predictability in war is often rather poor. If at some point in an industrial strike the participants are told it will go on for another three months, they will have a close idea of what this will mean. However, in a war, there is often doubt almost to the end as to what will happen. In the First World War, for example, many things seemed possible until the last few days. In the Second World War it had become clear who would win during the last few months, but prior to that there had been a lot of doubt. I suggest that this lack of predictability of both patterns and outcomes is the norm in war. This means that whether or not the projected costs are likely to exceed projected gains are much harder to estimate with any reliability. This alters the framework in which this analysis can be applied. In general when applying the model of Section 2 it would be supposed that the estimates of a rival's concession time would be arrived at by a consideration of the evidence. I suggest that when the evidence is vague and ambiguous one has to identify other factors such as 'optimism' or 'pessimism'. In principle these can also be related to prior events, and it is a mistake to think that it is impossible to formulate theories of them.

With the objections above, the basic rational actor model of decision can still be maintained. It is a bargaining problem with complications. There are two further factors which require its modification. First, when significant costs have been involved in a conflict, there is often the tendency to want to recoup these costs. This violates the proper 'economic' theories of rationality which assert that an actor should optimise from the present position. However, there are strong suppositions that, once costs have been incurred, demands increase to compensate for these costs. It is obvious that, inasmuch as this factor applies, the individual demands for a solution get further and further apart and create a sort of perverse learning. Clearly 'true learning' must at some point reassert itself or conflicts would never end, but this effect will delay the process. This 'sunk costs' problem probably occurs to a degree in a large number of bargains. However, because of the emotionally charged nature of warfare, there is a strong presumption that it will be much more significant there.

This brings us to the final point. The costs of war are the costs in lives as well as resources. The whole process of war involves the activation of very primitive and basic instincts and emotions which inhibit rational thought. These violent swings of emotion were partly analysed by Richardson (1948) though they are still poorly understood, at least at the social level, and the theories are inadequate even at the individual level. Classical economic theories of preference are poorly equipped to deal with them. These factors strengthen the resilience to negotiation by strengthening the sunk costs factor. That one might get a worse solution to a bargain after many people have died than one could have done if they had not, is understandably something which is emotionally hard to encompass.

These arguments do not invalidate the formal analysis of bargaining; indeed somewhat the reverse in that they clarify the problems and the issues involved. Pillar's work is a useful analysis of the way in which wars end, done in a bargaining framework. In the following sections I shall describe the characteristics of some bargaining models which seem to me to be useful. As approaches to theories (as opposed to models) they are clearly inadequate, but as devices for highlighting some crucial issues of classification they are extremely helpful.

2 Bargaining theory: the search for 'solutions'

Two problems are obvious issues in a bargaining problem. The first is whether, given the characteristics of a bargaining problem, we can define a solution. This involves clarifying the concept of a

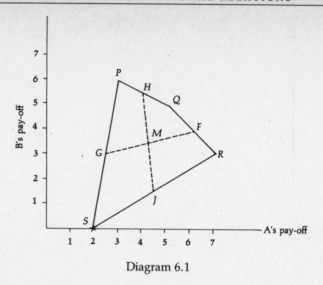

Diagram 6.1

solution beyond the rather bare statement of the previous section. The second is the process by which a solution is achieved. In discussing these two interdependent problems, I hope to clarify the nature of the bargaining problem as a whole.

Consider the chicken game again, which encapsulates the core of a great deal of conflict particularly in the international system. Two actors have a set of strategies A and B such that for any particular strategy pair A_i and B_j there is a pair of pay-offs (a_{ij}, b_{ij}). Consider an asymmetrical chicken game as defined in the following matrix:

Actor B

Actor A

	B_1	B_2
A_1	(5, 5)	(3, 6)
A_2	(7, 3)	(2, 0)

Represented as the corner points in Diagram 6.1 by:

$$\begin{bmatrix} Q & P \\ R & S \end{bmatrix}$$

A's pay-off is represented along the horizontal axis, and B's along the vertical. In this simple chicken game only the four points P, Q, R and S are achievable. However, if we extend the possible strategies such that A can play a *mixed strategy* of half A_1 and half A_2 then there are two new possible points for the game F and G, half way along QR and PS respectively. This mixed strategy can be interpreted in two ways.

106

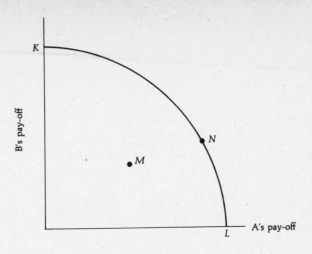

Diagram 6.2

Either it can represent the proportion in which A_1 and A_2 are used in an iterated chicken game or it is the probability with which the two are used in a single-shot game. If B also extends his strategies to a mixed half and half strategy we get the points H and J. If the two both use their mixed strategies, they will achieve a point M where the two lines GF and HJ intersect. This gives nine possible points which are illustrated in the matrix below:

	B_1	$[0.5B_1 : 0.5B_2]$	B_2
A_1	(5, 5)	$(4, 5\frac{1}{2})$	(3, 6)
$[0.5A_1 : 0.5A_2]$	(6, 4)	$(4\frac{1}{4}, 3\frac{1}{2})$	$(2\frac{1}{2}, 3)$
A_2	(7, 3)	$(4\frac{1}{2}, 1\frac{1}{2})$	(2, 0)

These pairs are represented in Diagram 6.1 above by the points:

$$\begin{bmatrix} Q & H & P \\ F & M & G \\ R & J & S \end{bmatrix}$$

It is clear that, if we allow the two players to use any mixture of their two pure strategies, that any point either on the boundary or within $PQRS$ is achievable. This set of points is known as the *bargaining set*. It is also referred to as the *attainable set* or sometimes the *negotiation set*. The attainable set of any two person game can be represented in this sort of way. A more general form is shown in Diagram 6.2 which will help us to make a few observations.

107

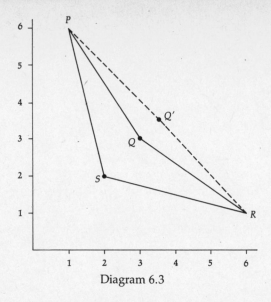

Diagram 6.3

First any point below the convex line *KL*, such as *M* represents a distribution of gains which can be improved upon by both parties simply by moving in a North-East direction on the graph. *N* is such a point which is better for both parties than *M*. However, once on the boundary, no such moves can be made. At point *N* for example, A could only improve his pay-off at the expense of B. Points where it is impossible for both to jointly improve their situations are known as *Pareto Optimal*. Secondly, I have defined the worst point in the game as (0,0). Any other point would do but this is convenient. As the pay-offs are utility terms which have arbitrary zero points this makes no difference to the problem in view. In the case of the chicken game which we considered above, to apply the same transformation would involve taking 2 units from each of the pay-offs of A giving the following matrix:

	B_1	B_2
A_1	(3, 5)	(1, 6)
A_2	(5, 3)	(0, 0)

The diagram which represents this game (and its mixed strategy extension) is simply Diagram 6.1 shifted two units to the left as in Diagram 6.4. It is clear that anything said about this diagram is exactly the same as anything said about the original except for the simple transformation of the pay-offs and that in some important sense it can be said to be the same game. The final point is that I have deliberately drawn Diagram 6.2 with a boundary which is convex to the origin. The reason for this, and for claiming that this is a widespread form of bargaining set, can be illustrated with another prisoners' dilemma.

	B_1	B_2
A_1	(3, 3)	(1, 6)
A_2	(6, 1)	(2, 2)

This can be represented by the Diagram 6.3.

The 'curve' made up of the two lines PQ and QR is now concave to the origin. If now the two players use *collusive* mixed strategies such that they play A_1B_2 half the time and A_2B_1 half the time then they can achieve the point Q' which is outside the original bargaining set. By appropriately varying the mixtures of their strategies they could achieve any point along the dotted line PR. The obvious issue about point Q' is that it is Pareto Superior to Q. This illustrates the more general point that, if the boundary of a bargaining set is concave, then it can always be expanded into a convex boundary (where we regard a straight line – the limiting case of either – as convex) by some appropriate set of mixed strategies. A set of points whose boundary is always convex is known as a convex set, and can be defined as a set such that a straight line drawn from any one point in the set to any other runs entirely within the set.[2]

The question now posed by bargaining theorists is whether it is possible to determine the 'solution' to a bargaining problem. A solution can be regarded either as the solution which in real life will commonly be found, or in some sense the solution which 'ought' to be the case according to some criterion such as fairness. There tends to be some ambiguity about the interpretation in many cases – though not in the case of one proposed by Braithwaite (1955) who makes it explicit that his suggestion is for 'fair bargains'.

In the next section of the chapter, I shall discuss approaches which consider the problem of actual solutions. For the rest of this section I shall consider a particular case of a 'fair' solution (or, more safely, 'a solution of ambiguous status') known as the 'Nash Point', and apply it to the chicken game I started off with. J. F. Nash is a mathematician who has made important contributions to this particular area. My motive in dealing with this rather abstract point is two-fold. First, the derivation of the Nash point is an interesting problem itself which

---

[2] Some writers (e.g. Rapaport and Chammah 1965) define a prisoners' dilemma such that its boundaries form a convex set thus excluding this case. It seems to me more convenient to define the prisoners' dilemma more broadly as I have done. The issue remains whatever the game is called..

illustrates one of the uses of mathematical analysis in demonstrating something which is not obvious. Secondly, it raises an issue of conflicting criteria in defining solutions, which is of more general applicability.

Let u denote the utility to A and v the utility to B. Nash proposes that the solution of the bargain should be that point (u^*, v^*) for which the product $u^* . v^*$ is the maximum of all utility pair products uv, in the standardised game where the starting point is the point which the parties can be sure of achieving. This is defined as $(0,0)$. Now, while this seems perfectly reasonable, there would seem to be many more solutions which would be equally reasonable. However, Nash goes on to show that this solution not only meets, but is the only one to meet, the following four requirements:

(1) A solution should be invariant with any utility transformations. Thus, if u is the utility of A in one representation of the bargain, then another representation in which $u' = ku + h$ $(k > 0)$ has the same solution. A solution which did not have this characteristic would be extremely limited.

(2) A solution should be Pareto Optimal. This is a common requirement which in general appears reasonable. It clearly is not met in many real world situations.

(3) Where appropriate a solution should be symmetrical. If a game is symmetrical between two players, then the solution should likewise be symmetrical. This would be a generally accepted principle of fairness.

(4) The 'independence of irrelevant alternatives' rule should be obeyed. First, I shall explain the principle. Suppose that we have a set of alternatives A, B and C from which a decision maker prefers B. Suppose that this set of alternatives is augmented to include D. It is possible that D will be the selected alternative. However, if it is not, then the principle states that the choice must be the original B and not shift to, say, A which was available before but not chosen. Another way of expressing this is to say that the preference ordering between two alternatives A and B should not be affected by what other alternatives are available for choice at the same time. This seems an innocuous principle which one would expect to find in general in choice situations.

These requirements all seem perfectly reasonable characterisations of a fair solution in the sort of highly structured situations to which they are applied. If one accepts these principles, then one necessarily accepts the Nash solution as appropriate. Nash's theorem is not in any way self-evident. (I do not prove it here. There is a proof in Luce and Raiffa 1957 and of course in Nash's paper.)

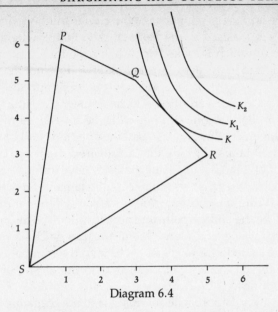

Diagram 6.4

Nash's theorem can be applied to the particular game of chicken presented earlier. The solution point is where uv is a maximum in the standardised game where the status quo is defined as (0,0). Let the value of this maximum be K. Hence we can construct a curve $uv = K$. This particular shape is known as a rectangular hyperbola. Further we could construct a family of curves for each different value of $K\,K_1\,K_2$ and so on which I shall call the *Nash Lines*. We could then represent the solution as the point where a rectangular hyperbola is tangential to the bargaining set. This is of course parallel to the construct in the theory of consumer demand using indifference curves. In this case we have established our curves, not by empirical observation, but according to a set of rules. We can easily demonstrate, in the example we have taken, that this point is (4,4) located on the line QR. These pay-offs result from B playing his pure strategy B_1 and A playing the mixed strategy of 0.5 A_1 and 0.5 A_2. We do this by showing that the line QR has the equation $b = -a + 8$, and then finding the maximum value of $-a^2 + 8a$. As this occurs in the interval QR, it follows from the convexity assumptions that this must be unique, so no equivalent point occurs on PQ). This is represented in Diagram 6.4.

The obvious point about this is that the Nash point is not at one of the corner points, and in particular it is not at the (3,5) point in the standardised game, or (5,5) in the original game. There is of course no particular reason why it should be so. If we had started off with Diagram 6.4, and not dwelt on its derivation from a chicken game, then the significance of the corner would not have stood out. Nevertheless there is some prominence to the corner solution, and this is in some ways emphasised in the basic chicken matrix where there is a crude sense in which it looks fair. While prominence is an intuitive characteristic and in the eye of the beholder, it does not mean that it is not a relevant criterion. If one accepted the (5,5) option in the basic chicken matrix then clearly it would have meant violating the Nash rules, specifically that one dealing with the invariance of the utility measure. However, this is not to say they should not be violated. A violation might be used to say that actors are foolish and in this case inconsistent, or it might equally be that they have different concepts of fairness. Nash argues that his scheme is both fair and predictive in that the actors, seeing what is fair, will have some 'rational expectation' that this will be the ending point and act accordingly. This in itself is an optimistic point of view. However, if a feature such as prominence were to be accepted as a relevant issue, then the rational expectation could be of the prominent point rather than the Nash point (at least where they differ).

There are several approaches of this sort to the bargaining problem. However, as I am not going to apply them directly, I shall not describe them but refer to the many excellent expositions elsewhere (Luce and Raiffa 1957, Rapoport 1970, Shubik 1982). They are the basis of bargaining theory, particularly those parts of it which derive directly from the theory of games. They illustrate both some strengths and weaknesses of formal approaches to the theory of conflict. They are very abstract and for this reason have limited application to a discussion of the international system. They raise the qualms which some have over the more extravagent flights of mathematical economics, that the intricacies of the mathematics are of greater concern than the substantive applications. However, while some of the results derived within the framework are of doubtful applicability for our purposes, the framework itself is of great value as a basis for analysing problems with more obvious applicability. It also illustrates that the conclusions of logical arguments are often not obvious and sometimes counter-intuitive. This is one of the great lessons that is to be learnt from formal analyses. The real world is more complicated than these simple models, and hence less, not more, likely to be understood by unaided intuition.

3 Bargaining as a process

In the study of international relations we are often interested in what happens rather than what ought to happen. We are certainly interested in distinguishing between the two. In this section I shall deal with a process of bargaining, and the way in which one point rather than another in fact might be selected as a solution, irrespective of any considerations of fairness or other ethical criterion.

The basic problem we wish to model is one where the two parties are able to make, and if necessary carry out, threats against each other in order to improve their positions. These threats involve a cost to the threatener. Now, in cases of perfect information, the recipient of a threat would know whether he would profit by resisting the threat or not. If he would, then the threatener would not make it, as he would lose. Conversely, if the recipient loses more by resisting than giving in, he will not resist. However, the world is full of situations where parties are in conflict with each other and persist at Pareto sub-optimal points in the hope of making the rival accede to a better final position. Strikes are common in domestic relations, while trade wars and competitive currency devaluations are the commonplaces of the international system. It would seem in particular to characterise a lot of warfare, as argued in the first section. When the conflict is over, a solution point is reached, but this solution could have been obtained without the costs of the conflict if the losing party could have foreseen that his rival would not give in to his wishes. Thus the failure to correctly perceive the stubbornness of the rival is a crucial element in this analysis. We want to clarify this in the context of rational but misinformed actors.

Consider again the chicken game of Section 2. Let us regard this as the basic matrix in an iterated game. If there is a discount parameter of w per period, then there is a matrix for the whole game spread over the indefinite future of $1/w$ times the elements in the basic matrix. In terms of the diagram, this means increasing it by a factor of $1/w$.

Suppose that the current position is (5,5) or Q on Diagram 6.1. Considering the problem from the point of view of B, he would prefer (3,6) which is represented by point P in the diagram. Then B plays the strategy B_2 and initially achieves (3,6). A can respond by playing A_2, forcing them both down to (2,0) which is Pareto sub-optimal. However, A will only do this if he thinks that the final solution will be better than (3,6), otherwise he simply loses by the act. Suppose that A believes that B will concede defeat at point $t = k$ and return to strategy B. The pay-off in the over-all bargaining problem will be

$$2 + 2w + 2w^2 + \ldots + 2w^{k-1} + 5\,w^k + 5w^{k-1} + \ldots$$
$$= 2\,(1 - w^k)/(1 - w) + 5w^k/(1 - w) \qquad (6.3.1)$$

The consequence of not responding will be

$$3(1 + w + w^2 + \ldots) = 3/(1 - w) \qquad (6.3.2)$$

113

It follows that if (6.3.2) is greater than (6.3.1), A will accept B's action and put up with (3,6) whereas if the opposite is the case he will respond and play his own aggressive act.

Suppose that A did in fact respond but that at point $t = k$, B does not concede as A had supposed. A must now revise his estimate of B's concession time. Suppose this is now k_1 from the time of revision (i.e. $k + k_1$ from the original starting point). A now simply replaces k with k_1 in expressions (6.3.1) and (6.3.2) and persists with the conflict if the revised version of (6.3.1) is greater than the revised version of (6.3.2). If B never in fact gives in, then A will persist until his estimate of B's concession point from the *current* point has increased to the point that expression (6.3.2) above becomes greater than (6.3.1). There are two issues to keep clearly in mind. First, discounting takes place from the current point in time which enables us to repeatedly use expressions (6.3.1) and (6.3.2). Secondly, and more important for our analysis, past losses are over and done with. In this model, as in all standard optimising models, the actors do not attempt to recoup past losses. While this is a convenient assumption which might often hold, it should not be held inviolate as a description of actual behaviour. This means that it is quite possible for A to rationally persist to $(k + k_1)$ even though it would not have undertaken it if it had realised that it would require $(k + k_1)$ in the first place.

The analysis of whether B will make this aggressive move in the first place is analogous. Suppose that h is B's estimate of A's concession time. If B were to have perfect insight into A's perceptions, and A concedes at the ith disappointment in the above process, then $h = k + k_1 + \ldots + k_i$. B will make the move if

$$5/(1 - w) < 6w^h/(1 - w)$$
$$\text{or } 5/6 < w^h \tag{6.3.3}$$

Again, by the same sort of argument, if B is disappointed at h, he will revise his estimate of A's concession by h_1, and either concede himself or go on.

The crucial thing about this analysis is that at least one, and possibly both, of the participants are mistaken about the concession point of the other if this sort of conflict is to take place. Let K be the actual concession point of B, and H be the actual concession point of A. If $K < H$, then B will lose and be forced back to the original starting point. However, in the period $t = 0$ to $t = K$ he will have been losing and would in fact have been better off not initiating the action at all. Conversely if $H < K$, A would have been ill-advised to respond, to B's attack. He is going to lose in any case and the response involves a cost beyond that of the point which B has sought to impose on him. Thus, in this particular model, a conflict will only take place if one or both of the actors incorrectly predicts his rival's concession point. If concessions were appropriately estimated, then there would be an immediate concession on the part of the weaker party.

The assumption behind this analysis is that a solution in terms of the basic pay-off matrix will be Pareto Optimal. In the basic chicken matrix three of the points P, Q and R are Pareto Optimal in themselves. Thus the boundary of the mixed strategies PQ and QR are likewise Pareto Optimal. However, in the expanded pay-off matrix this is only so if a concession is made immediately. If there is a conflict prior to the concession point, such that in a number of the basic matrices a non-Pareto Optimal point is achieved, then this means that in our over-all matrix, the solution will deviate from the Pareto Optimal boundary. The longer the conflict goes on, the further from the boundary will this point be.

In this analysis, the Nash point has no particularly privileged position. Even when no conflict is acted out, such that the solution in terms of the over-all pay-off matrix is Pareto Optimal, there is no particular reason to assume that it will be the Nash Point. As issues such as mutual perceptions have been introduced into the analysis, which have nothing to do with fairness, this is not surprising. While this does not invalidate such approaches as Nash's to analyses of fairness or other normative issues, it raises doubts as to how practically relevant they are to the analysis of actual conflicts. However, if the actual solutions are not Nash solutions, they violate the Nash postulates. This is an issue of logic. If these postulates are regarded as ethically proper then it follows that the actual solutions of conflicts, if they are conducted in the manner that I postulate, are not ethically proper.

7 A WORLD OF MANY ACTORS: ALLIANCES

1 The potential complexity of alliances

The analysis in Chapter 3 was largely restricted to two actors. While this enabled a number of conceptual points to be more clearly discussed, and aspects of some 'real world' problems can be fruitfully looked at in this way, importantly a number of problems in the super-power relationship, it is clearly very restrictive as far as a more far-reaching analysis of the international system is concerned. The techniques would lose a great deal of their significance as explanatory tools if the range of application could not be extended.

There are two different types of system behaviour where there are more than two actors. I shall call them *parametric systems*, and *actor-dominant systems* respectively, which roughly, though only roughly, correspond to Kaplan's concepts of system and subsystem dominance (Kaplan 1957). A parametric system is one where the membership is large and no single actor can significantly alter his environment. Further it is not possible (perhaps because too costly) for any sufficiently large group to combine to affect the parameters of the system. All each actor can do is adjust to the parameters of the environment. The group, acting as an unconscious collectivity, determines the environment in some critical respects, but no individual can do anything about it. This is the basis of the economic model of perfect competition as well as of some biological systems. For the most part this does not apply to the international system where there are a relatively small number of actors and some of the major ones all too clearly determine the environment. However, there is one aspect of it which may be of some interest for the international relations theorist. A small country in a world of large states usually cannot determine the environment but must adjust to the situation. The range of options may be broader than it superficially appears – the world is full of small states which have successfully defied a larger power's manifest wish that it should behave otherwise. Nevertheless, it can do relatively little

116

about determining the nature of the system as such. The actor-dominant systems can be conveniently divided into two, the large and the small – terms which are to be defined more by patterns of behaviour than numbers. In the case of the small system the behaviour of the system is determined by the interactions of the actors and the actors are aware of this. A knows that the behaviour of B towards it is at least in part determined by its own behaviour towards B, and that changes in A's behaviour will bring about changes in B's. This sort of interactive or strategic behaviour is the province of game theory. Now this sort of interactive behaviour can also take place in large systems under certain conditions. If the interaction between two actors in a system does not affect other members particularly, then they will not be disposed to intervene in such an interaction. The strategic behaviour can go along more or less unhindered and there will be no particular pressure for alliances. Now it may be that the over-all effects of certain types of strategic choice will determine the over-all characteristics of the system in much the same way as in the parametric case but the analysis of how these choices are made is still done in strategic terms. I think that this sort of approach is needed to interpret the various results of Axelrod (1984).

This chapter will be mainly considering the actions of self-interested actors in a conflictual environment. To a considerable degree we will be considering the underlying structure of systems in a rather abstract way and the analysis can be applied to a wide variety of social systems. It is very easy to consider the actors in the international system as being states. The coalitions[1] which are most publicly talked about are interstate treaties and official alliances such as NATO where the actors are states (or governments). Clearly interstate alliances are very important. However, many of the interesting alliances are between actors which cross state boundaries. Thus multinational corporations are non-state actors, but make alliances with each other and with governments over issues which are clearly central to any understanding of the international system. Thus, I stress again the point made earlier, that the actors in the international system, aspects of which are modelled here, are often states, but by no means always.

While I have suggested that it is inappropriate to regard the problems of systems with more than two members as identical to the problems of alliances, clearly the issue of alliances is very important.

[1] An *alliance* is a group which acts together over a number of issues, involving a general agreement to act together. A *coalition* is a group which has come together for some specific purpose only (OED). A large number of cases seem to be ambiguous – an ambiguity reflected in my usage of the terms.

117

In the two person case we were able to dodge it in order to concentrate on other forms of analysis. Unfortunately the analysis of alliances is not easy. That it is likely to be a problem is indicated by the sheer numerical size of the possibilities. I shall illustrate the problem (and the general mode of analysis for working out the number of possibilities in dealing with issues like this), by considering the number of ways in which the four unitary actor states A, B, C, and D can form alliances. At one extreme is the *universal alliance* where all four combine together. This will be denoted by $\{A, B, C, D\}$. Notice that in this formulation it does not matter in which order the letters are arranged. It is not a vector where the ordering is crucial. At the other extreme is the case where no alliance forms. It might be assumed that the actors engage in a war of all against all if one is a pessimist, or mutual indifference if one is an optimist. This is denoted by $\{A\}, \{B\}, \{C\}, \{D\}$. Next consider the options where the four divide into two coalitions. One possible structure is of one versus the other three of which $\{A\}, \{B, C, D\}$ is an example. There are clearly four possibilities in this category, with each being the isolate in turn. Another possibility in the two-coalition structure consists of two sets of two such as $\{A, B\}, \{C, D\}$. In this A could be with any of the three others, but this totally exhausts the possibilities as the remaining two have to go into the final alliance. The final structure is of three possible coalitions where $\{A, B\}, \{C\}, \{D\}$, is an example. There are three possibilities with A as a member of the pair. There are similarly three possibilities with B as a member of the pair. However, as one has already been counted in when considering A this gives two new possibilities. With C there is one hitherto uncounted possibility and when we come to D, all the pairs which it was in have already been counted. Thus there are six different ways in which the four states can be divided into three alliances. We have now analysed all possible alliance structures and come up with a grand total of fifteen different ways in which a system of four can be divided (thirteen if we ignore the universal alliance and the general independent actor situation). This raises fears that for larger numbers of states the number of possible alliances become astronomical. These fears are entirely justifiable. For a still modestly sized system of only ten members the total number of ways in which they can be formed into alliances is 115,975 which can be slashed to 115,973 if the universal and the general independent actor possibilities are excluded. The number of ways in which two alliances can be formed out of ten actors is a modest 511. The division into two is of considerable interest as in violent conflicts there seems to be some tendency for this to happen. Another interesting categorisation is into three groups interpreted as two rivals plus the neutral. There are 9,330 in this category.

The precise numbers cease to be important. We have demonstrated that they are very large and that the process of predicting which single alliance pattern will form requires some drastic cutting out of alternatives. That even modest constraints of a sort directly applicable to the real world manage to cut the options down significantly is illustrated in the first example given. Suppose that the relations between A and B are such that they cannot be in the same alliance. This reduces the number of possibilities from 16 down to 10. A few constraints of this sort can bring down the number of possibilities to much smaller, though still quite large levels. It suggests that the appropriate problem for the alliance theorist should not be to consider the set of possible alliances in the abstract but to ask whether the *given* structure of alliances such as the present one is stable and, if not, in which direction it is likely to move. This is likely to be a more tractable problem and just as interesting as far as any possible application of the theory is concerned.

A conundrum in the theory of alliances is illustrated by the following simple example. Suppose there are three actors A, B, and C who can form any alliance they choose. This includes forming no alliance or the grand alliance of all three. Their problem is to divide twelve units of benefit amongst themselves. Any two can impose their solution on the third, though they can negotiate, and imposition is not required.

Assume that initially the actors have an equal distribution of the benefits. This is represented by the vector (4, 4, 4) in which the first entry is the pay-off to A, the second to B and the third to C. Such a pay-off in the *n*-person game theory literature is called an *imputation*. Now it is clearly possible for A and B to get together and impose a settlement of 6 each for themselves and 0 for C; that is, the imputation (6, 6, 0). C, unhappy with this result, can propose an alliance to B in which B gets 8 and C gets 4, that is the imputation (0, 8, 4). As they can impose it, and it is clearly better for both parties than the preceding imputation, then self-interested actors will adopt it. However, A can now propose to C the imputation (6, 0, 6) which gets us in to the position we were in immediately after the break from equal division except that C has replaced B. Clearly we can go on indefinitely in this way and there is no stable coalition which cannot be won over by the outsider making a better offer to one of the insiders. In formal terms, this simply states that, when the sum of the pay-offs is constant, no imputation can dominate all other imputations, but there is a circular process of domination.

As alliances in the international system in fact seem to enjoy a considerable measure of stability, it would seem to indicate that this model is lacking in some crucial feature. Perhaps the zero sum model is inappropriate, or perhaps there are some other features of alliances, such as that there is a cost to alliance-building. These objections are both legitimate, and we should beware of drawing strong conclusions from static models. The above model shows that there is always another imputation which can dominate any given imputation. It says nothing about the speed at which this process will proceed. Thus an observation that a process in the real world is slow, does not mean that a system is in equilibrium.

Not all conflicts of interest in the international system are zero sum. Of three basic sorts of model which are relevant to discussing alliances one is zero sum, namely when alliances are *distributive alliances*; a zero sum game is essentially a procedure for distributing a fixed amount. Secondly, alliances are formed in non-zero sum games which can be termed *productive alliances*; in a non-zero sum game new benefits can be created, and the formation of the alliance can actually create something new and is not only a procedure for distributing what exists. However, games are normally distributive as well as productive, though games of pure coordination in which the interests of all actors totally coincide do exist, for example at times in personal relationships. Exhibiting the same principles in reverse is the destructive alliance, but I shall continue to look at the optimistic variant. The final sort of alliance is the *alliance with externalities*. In this case the existence of the alliance not only creates benefits for its members but also for other actors who may be unwilling or unable to join it. The crucial point is that the outsiders cannot be deprived of the benefits by the members of the alliance. This last characteristic is known as *non-excludability*, and the over-all benefit produced by the alliance is known as a *collective good*. These problems are widely discussed in the theory of domestic behaviour, but have also unexpectedly great significance in the international system, for example in connection with collective goods such as defence (Olson 1971).

2   When alliances form

The problem of alliances as a theoretical problem was first approached in the context of game theory in an attempt to derive a theory of the *n*-person game. More than half of Von Neumann and Morgenstern's *Theory of Games and Economic Behavior* in fact dealt with what is effectively a theory of alliances. Most subsequent attempts at formulating a theory of alliances derive in one way or another from game theoretic origins. This will be clear throughout this chapter.

It is convenient to describe some of the basic concepts in terms of an artificial three person constant-sum game. Once again this is a game of

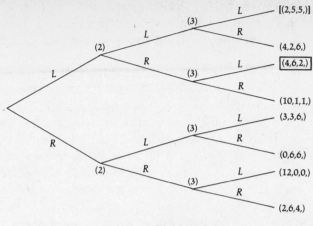

Diagram 7.1

the division of twelve units of benefit, though with rather more restrictive rules than we had in the earlier version. This particular game has no direct interpretation in terms of international relations; it is purely for the purposes of clarifying some of the conceptual points by the traditional process of discussing the simplest possible situation.

Consider a game in which each of three players, named (1), (2), and (3), chooses between two alternatives, Left L and Right R. They choose in sequence with (1) being the first, and where (2) and (3) know what the past choices were. The final pay-offs are determined by the pattern of Ls and Rs and again are known to the players, so the game is a game of full information. The game and the associated pay-offs is illustrated in the game tree above. The triple of numbers at each ending point represent the pay-offs to (1) (2) and (3) respectively (See Diagram 7.1.)

First let us consider what is likely to be the solution of the game if the players do not form coalitions. Consider the problem of player (1). If he plays L then the top half of the game tree is relevant, and he must consider what the other two players will do in this case. He would look at the situation from the point of view of (2) who in turn will consider (3). If (2) also chooses L then he can expect that (3) will choose R giving (2) 2 units and (1) 4 units. If he plays R then (3) will choose L giving (2) 6 units and (1) 4 units. Thus, if (1) chooses L he can expect the final imputation to be (4, 6, 2). By a similar analysis we can show that if (1) chooses R the imputation will be (2, 6, 4). As the first is preferred to the second by (1), and, as he initiates the game, this then can be regarded as the solution. It is blocked in the diagram.

Suppose now that (2) and (3) agree to coordinate their strategies to

121

get the maximum between them, which they will then divide between themselves. As this is a constant sum game, maximising the coalition's pay-off is the same as minimising (1)'s. Suppose (1) were to choose L. The coalition will then agree between themselves to both play L so (1) will get 2 units and the coalition between them will get 10. If (1) were to choose R, (2) and (3) would choose L and R respectively, so (1) would get 0 and the coalition 12. Consequently (1) will chose L, but will receive a lower pay-off than if the other two were not in agreement with each other. This is represented in blocked brackets. Notice however that the division should not be equal between (2) and (3) otherwise (3) would do less well than if he had acted on his own. However, we shall not concern ourselves with division within the coalition at this point.

One way of approaching the theory of n-person games is to assume that they divide themselves up into two rival coalitions and then see how well the coalitions do in conflict with each other. In the three-person game there are just three coalition structures for which this is possible, namely $\{12\}$, $\{13\}$ and $\{23\}$ each against the remaining coalition of one member. The game can then be described by the pay-offs each coalition receives if it plays rationally against the opposing coalition which also plays rationally. This description is known as the *characteristic function* of the game. In the case of the game above the characteristic function is therefore

$$v(1) = 2 \quad v(2) = 3 \quad v(3) = 2$$
$$v(12) = 10 \quad v(13) = 9 \quad v(23) = 10$$
$$v(0) = 0. \quad v(123) = 12 \tag{7.2.1}$$

$v(0)$ is the value of the 'empty' coalition, or the amount which might be thrown away. That this is 0 indicates that all the benefit units are distributed to one or another of the players. $v(123)$ is the value of the universal coalition when a conflict does not take place.

The characteristic function has three qualities, most easily illustrated in the case of the zero sum game with N players.

1. The value of the universal coalition will be zero as the gains of one player are the losses of another. Similarly, as above, the value of the 'empty' coalition is zero. Thus

$$v(0) = 0 \quad v(N) = 0 \tag{7.2.2}$$

2. If S is a coalition formed by some of the N players (i.e. S is a *subset* of N), $-S$ is called the *complement*, that is the coalition of all those members of N which are not members of S. In this case

$$v(S) = -v(-S) \tag{7.2.3}$$

This follows directly from the definition of the game as zero sum.

3   If S and T are two coalitions (subsets of) taken from N which share no common member, then

$$v(S \cup T) \geq v(S) + v(T) \qquad (7.2.4)$$

This is an assertion that if two coalitions join together then they can do at least as well together as they could individually. This quality, illustrated by the above inequality, is known as *super-additivity*. It seems an almost trivially obvious quality. The members of coalition $(S \cup T)$ can always do what they would have done had they not been aligned which would seem to guarantee at least the equality. Further they might be able to do something which they would not have been otherwise able to do for their mutual benefit, which makes the inequality possible. Remembering that S and T can consist of the limiting case of coalitions of one member, the inequality relationship must hold for at least one pair of actors for there to be any prospect of alliances at all. Games without this property are called, somewhat dismissively, *inessential games* in game theory terminology, as distinct from the *essential games* which have this property. They are inessential in that no coalitions can fruitfully form, and uninteresting in this particular mathematical context. However, this should not be interpreted to mean that they may not model very interesting, if possibly rare, social situations, though in fact I shall not be dealing with such situations in this book.

Next let us consider the three person prisoners' dilemma as represented in the following matrix:

			Player 3	
			C	D
	Player 2			
	C		(7,7,7)	(6,6,10)
C				
	D		(6,10,6)	(2,8,8,)
Player 1				
	C		(10,6,6)	(8,2,8)
D				
	D		(8,8,2)	(4,4,4)

The first number in each of the triples in the matrix represents the pay-off to player (1), the second to player (2) and the third to player (3). It can easily be shown that this game has a good claim to be regarded as the three party equivalent of the two party prisoners' dilemma. Suppose we start off with the players all playing the cooperative act, gaining (7,7,7). If player (1) defects while the others cooperate, he will gain 10 while the others go down to 6 each. If (2) also defects, (1)'s gain is reduced to 8, but (2) will move up from 6 to 8 leaving (3) with only 2, the worst outcome in this game. He can then be expected to respond and move up to 4 and (4,4,4) is the solution of the game if there is no agreement. As in the two party prisoners' dilemma this solution is not Pareto Optimal.

Let us consider the formation of coalitions. Suppose the coalition {12} forms. What happens depends on whether the pay-offs are tradeable or not, that is, if it is possible for one player to compensate the other for playing a jointly beneficial strategy, at the expense of the individual pay-off to that player. I shall assume that in fact this is possible. In most international relations situations some form of compensation in the inter-relationships would seem to be plausible. The best the members could do for themselves if {3} played the cooperative strategy would be to play CD or DC and for the D player to compensate the C player. However, against this {3} will defect as it gives 8 instead of the 6. With tradeable pay-offs, the best that the coalition can do now is revert to its joint collaborative strategy and endure the suckers' pay-off. The three party prisoners' dilemma is thus rather similar to chicken, and indeed can be regarded as a slightly extended version of chicken (Taylor and Ward 1982). This is made clearer if we regard {12} as a single player by adding together their pay-offs and regarding CD as equivalent to DC. We then get the following pay-off matrix:

		Player 3	
		C	D
	CC	(14,7)	(12,10)
Player 1 and 2	DC/CD	(16,6)	(10,8)
	DD	(16,2)	(8, 4)

Clearly if {3} defects, as any rational player is bound to, then {12} has the choice of two even worse outcomes, in place of only one in the simplest version of chicken. Neither has much to recommend it.

At first sight it seems paradoxical that, starting from a three way symmetry, a coalition does worse than an isolate. However, before wallowing in paradox there is one redeeming feature. Given that {3} has defected, {12} does better as a coalition than they would have done as isolates. Consider the two party game between {1} and {2} after the defection has taken place. We get the following matrix:

		Player 2	
		C	D
Player 1	C	(6,6)	(2,8)
	D	(8,2)	(4,4)

This is a straightforward prisoners' dilemma in which it is better if the two parties can agree and obtain the mutual collaboration pay-off.

The paradox is more apparent than real. The problem with a three person prisoners' dilemma is that it turns into a chicken game of any one versus the rest. The defector has to win against both the other two players, and hence an alliance with one of them restricts a potential defector's freedom of action to exploit all the other players. Given this sort of structure, it is not particularly odd that the alliance cannot profitably form, though again I stress that, once the defector has defected, the two remaining players do do better by coordinating their strategies. In the next section I shall show that extensions of this problem are interesting, but not particularly paradoxical.

The problem reveals itself again in the characteristic function. The characteristic function for this game is

$$v(1) = v(2) = v(3) = 10$$
$$v(12) = v(13) = v(23) = 6$$
$$v(0) = 0. \quad v(123) = 21$$

Clearly as $v(1) + v(2) < v(12)$, with similar relationships for the other pairs, the super-additivity condition does not apply, though this is effectively just a restatement of the problem.

As a technical device, those non-zero sum games which do not have the property of super-additivity can always be made zero sum, with a properly defined characteristic function, by inventing a 'dummy player' who wins or loses the balance left around some arbitrarily defined constant. This has an interpretation if any coalition is intent on minimising its rivals' pay-offs rather than maximising its own (for in a zero sum game, minimising the rivals' benefits is, by definition, the same as maximising one's own). However, this is not the most helpful way of proceeding for tackling the problems which are relevant for the theory of international relations. I shall accordingly proceed along more informal, but I trust more fruitful paths.

3 The size of alliances

Clearly one of the crucial questions in the theory of alliances is what determines an alliance's size. In one of the earlier seminal modern works on formal political theory, Riker developed a theory of alliances which was based on the proposition that an alliance would increase its membership to the point where it could win the conflict, but stop at that point. If it acquired additional members, the benefits of the alliance would have to be distributed amongst a larger number of actors, meaning less for each individual member.

We can illustrate this by a simple example, which is a slight extension of the case examined in Section 1. Suppose there are sixty benefit units to be distributed amongst five players. Any majority coalition can impose the settlement. Thus an alliance of three could impose the settlement of

$$(20,20,20,0,0)$$

If the coalition added a member then the egalitarian settlement within the alliance which could be imposed is only

$$(15,15,15,15,0)$$

Any distribution within the expanded alliance would have to involve the reduction of the pay-off to at least one of the original coalition members in order to provide something for the new member. Hence, the argument runs, the alliance will not expand beyond the *minimal winning alliance*. In this example the solution is vulnerable to perpetual readjustment of alliances, as disgruntled excluded members try to bribe alliance members to join another alliance, but is not an inherent characteristic of the minimum winning coalition theory.

The most obvious interpretation of this model is in terms of voting situations. A vote determines who wins and who loses, where the biggest coalition wins. In many voting situations, the aggregate pay-off for winning is the same irrespective of the size of the majority of votes over the losers. Thus, anything beyond the bare majority is superfluous for determining the winner, but those who contribute still require a share of the proceeds, and hence are costs for the other coalition members. Riker's main application in the original development of the theory was to voting in legislatures, though he discussed its application to the international system. The question is whether the model from which the minimum coalition theory is derived is applicable to the international system, and if not whether there are still insights to be gained from it in looking at international alliances.

Let us have a brief look at the Riker theory. Riker proposes his theory strictly in terms of the theory of games. There are four relevant characteristics of the problem for our purposes. First, Riker considers situations which are zero sum, arguing that there are a large class of cases where there are 'win–lose' outcomes, which can be reasonably looked at in this light. In many legislative situations, the problems are 'cake sharing' or distributive problems. Secondly, it must be possible for the distribution of benefits (and losses) to be 'determined' at some point in time. By this I mean that if a coalition wins there must be a date or hour when it knows it has won. Prior to that point there is negotiation, conflict or whatever, and nobody has won. After the distribution is determined, the game is over and a new problem of division can face the actors. Thirdly, in the simple versions of this theory, as with most other coalition theories, actors are homogeneous in the relevant respects. This is obviously appropriate when we are discussing voting situations where one person has one vote. Finally, coalitions can be divided into three groups, *winning coalitions*, *losing coalitions* and *blocking coalitions*. From a set of members of a social system, N, let S be a subset and $-S$ be the complement of S (that is, those members of N which are not members of S). If S is a winning coalition then $-S$ must be a losing coalition. If S is a blocking coalition it means that it can stop $-S$ from winning, but cannot win itself. Thus the complement of a blocking coalition is itself a blocking coalition. A blocking coalition is therefore one which can prevent the conflict being determined.

There are two issues which are crucial in considering alliances in the international system – the uncertainty which prevails in the system and the lack of the zero sum characteristic. Uncertainty also exists in the domestic situation and is discussed by Riker. While in a voting situation the rules which decide who wins and who loses are normally clear, it is often unclear precisely who in fact is going to vote on which side. People might switch allegiance just before a vote, they may have an accident on the way to the legislature, they may have been ambiguous in their promises. Even in well disciplined legislatures like the British House of Commons, the party whips, whose job it is to turn out the vote, have a difficult job. In situations where the determination of who wins and loses is less clear cut – a war being perhaps the other extreme – then what constitutes a minimum winning coalition can be very problematic. Thus if there is a coalition which is seeking to be a winning coalition (called a *proto-coalition* in Riker's terminology) then, within certain ranges, the addition of a new member increases the probability of the coalition being a winning one. The size of the coalition is increased until the probability of success has reached the level required by the members of the coalition.

The non-zero sum condition raises some more fundamental problems. Alliances, whether economic or military, are not typically formed in situations which are zero sum, that is, they are normally productive as well as distributive. A new state joining a military alliance brings something with it as well as taking something out of it. Suppose, in a rather simplistic framework, that an alliance is being formed for aggressive purposes. It may already be at the point where it is a winning alliance. However, a new member might make it win more quickly, reduce the costs of the war, and hence contribute at least as much to the benefits of the alliance as it needs to be paid to become a member. Thus, 'winning' can involve various degrees of winning and is not simply the case or not the case as it is in the voting situation.

The non-zero sum quality of many of the situations we are dealing with in the international system highlights another difference. In the zero sum situations, it would normally be supposed that an actor would rather be a member of a winning coalition than of a blocking coalition and of a blocking coalition than a losing coalition. However, suppose we are dealing with a military alliance. Wars are costly, and winning may in fact be perceived as being worse for an actor than not fighting at all. Hence, the aim might be to form a blocking alliance rather than a winning alliance and attempt to avoid the determination of the conflict. This would seem to be the natural interpretation of deterrent alliances. However, this is inconsistent with regarding the situation as zero sum.

Can we say anything about the size of deterrent alliances viewed as blocking alliances? Whether a given military alliance is an effective size for a blocking alliance is a probabilistic matter. Suppose its members, k in number, believe it is a blocking alliance with probability p over some period of time. In more conventional strategic language, it is a deterrent alliance, where the probability of the deterrent failing is $(1 - p)$. A new member will provide increased resources to the alliance and increase the probability of the alliance succeeding to q, where $q > p$. Alternatively the k original members of the alliance, providing R units of resources, may believe that this already provides a sufficiently high probability of it being a blocking coalition. If a $(k + 1)$ member joins the coalition, then the costs will be shared amongst a larger number of members and will therefore still be to the benefit of the existing members. There may be costs in increasing the size of an alliance, such as for example having to tolerate an ideologically uncongenial partner whose military value may be undeniable – a situation which has arisen over South Africa on many occasions. However, in general, the costs involved in expanding a blocking military alliance are relatively small and, from the point of view of the alliance itself, the goal will be to expand the alliance size without the sort of constraint there is in the winning alliance.

However, looked at from the point of view of the putative entrant, E, who has to provide the resources, the story might look rather different. The crucial issue is whether the alliance provides a collective good or not. If the alliance can feasibly exclude E from its defensive arrangements, then the probability of E being attacked will be higher out of the alliance than in it. Thus, it can buy the lower probability of attack by means of devoting some resources to the alliance. This indeed may not be more resources than was being used in any case for military purposes – indeed it is easy to envisage situations where it may even be less. Thus, when an alliance can exclude outsiders from the benefits, there is a presumption that outsiders will want to join. If both existing members want the alliance to expand, and new members want to join, there is a further presumption that such an alliance will expand.

If the alliance provides a collective good the story is rather different. Clearly the existing members of the alliance will want E to be a member in order to lower the costs of a given level of security. However, if E gets exactly the same level of security as it would have done in any case and there is a cost to joining the alliance it will not do so. Hence, the constraint on the size of the alliance comes from the reluctance of new members to join (and the temptation of existing members to leave) and will result in a size which is the minimum necessary to guarantee 'adequate' security.

4 Alliances and collective goods

Much of the discussion about alliances revolves around the issue that alliances often provide a *collective good*. This term is used technically to mean that whatever it is the alliance produces, such as security, is also of value to other actors who are not members but who cannot be excluded from its benefits. They may be asked to contribute to the cost, but they cannot be compelled to do so. Thus, if a country is appropriately situated geographically, then the endeavours of other countries to defend themselves, necessarily involve the defence of this country. Thus, for example, it is widely believed that, though Sweden is not a part of the NATO alliance, it is in fact defended against a possible Soviet attack by the collective good of deterrence whether Nato, the Swedes or the Soviet Union, like it or not. The problems of collective goods raise many intriguing issues in general, but in the case of the international system in particular. The basic problem is that if any particular actor can get the benefit of the alliance without paying for it, then, if he is a rational actor, he will do so and be what is known (often with pejorative disapproval) as a 'Free Rider'. However, everyone wants to be a free rider. Hence, it is possible that a collective good will not be provided at all, or if it is, it will be provided at sub-optimal levels (Olson 1971).

Initially it is convenient to consider the problems of collective goods in terms of the simple two choice games. It is commonly supposed that the collective good problem is most appropriately modelled by the prisoners' dilemma. As Taylor and Ward (1982) have shown, while this is sometimes the case, a chicken game often appears from what looks initially like a prisoners' dilemma. This is particularly true for 'lumpy' goods which are those goods which, to be useful at all, have to exist in a certain minimum quantity. For example, an aircraft detection system is of this nature. It needs to be of a considerable level of complexity (and expense) to work at all, but then it basically either works or does not work.

First, let us consider the case of just two countries who are so inextricably thrown together by geography that the defence of one is automatically the defence of the other. Thus any defence expenditure by one automatically benefits the other by as much. Suppose that some military programme such as an aircraft detection scheme is proposed. The total cost of providing this scheme is 4 units and the benefit 3 units each. In this case, the utilities are not tradeable, as it is the utility each receives from the same thing. With these figures neither side would be prepared to install the system on its own. However, if they were willing to collaborate in an alliance together, they could share the cost and it would be worthwhile. This can be represented by the following game which is clearly prisoners' dilemma in structure:

	B	
	Contribute	Not contribute
A		
Contribute	(1, 1)	(−1, 4)
Not contribute	(4, −1)	(0, 0)

The prisoners' dilemma is not the inevitable result. Suppose it would pay either of the parties individually to carry out the scheme, though they would obviously prefer to share the costs. An example of this would be if the benefit were 4 to each of the parties and the total cost 2. This would give the matrix below which is clearly chicken.

	B	
	Contribute	Not contribute
A		
Contribute	(3, 3)	(2, 4)
Not contribute	(4, 2)	(0, 0)

This argument can be generalised. Let us suppose that, to provide some collective good, it requires at least k of n possible actors to participate. Participation costs 1 unit per actor irrespective of the actual size of the alliance. The gross benefit of there being an alliance is 2 to all of the n actors whether they are actually contributing members of the alliance or not. I shall call a group which is the minimum size to generate the collective good a *k-group*. Let us now suppose that at some point in time there are $h > k$ members of the alliance who will receive a net pay-off of 1 unit each. The remaining $(n - h)$ members are known as the *privileged group*, as they are in the happy position of receiving the pay-off of 2 without having to contribute towards the costs. It follows that it will occur to any alliance members that, if they were to leave the alliance, they would automatically join the privileged group. However, if all the members of the alliance give in to this obvious temptation, then the alliance will collapse, the collective good will not be provided, and everyone will have a pay-off of 0. This is the classic problem of the free rider, which is the core of the problem of collective goods.

Suppose the alliance has exactly k members. If the kth member leaves, then the alliance will break up, and everyone, including the kth member, will receive nothing. The choice for this member is thus a choice of 1 or 0. Clearly, he will remain in the alliance, however much he resents the members of the privileged group who are getting the benefits free. This is a more general form of the three person prisoners' dilemma discussed in the last section. If $k = 2$, then we have the same case discussed above, where the k-group ends up in a chicken game with the defectors. The earlier analysis therefore extends to cases where $k > 2$ and $(n - k) > 1$.

Finally suppose that the alliance consists of $(k + 1)$ members. If two members of the alliance are in some sense marginal, then, in effect, they are involved in the following game with each other, a game which is clearly almost a chicken game, and called by Rapoport 'degenerate chicken':

	B	
	Contribute	Not contribute
A		
Contribute	(1, 1)	(1, 2)
Not contribute	(2, 1)	(0, 0)

This lay-out of the argument illustrates the structure of the situation. From it we cannot say how the situation will be resolved for, as we have argued, neither prisoners' dilemma or chicken offer solutions deduced from optimising, or any other behavioural assumptions.

Despite this, we can offer some comments, according to whether we can draw distinctions between the different members of the group. If all members of a group of n members get the same benefit from the alliance, and pay the same cost, then there is no particular order in which we can arrange the members. When there is no particular reason to pick out one member of a group as being distinct from another, I shall call the group *undifferentiated*. Voting groups are sometimes, though not necessarily, undifferentiated groups. In order to win some particular vote, let us suppose that it requires that k of the n members of the group who are known to be sympathetic to some motion to participate. The number of people casting a vote is denoted by v, so the condition for winning is expressed as $v \geq k$. The benefit of the motion being passed is 4 units to each member of the group. Each person who actually casts a vote incurs a cost of 1 (perhaps in the inconveniences of travel), but the non-voters incur no cost. The decision problem facing any voter, i, in contemplating whether to vote or not is as follows:

	v, the number of voters		
	$v \geq k$	$v = k - 1$	$v < k - 1$
Voter i			
Vote	3	3	-1
Not vote	4	0	0

Actor i benefits only when exactly $(k - 1)$ other voters vote, and he becomes the *pivotal voter*. If p is the probability of this happening, then he will vote if $p.3 > (1 - p).1$. Other things being equal, the probability of this being the case decreases as the number n increases. In small groups, the required majority is more likely to be provided than in large ones, simply because the expected value to any individual of voting is more likely to be positive. This result is also likely in the chicken game above. If there were two marginal members, for example if $k = 1$, then a resolution of the chicken game, in terms of both subscribing to the alliance, is more probable than if there were a large number of actors wondering whether to continue their membership. Here again, the likelihood of the collective good being provided in a large group is less than it would be in a small group. Notice that this assertion is an assertion about how the world behaves based on a consideration of the structure of the situation. It is derived neither from prior postulates of behaviour nor from a wealth of (or even a few) empirical observations. It should thus be treated with caution.

In the above example, the members were assumed to be undifferentiated. One person's vote was the same as anyone else's and the costs and benefits were the same to all. Each member was thus assumed to be as likely as any other to vote. However, in the international system, the members of groups are likely to be differentiated. In a military alliance, it is not any group of k which will be able to provide the collective good, but a particular group. There may be some flexibility, but not as much as implied in the above examples, where one person's vote was the same as another's. Consider the formation of an alliance which benefits a particular set of N states. We can crudely categorise the members of N into three groups. There are the *crucial states*, C, without which the alliance would not work at all. There may be just one crucial state, but there will often be more. There are then the *significant states*, I, some of which must join the alliance for it to work and provide the collective good, but not all are necessary. Finally there are the *remainder states*, R, who benefit from the alliance but whose participation does not increase the quantity of the collective good. However, if they contribute towards providing the collective good, it will lower the cost for each of the existing members. Obviously, the alliance will only exist at all if the C members participate, and will only start at all if they individually benefit from it. If it exists at all, they will be members. At the other extreme, the R members are in a strong free rider position, in that they can all defect and still get the benefits. The presumption is that they will stay out, or possibly participate minimally. The I group are the ones for whom the above chicken analysis applies. In the sort of cases which are of interest to scholars of the international system, the numbers here can typically be assumed to be small so there is a presumption that the collective good will be provided. That is, in general, mutually beneficial alliances will normally exist and not break up, even though the chicken situation exists. However, there is a supposition that the alliance will be hovering near the minimum necessary alliance. Above that point there will be members in whose self-interest it is to leave. If they can do so while the rest of the alliance remains intact, then they will do so. Thus there is pressure towards the minimum.

The analysis of this structure has some direct interpretations. Taylor and Ward discuss the case of whaling. While there is some controversy over the level of whaling which can go on without making various species of whale extinct, it seems to be generally agreed that it is a fairly low level. However, one or two countries can defect – Japan and the Soviet Union being the traditional culprits – and the whale stocks still be maintained. If anyone else joined in, the whale stocks would be exhausted, and everyone would be worse off. Thus the non-whalers are members of the k group, and the situation is relatively stable.

Another example is the problem of nuclear proliferation. In the nineteen sixties it was widely believed that there were many aspirant nuclear powers and that widespread nuclear proliferation was imminent. This has not happened, though there is the constant uneasiness that it is about to. There have not been unexpected technical difficulties which have slowed down the process – it is almost certain that the level of proliferation envisaged could have occurred. The various possible proliferators took decisions, which must have been explicit, not to do so. Conventional military wisdom would suggest that a state is always better off if it has its own nuclear forces than if it does not; if just one other state is considered, the implicit model is therefore prisoners' dilemma.

$$f = \text{non-proliferators}$$

	$f > k$	$f < k$
Potential proliferator		
Remains non-nuclear	10	-5
Goes nuclear	20	5

On this basis one would expect proliferation to have been widespread. That it has not been suggests that the nuclear aspirants failed to aspire because they appreciated that the long-run consequences would be that a lot of other states would enter the nuclear club. This is widely perceived as leading to a general decrease in security (though not universally, Waltz, 1981 disagrees, arguing that proliferation induces caution). In terms of the matrix, this means that the long-run pay-offs are seen to be 5, despite the short-run gains of 20. Thus, potential nuclear aspirants appear to think that the number of defectors who currently make up the nuclear oligopoly can be held at about the present level, and that the existing members of the non-nuclear cooperators are at, or close to, the k-group. This would not necessarily lead to a chicken game – it could quite easily be a prisoners' dilemma. The significance of the k-group is that it is perceived as being a situation where defection from it leads to the alliance collapsing, whereas defections prior to that do not.

One final point about the proliferation problem concerns the speed with which a member of the k-group could abandon its membership if the size fell below k. By the arguments of Chapter 3, the more rapidly an actor could divest itself of these costs, the readier it would be to stay within the group. It is of interest that many states such as Canada and Sweden could probably acquire nuclear weapons quickly if they wished (Meyer 1983). It is unlikely that there are any substantial technical problems for them to solve, and they have stayed some way short of becoming nuclear states by decision and not lack of ability. As argued earlier, this fast reaction time makes the cooperative solution much more stable, and induces a greater readiness to stay within the k-group.

The structure analysed above suggests why the almost universally held views of the nineteen sixties were proved wrong in the event. In many ways it still seems surprising that the expected proliferation did not take place. This analysis suggests a structure in which the observed behaviour can be seen as a possible consequence of individual maximising assumptions. I emphasise that all that has been shown is the framework for analysis. I have not laid down behavioural principles from which this follows deductively as a conclusion. Thus we have a mathematical picture which illustrates the possibilities, not a deductive model which, within the framework of its assumptions, provides necessities.

5 The contribution of members to an alliance

So far the argument has been entirely in terms of whether an actor would or would not be a member of an alliance. I shall now briefly consider the question of the degree of participation; that is, given that an actor is a member of an alliance, how much does he contribute to the cost of providing the collective good – in this case supposed to be military expenditure? In an important paper, Olson and Zeckhauser (1966) argue that, in an alliance, there is a tendency for larger members to contribute not only more resources in absolute terms (which is to be expected) but also a larger *proportion* of resources than smaller members. This is a particularly important point of some practical significance. It conflicts with one's immediate intuition and perhaps also with some concept of fairness. I discuss the issue in the context of a slightly more general analysis of the problems of contribution.

The conceptual issues can be illustrated by a simple example. We consider both the increasing efficacy of military expenditure and its increasing costs as more of the Gross National Product (GNP) is devoted to it. Suppose we think of a 'standard military unit' such as an army division. In purely military terms it is reasonable to assume that the more divisions there are the better. However, the added effectiveness of additional divisions decreases the more of them there are – the addition of the ninth to the eighth adds more than the twenty

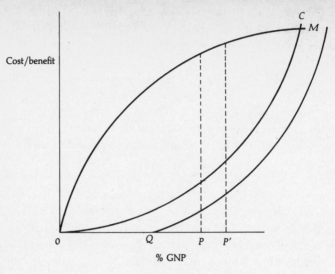

Diagram 7.2

ninth to the twenty eighth. This is due to the more urgent military tasks being attended to by the initial number of divisions, as there must be some heirarchy of military priorities. This is merely an interpretation of diminishing marginal productivity or utility which applies to military as to most other matters of resource allocation. A military effectiveness curve with respect to percentages of the GNP is represented by the curve *OM* in Diagram 7.2.

Now consider the costs, regarded as 'opportunity costs', which are costs in terms of alternative civilian expenditure which could have been made if the resources had not been devoted to the military. It is plausible to assume that the higher is the proportion of GNP spent on defence so the desirability of these foregone alternatives increases. Thus the added burden of moving from 9% to 10% of the GNP is greater than moving from 2% to 3% in that more desired social alternatives are not being taken up. This effect is aggravated if we also assume that the effectiveness of divisions decreases due to having to use less dedicated soldiers (e.g. unenthusiastic conscripts, older troops and so on). Thus an added 1% of GNP buys less military capability on top of being more 'costly' in terms of opportunity cost. This phenomenon is represented by the curve *OC* in Diagram 7.2.

Under these conditions the proportion of GNP devoted to military purposes will be where the gap between *OM* and *OC* is the greatest, for this is the point of maximum net benefit. On the diagram this is *OP*, determined by the point where the tangents to the two lines are equal.

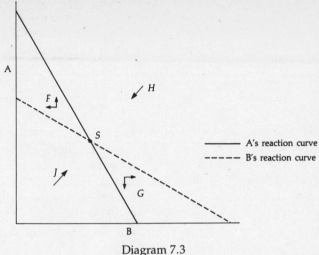

Diagram 7.3

Now suppose that two states, A and B, form an alliance. The weapons of B are now added to those of A, and, even if they are not regarded as equivalent to its own, they are still of some assistance. Consider Diagram 7.2 to relate to A, and suppose that the armaments of B are such that their value to A is the same as that which could be bought for OQ. The cost curve is now shifted over to start at Q instead of O, giving a new optimum point of P' involving an expenditure of QP' (in terms of proportions of the GNP). As the curve OM is constantly sloping less and less steeply while OM (and QM) have constantly increasing slopes, it follows that the point of tangency of the moved cost curve will occur with the benefit curve sooner than in the case of the original cost curve. Thus $OP > QP'$. That is, there will be a reduction in A's expenditure (which is hardly surprising). However, B will be similarly affected by A's expenditure and reduce its expenditure accordingly which will again revise A's view of the optimum, and so on, in a manner reminiscent of the Richardson model of the arms race, though in the opposite direction. However, as this is an alliance, it would seem improbable that there would be a sequential reactive process as presumably the actors are on speaking terms and can make agreements about the final level. The question is, what would be a mutually acceptable agreement?

Let us draw 'reaction curves' for the two actors, illustrated in Diagram 7.3.

The continuous line represents the optimum level of arms for A for any given level of B's arms. The broken line is the equivalent curve for

137

B. The lines are drawn to intersect at S, though from the assumptions they are not required to intersect. However, when S exists it is clearly an equilibrium, in that if the system is at that point, both sides will be content. Now consider what will happen if an agreement is made in area F. A will want to increase his arms while B will want to decrease his. If B succeeds, then this will make A's desire for arms all the stronger. The converse happens in G where it is B who wants to increase arms and A decrease them. Thus there is a pressure in the system in these areas to move away from S. One can predict that if an agreement is made in either of these areas that there will be constant bickering in the alliance as one party appears to want to relinquish its burdens while the other looks like taking on the lot. The system is more likely to start off in area H. In this area both parties will want to reduce arms. If an agreement were signed in this area both would be want to modify it in the same direction, so this would presumably happen. This would suggest that an agreement in H would be unstable but amicably so, leading to shifts in an agreed direction. A similar amicable instability will prevail in area J. It would clearly be important for the treaty revisers to make the final agreement at S and not reach any of the boundaries of either F or G, for in these areas the distribution of contributions to the alliance is in opposite directions, and will result in one or the other state providing the whole of the military effort for the two of them. We should notice, however, that it could happen to either of them, providing that S exists, which is a slightly unexpected conclusion.

Now let us consider the situation when the two alliance members are significantly different in size. Suppose that A and B have exactly the same cost curves, attitudes to arms and so on and, prior to the alliance, devoted the same percentage of their GNP to arms. However, A has twice the GNP of B. For simplicity we shall assume that both countries evaluate the other's arms as equivalent to their own. Now 1% of GNP of A buys the amount of arms of only $\frac{1}{2}$% of A's. This is the core of the issue. In Diagram 7.4B below, which refers to B, the point Q_a which denotes the level of arms of A prior to the alliance, is well to the right. If A were to continue to produce its original level of arms this would indicate B will produce very few arms for itself. However, in Diagram 7.4A Q_b is well to the left as the contribution of B is proportionately smaller. In the diagram $Q_aP' < Q_bP'$. Thus A will initially want to reduce the percentage of GNP devoted to arms very little and B a lot.

The issue now is to find out whether an equilibrium point also shares this attribute. Diagram 7.5A and 7.5B represent the two

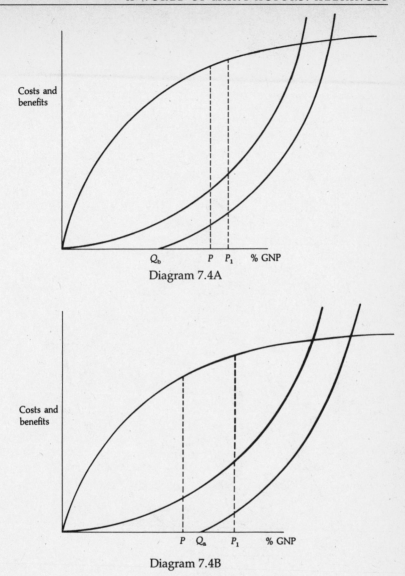

Diagram 7.4A

Diagram 7.4B

countries at equilibrium. We do not need to assume that the arms of A are equivalent from B's point of view to its own arms, but we do need to assume that the two countries 'discount' the others arms equivalently (that is, if a division of A is worth half a division of B to B, then a division of B is worth half a division of A to A).

$P_b - Q_a = c$ is the percentage of B's GNP devoted to arms B depicted in Diagram 7.5B. In diagram 7.5A b is the amount saved by A because

139

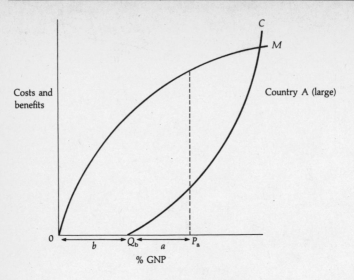

Diagram 7.5A

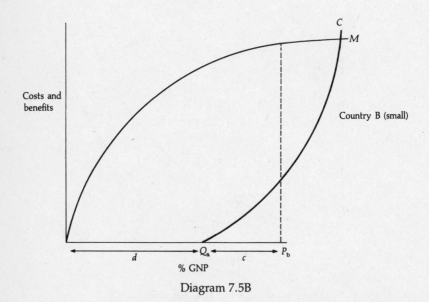

Diagram 7.5B

of B's arms. From our assumptions $b < c$. Similarly a of A saves d of B's production, where still numbers are representing percentages of the GNP. It follows from our assumption of equivalent discounting that $c/b = d/a$ or

$$c/d = b/a \tag{7.5.1}$$

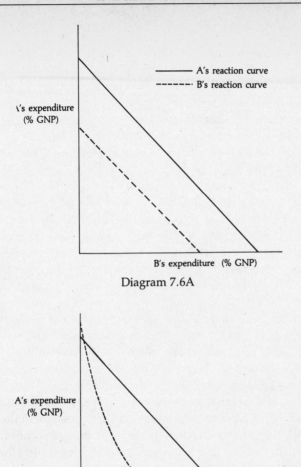

A's reaction curve

B's reaction curve

A's expenditure
(% GNP)

B's expenditure (% GNP)

Diagram 7.6A

A's expenditure
(% GNP)

B's expenditure (% GNP)

Diagram 7.6B

From the size assumption, $d > b$ as B's cost curve is shifted further to the right than A's. Thus, because the cost curve starts at a point where the benefit function is flatter, it follows that the percentage points to get to equilibrium for B are smaller than those for A, that is

$$c/d < a/b \qquad (7.5.2)$$

Hence $b/a < a/b$, and thus $b < a$. As $c \leq b$ by assumption, it follows that

141

$$c < a \qquad\qquad (7.5.3)$$

That is, in the equilibrium position, under these assumptions, the larger country is devoting a larger proportion of its GNP to military expenditure than the smaller, where both are adopting completely rational responses to each other.

It is clearly quite possible for Q_a to be moved so far to the right that B does not want to produce any arms at all. This is represented on the Diagram 7.6A by A's reaction line lying completely outside the dotted line, meaning that there is no point S as there is in Diagram 7.3. Examples where this could happen are not hard to find. For example, any defence of Western Europe is necessarily a defence of Belgium, whether it is direct defence or deterrence. Thus Belgium would have a reaction curve lying totally within the curves of several other countries. Is it then irrational for Belgium to have any armed forces? There are three reasons for arguing it is not so. First, there is a certain amount of arms which most countries need for purposes separate from those of the alliance (even if some could more properly be attributed to the Ministry of Tourism than to the Ministry of Defence). Secondly, a certain minimum of arms is necessary in order that the country should have some autonomy within the alliance and have influence on its policies. (Illustrated in Diagram 7.6B for those points where B's reaction curve rises above A's – at least at low levels of arms). Finally, there may be feelings that to be an extreme free rider is 'unfair'. The criticism of other NATO countries made by many people in the United States is of this nature. The beneficiaries of this unfairness are not totally insensitive to the charge, sharing an intuitive feeling that states should contribute in equal proportions to the costs. However, such a principle conflicts with the principle of self-interest, and some vague compromise seems to be the consequence.

In a slightly different dress, this is the core of the argument Olson and Zeckhauser use to explain why the larger members of NATO, particularly the United States, spend a larger proportion of their GNP on military expenditure than the smaller states. Clearly it is not specific to NATO but applies in general to any group providing a joint collective good where the members have different capabilities and valuations. The analysis is undeniably very suggestive and, if treated with caution, is insightful. The caution stems from the use of a model formulated under extremely restrictive assumptions for directly interpreting a specific instance of a phenomenon in the real world. For example, cost and benefit curves are unlikely to be as clearly defined as in this model; different countries have different attitudes to military expenditure, and a greater perceived threat can make a state value military expenditure much more highly than another state might. This is all apart from the assumption that governments decide about defence expenditure in a manner which is closely comparable to that of an individual deciding about his expenditure on potatoes. However, these caveats aside, this model is illuminating in that it indicates pressures which push in one direction rather than another. While the factors discussed in the model might well be overwhelmed by other factors when the countries are close in size, in the case of big discrepancies, the factors in the model are likely to assert themselves.

6 Strategies in groups: tacit alliances

Earlier I discussed the significance of the TIT-FOR-TAT strategy in Axelrod's two person computer tournament, and its surprising efficacy. Its significance would be muted if it could not be extended beyond this, but fortunately it can.

The basic question is what strategies become dominant in a group whose members are involved in a prisoners' dilemma with each other. Notice I talk about strategies in the sense of a principle of choice, thus shifting the question. The earlier question was an examination of the conditions in which an actor or group of actors, choosing a simple cooperative act, can survive in an environment where some are defectors. Now I am asking a more general question of what strategies can survive, where the pure cooperative strategy is a special case. In particular, does the TIT-FOR-TAT strategy remain effective when played against more than one opponent.

To consider this problem, we can examine a group of actors playing TIT-FOR-TAT, and see if a new actor entering the group and using a different strategy is able to secure dominance. If it does, then the original members of the group may imitate it but not necessarily. To consider this problem, we introduce the concept of *collective stability*. A strategy is *collectively stable* in a group if no new strategy can replace it, or to use the more precise terminology, if it cannot be 'invaded' by another strategy. Let us consider the possible invasion by what would intuitively appear to be the most potent alternative strategy, namely 'Always Defect'. Prior to the invasion we assume the players to be playing benignly and all using C. Thus, the typical member of the group, g, gets the pay-off per period of b. The invader, i, plays D initially and therefore gets a in the first period. However, in the second period he gets c when the other actors have responded, and will continue to get c in all subsequent periods. Thus, the expected value of the D strategy amongst a community of TIT-FOR-TAT players is

$$a + w\,c + w^2c + \ldots = a + wc/(1 - w) \qquad (7.6.1)$$

If i were to play the TIT-FOR-TAT strategy, he would get

$$b + w\,b + w^2b + \ldots = b + w\,b/(1 - w) \qquad (7.6.2)$$

Thus, he will play the defect strategy if (7.6.1) is greater than (7.6.2) and conversely. This is the case when

$$w < (a - b)/(a - c) \qquad (7.6.3)$$

Given the pay-offs this depends on the size of the discount rate. If this is 'low' then the defect strategy will be the most profitable, and if it is 'high' then the TIT-FOR-TAT strategy will be the most profitable. Put a little more carefully, and noting that both sides of inequality (7.6.3) are between 0 and 1, we can state that for any set of pay-offs obeying the prisoners' dilemma restrictions, there exists some value of $w = w_0$ such that for $w > w_0$ TIT-FOR-TAT will dominate, and for $w < w_0$ Always Defect will dominate. Axelrod shows that this proposition applies to all possible strategies. If w is sufficiently large, a population playing TIT-FOR-TAT cannot be invaded.

It will be noticed that this proof made no reference to the size of the group. Indeed, it could easily be interpreted as applying to a group of 1, known to be a TIT-FOR-TAT player, being 'invaded' by another player. Thus the expansion from individual to group TIT-FOR-TAT makes no essential difference to the argument.

Now consider a group in which the players all discount the future very heavily. The discount parameter w is therefore small, and we shall assume that it is sufficiently small for them all to play the D strategy. An invader appears with a much higher discount parameter, such that, in a group of like-minded players, TIT-FOR-TAT would be the appropriate strategy. It is fairly clear there is nothing much he can do. A cooperative play in the first period will give him the sucker's outcome. There will be no response to his initiative, and the best he can do is follow the others and play D. What happens now depends on the structure of the situation. One significant possibility is closely analogous to the earlier discussion of the k-group. Suppose we have a group of n members $(n - 1)$ players are using TIT-FOR-TAT but the nth player is using all D perhaps because his discount parameter, w, is very low, such that he rationally defects. If we suppose the interaction always takes place between pairs in the group, where any actor i meets any other actor j on a random basis, then it follows that i will meet n on $1/(n - 1)$ interactions. Assuming that i cannot identify n in advance, then his average pay-off per interaction will be $[(n - 2).b + d]/(n - 1)$. If this is greater than c, he will continue to play TIT-FOR-TAT providing that he assumes that his fellow players will also do so. Extending this, suppose there are h players, of which i is one, who use TIT-FOR-TAT and $(n - h)$ players who are defectors, i will continue to play TIT-FOR-TAT, on the assumption that his fellow will also do so, if

$$[(h - 1)b + (n - h)d]/(n - 1) > c \qquad (7.6.4)$$

If $h = k$ is the minimum size for which inequality (7.6.4) holds in the required direction, then for any $h > k$ we are in the same situation as we were in the collective goods case. If a player continues to play TIT-FOR-TAT in a group, despite there being some defectors, then it is more profitable for him to join the ranks of the defectors, who have become a privileged group. Exactly the same arguments now apply as they did in the earlier discussion of k-groups. There will be a tendency for players to move over to the all D strategy, until there are just k left playing TIT-FOR-TAT.

The argument has assumed that player i cannot distinguish between players' styles of play in advance – or indeed even identify them having played with them – and so avoid a second experience of defection. In large groups this is reasonable. The probability of interacting twice with the same player in a large group is small. However, in the small group this is not so. If i learns that some players are TIT-FOR-TAT players, and some are D players, then he will obviously select the former to play with. In this case the group will split into two, though the D group will have a constant interest in concealing their identity from the rest. This gets harder the smaller the group. To explore this, it is by now clear that we would enter into a new sphere of strategic interaction which is beyond the scope of the present section.

Though this argument was initially expressed in terms of random bilateral interactions, it clearly applies to the case of a collective good of which the costs are born by the cooperators. k now becomes the critical minumum such that, if $h < k$, the costs of producing the collective good for the cooperators is greater than the benefit they derive from its existence. The extension to lumpy goods is equally obvious.

Taylor (1976) uses a similar argument to Axelrod but in a slightly different way. In discussing membership of a k-group, he conceives of the marginal members playing TIT-FOR-TAT as a strategy for retaining the k-group. A member of the k-group, if it is at the critical size, can punish other players by defecting and dissolving the group. In effect they are then playing the game of 'I'll be a member if you'll be a member'. In this respect, as in many others, Axelrod's analysis is close to Taylor's.

A number of features are of particular interest in relation to Axelrod's work. First, the thrust of the argument is almost as clearly turned towards biological problems as it is towards the problems of political science. It is a relative of the work of Maynard Smith (1982) who has interpreted evolutionary theory in terms of the theory of games. This is particularly interesting in view of the continuous links there appear to have been between theoretical biology and theoretical political science. The links are clearly continuing in a manner which it is hard to think of as purely fortuitous. Despite his own background as a political scientist, Axelrod's approach sometimes leads to a certain distancing of the analysis from the problems of international relations. Most of the significant problems in international relations are about inter- actions between a relatively small group of named players. In biology most of the interactions take place between large groups of anony- mous players. The theory of games was initially thought of in terms of the first sort of problem, but it has proved very fruitful in both its extensions to anonymous groups in biology and large group com- petition in economics.

Secondly, in trying to take the sting out of the prisoners' dilemma there is the recurrence of the strategy of TIT-FOR-TAT. It appears in Taylor's work, though not in a central role. It appears crucially in Howard's very different analysis of the problem. It is prominent in Axelrod's analysis. Its recurrence in very different styles of work suggests a central role in the analysis of cooperative behaviour in conflictual environments. It is interesting to observe that it was Anatol Rapoport, an admirer of Howard's work, who suggested the TIT-FOR- TAT strategy for Axelrod's computer tournaments.

Thirdly, the results of this work are surprisingly optimistic for people whose prejudices are towards cooperative behaviour. The prisoner's dilemma seemed to present a gloomy view of the human condition, whereas this analysis seems to suggest that things might not be so bad after all, providing some consolation for the beleagured optimist.

8 MODELS OF THE ARMS RACE

1 A simplified Richardson model

In the introductory chapter I discussed the work of Lewis Fry Richardson and its seminal significance as far as the social scientific study of the international system was concerned. In this section I shall describe a simplified model of Richardson's theory of an arms race, and in the next section a somewhat more elaborate one. As I earlier commented, the Richardson model is the earliest attempt at formal hypothetico-deductive reasoning applied to the international system and, apart from its continued relevance, is a classic in the field.

A simple definition of an arms race is that it is a reciprocal pattern of behaviour, generated between two or more states, perceiving each other as hostile, such that the level of arms of one of the states is a factor which effects the aspirations and subsequent behaviour of the others. The Richardson model is not a model of decision making processes as such. It simply asserts a behaviour rule which is derived from this general statement alone.

Let us suppose that the decision makers of state A act as follows. The level of arms is denoted by x and those of state B by y. We initially assume that there is nothing problematic about the measurement of the level of arms. The higher is the level of arms of B the more A wants and takes steps to achieve this. However, armaments cost money. More directly, resources used for making arms are not used for making peaceful products which are also desired. Hence the level of arms which a state has is a dampening factor on its desire for further arms. The desired level of arms is thus a balance between these two factors which pull in opposite directions. The simplest expression for such a relationship is the linear equation

$$x_d = a_1 y - b_1 x + c_1 \tag{8.1.1}$$

x_d denotes the desired level of arms of state A. By making a parallel set of assumptions for B we can formulate an analogous expression

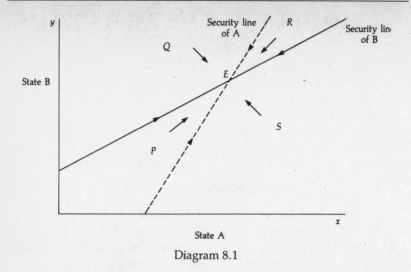

Diagram 8.1

$$y_d = b_2x - a_2y + c_2 \qquad (8.1.2)$$

Of particular interest are the points where the existing level of arms is regarded as adequate by the states. For A this is when $x = x_d$. By subsituting in (8.1.1) and rearranging such that y is on the left hand side we get

$$y = (1 + b_1) \cdot x/a_1 - c_1/a_1 \qquad (8.1.3)$$

I shall refer to this as the *security line* of A. By a similar process we can derive the security line of B which is

$$y = b_2x/(1 + a_2) + c_2/(1 + a_2) \qquad (8.1.4)$$

These are illustrated in Diagram 8.1, where the broken line is A's security line, representing equation (8.1.3), and the continuous line is B's security line.

Consider the case of B when the system is away from its security line. Clearly anything below the line is regarded by B as being inadequate. B has the option of moving either upwards or downwards on the graph and in this case will move up towards the security line; that is, B will increase its armaments. Conversely, if it finds itself above the line, it will reduce its level of arms in that it regards itself as paying too much for security in the light of the level of its rival's arms. By exactly the same reasoning, we can deduce that A will move towards the right if it is to the left of the security line and towards the left if it is to the right. Clearly there is one point only where both sides are fully satisfied, namely the point of intersection between the two

148

lines, denoted by E. This point will be referred to as the 'equilibrium point'.

This happens in the positive quadrant because of the slope and the position of the lines. In turn it reflects assumptions about the armaments decisions involved. Consider state B. The line starts above the zero point on the graph which implies that, even if A had no arms whatever, B would feel that it needed some. However, beyond this point, B does not react very vigorously to the acquisition of arms by A. The line is drawn less than forty-five degrees which implies that at least beyond this minimum security level indicated by $c_2 (1 + a_2)$ B reacts moderately at A's arms acquisitions. If B adopts a genuinely defensive stand, then this is a very plausible assumption. It is a commonly asserted proposition that attack requires more than defence. Thus, if B is merely defending itself against A, it would follow that it would need to devote less resources to the military than A. Hence, the assumption of a not over vigorous responsive security line is likely to be descriptive of some genuinely defensive systems.

I shall now examine more carefully what happens in each of the four areas P, Q, R and S.

In area P both parties feel their level of arms is inadequate. Hence A will increase the value of x and B the value of y resulting in a general move upwards in a north easterly direction. This will continue up to the equilibrium point E where the process will stop. Notice that there is no reason for the system to cross the security line of either state, so, once in this area, the system will remain within it.

In area R the opposite will happen. Both states are above (or to the right) of their security lines and both will reduce their level of armaments. This process will likewise come to a halt when the equilibrium point is reached.

Suppose now the system is in area S. B is dissatisfied so will increase the value of y, but A has more than enough arms and will reduce the level of x. Thus the system will move in a north westerly direction until it meets one of the security lines. It is not possible to say which one without specifying where the system is within area S, and even more crucially some more precise rules of movement. In this simple model I shall not specify such rules. I shall show later that such a specification represents the major difference between this and the 'classical' Richardson model. Assume that the system meets A's (the broken) security line first. It has now effectively entered the edge of area P and will turn to move upwards in that area towards the equilibrium point. Now, assume that it meets B's (the continuous) security line first. In this case it moves to the edge of area R, and likewise moves towards the

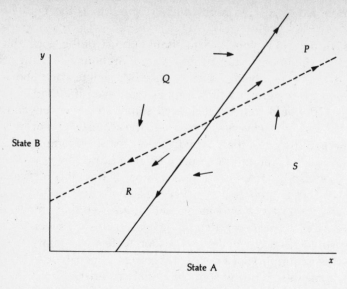

Diagram 8.2

equilibrium but this time in a south westerly direction. In either case it moves down towards the equilibrium.

From a point in area Q the movement is analogous to movement from within S. The system will move down to either area P or R and from then on move towards the equilibrium point.

It is clear that the system is extremely stable in that from any point within it, it moves towards the equilibrium point. Within P there is an arms race but it is a restricted one which arrives at E and then stops. From any other point the system moves towards the equilibrium, which is known, unsurprisingly as a 'stable equilibrium'.

Now let us make some alternative assumptions about the security lines which are drawn in Diagram 8.2 using the same convention that the continuous line is B's security line and the broken one A's.

The assumption about B is that A can have $-c_1/b_1$ armaments without B responding at all (c_1 is a negative number so this expression is positive). Beyond this point, however, B reacts strongly to any further increases in A's armaments which is indicated by the steep slope of the line which is more than 45 degrees. This sort of behaviour could be the result of B believing that A had a need for arms for internal security, to cope with an obstreperous neighbour or to keep down an empire and thus a certain level of arms posed no risk to B. Beyond that level, however, a risk appears and is perceived as a serious one requiring vigorous response.

150

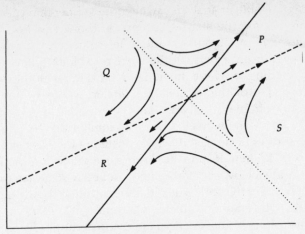

Diagram 8.3

Exactly the same assumption is made about the responses of country B creating a system similar to the first one except that the two lines are placed in different positions and, what is crucial, differently in relation to each other.

A similar analysis to the above can now be carried on with this system. Consider now a point in area P which like the former P in the former diagram is an area below the continuous line and to the left of the broken line. Both sides feel inadequately armed and will increase arms. In the diagram this means there is a move upwards and to the right to a point yet further away from equilibrium. This argument can now be applied to the new point the system has reached. The system moves steadily away from equilibrium, at each point the situation becoming less and less satisfactory for both parties. We now have a runaway arms race.

Now consider area R. Both parties are above their respective security lines and hence wish to disarm. This will lead them further from the equilibrium point, but now in what would commonly be regarded as a benign direction. We have now a disarmament race which will end with everyone being disarmed.

What happens in areas S and Q is more complex and it is more easily seen in Diagram 8.3, which is an elaborated version of Diagram 8.2. Consider a point in the area S, drawn to the right of the dotted line below the continuous line. As in the earlier cases a point in this area will move towards the two security lines. Above the starred line I assume that the system will move into area P and result in a run-away

151

arms race. Below the line I assume that it moves into R and thus to total disarmament. A similar analysis can be carried out with respect to area Q. We can assume the starred line exists, though without making some stronger assumptions we cannot determine exactly where. It is of greater significance here as the system exhibits totally different patterns according to where the initial point is in relation to the line.

The conclusion of this is that this version of the system is very unstable. Apart from when it is actually at the equilibrium point, there is pressure to push it away from the equilibrium to one of two extremes. Further, a small shift in the position of the initial point can produce very different results. For example, a small shift from slightly above to slightly below the starred line at an early stage can produce a remarkable shift in the path which the system adopts. An equilibrium of this sort is called an 'unstable equilibrium'.

The conclusions of this analysis are disconcerting. Clearly the two models are simply different versions of each other. Despite this, we have shown that, for relatively modest variations in the precise assumptions, the system behaves in two very different ways, from the highly stable to the highly unstable. This conclusion is not self-evident and I find it hard to believe that anyone, unless possessed of unusual mathematical intuition, could have reached such a conclusion without an analysis on the lines conducted. It is not very helpful to say that this is an extremely simple model and might be expected to give a rather curious picture of the real world. To derive comfort from this, one would have to assume that an increase in complexity leads to an increase in stability, a proposition for which neither mathematics nor life offers much support.

Obviously there are many different sets of assumptions which would give different security lines, which need not, incidentally, be linear. However, the different assumptions will produce cases which will all fall into the above two patterns, where the crucial issue is whether the continuous line cuts the broken line from above or below. I illustrate just one case as it also serves to make a point about formal modelling. In the second model which produced the possibility of a run-away arms race we left the system moving further and further away from equilibrium presumably going off to infinity. This however is absurd. There is some limit to what can happen even if armaments bump into the constraint of using up the entire Gross National Product. One possibility, which was that assumed by Richardson, is that at some stage the runaway arms race was interrupted by the onset of war. Clearly it could happen and sometimes does, though whether there is a systematic tendency for this to happen is an active current

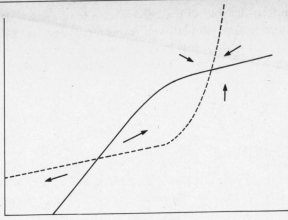

Diagram 8.4

issue of controversy and research (Smith 1980, Wallace 1979, 1982). Another plausible possibility is that, while the cost parameter is a constant for relatively low levels of armaments measured as a percentage of the GNP, for higher levels it begins to increase, meaning that it itself becomes a function of y and the equation is no longer linear. The result of making parallel assumptions of this sort about the two states gives the model pictured in Diagram 8.4.

In this case we have a system which is unstable with respect to one equilibrium but stable with respect to the other. The direction of movement within the model is illustrated by the arrows.

It is not uncommon in making models of social processes to find that a model indicates an explosive system in which variables go to plus or minus infinity in a way which clearly cannot describe a real life process (though some hyperinflations seem to have had a good try). It indicates to the modeller that within a certain domain the model can be quite adequate, but at some point it must break down and different assumptions must be made. There are often implicit restrictions on the domain to which a model applies which lie behind the apparent mathematical generality. When variables 'go to infinity', this point is made particularly clear.

2 A more complex Richardson model

The model discussed above started with the assumption of the existence of the security lines and worked backwards to see how the system behaved in relation to these. In the more conventional version of the Richardson model the starting point is somewhat different. The

153

basic dependent variable whose behaviour is to be analysed is the rate of rearmament or disarmament. For A this rate is denoted by dx/dt (see mathematical appendix). It is hypothesised that this is stimulated by the opponent's level of arms and damped by the cost of one's own. For A this equation is thus

$$dx/dt = ky - \alpha x + g \qquad (8.2.1)$$

and for B

$$dy/dt = lx - \beta y + h \qquad (8.2.2)$$

If A has a level of armaments such that it feels secure without spending too much, it will not alter its level of arms. This is represented as $dx/dt = 0$, which gives the expression

$$0 = ky + \alpha x + g \qquad (8.2.3)$$

Now this must also be the security line, for the definition of the security line is the set of points where the relevant country does not want to alter its level of arms for the given level of its rival's. There is an equivalent line for B where $dy/dt = 0$, namely

$$0 = lx - \beta y + h \qquad (8.2.4)$$

The coefficients in this model and its simpler predecessor are obviously directly related to each other. In the case of A's equation, $k = a_1$, $\alpha = (1 + b_1)$, and $g = c_1$ with similar relationships between (8.1.4) and (8.2.4).

The important alteration in this new version of the model is that the security lines are derived from an assumption about the way in which armaments levels change, whereas in the simpler case the assumption was directly about the security lines as such.

In this light let us briefly return to the stable version of the model illustrated in Diagram 8.1. In the area P, both $dy/dt > 0$ and $dx/dt > 0$. It is possible to go further, however. If a point p is further away from both security lines than is p' then according to the Richardson postulate the rate of rearmament at the former is greater than at the latter. In the simpler model all that could be specified was the direction in which the system moved, whereas this version of the model is richer in that it is possible to specify not only directions but also the rates of change. This becomes of particular significance for analysing behaviour in areas Q and S. It now becomes possible to say of a specific point whether it will move into area P or R. In the stable version of the model this affects the path of the armament process but not the final ending point. However, in the unstable version of the model, it critically determines the whole direction in which the system moves and whether it will end up as a runaway arms race or a move towards disarmament. The unstable model was illustrated in Diagram 8.3 where now we could (in principle) determine the starred line.

Whether the model is stable or unstable still depends on the relative slopes of the two security lines just as in the simpler version of the model. The condition for this is determined by the coefficients of x when the equation is written in the standardised form of $y = mx + c$. The slope of the line is m and c is the intercept on the y axis. For the security lines as represented by equations (8.2.3) and (8.2.4) the condition that the stable version of the model obtains is that $\alpha/k > l/\beta$ or, with rearrangement

$$\alpha.\beta > 1.k \tag{8.2.5}$$

The simpler version of the model explained first is more general than the more complex 'classic' version. The differential equation model makes a precise set of assumptions about movement through time, whereas the simple model is content with specifying whether one event comes before or after another. Indeed, the basic postulates of the complex model are movement rules. These are consistent with the simpler model but other quite plausible assumptions would also be equally consistent with it. Thus, the second model is consistent with a narrower class of possible behaviours than the first, which makes it more powerful but also more vulnerable. Whether at this stage of development of a theory such vulnerability is a virtue, as is claimed for more developed theories in the natural sciences (Popper 1959), is open to question. When Richardson first developed his theory of the arms race, the initial postulates of the system were the pair of differential equations (8.2.1) and (8.2.2). However, as was argued earlier, it is to some degree arbitrary where we step into a system for analysis.

Clearly we would be justified in taking the Richardson postulates seriously just on their face-value plausibility. However, if it can be shown that the postulates can be derived from some prior set of postulates, then this strengthens our faith in their suitability. I shall now discuss some forms of behaviour which were shown by Abelson, rather surprisingly, to imply the Richardson equations.

Let us temporarily put armaments aside and use instead the concept of 'hostility' – assumed to be a measurable concept. At time τ actor A takes up a hostile stand of a degree $A(\tau)$. This provokes a reaction in hostility by B of

$$B(\tau) = bA(\tau) \qquad (8.2.6)$$

However, this hostile response declines with time and the further in the past the hostile act is, the lower is this hostile response. Thus, at the later time t the response has declined to

$$B(t) = e^{-\lambda(t-\tau)}\, bA(\tau) \qquad (8.2.7)$$

$e^{-\lambda(t-r)}$ simply represents a decay or discount function which gets progressively smaller as the interval of time between now and the offending act, $(t - \tau)$, gets larger. It is like a discount factor operating backwards in time, and reflects the notion that the further away in time are events from the present in either direction the more they are discounted.

Now equation (8.2.7) represents the response at time t to a single event at time τ. However, if there is a succession of hostility generating acts or conditions (such as the possession of armaments) during the period from the initial time τ up to the present, then these will all be felt at time t, each reduced according to how long before t they occurred. The total hostility felt by B towards A at time t is therefore the sum of these factors. If there has been a continuous expression of hostility towards B by A during this period of $0 \leqslant \tau \leqslant t$ then the hostility felt by B at time t will be represented by

$$
\begin{aligned}
B(t) &= \int_0^t e^{-\lambda(t-r)} bA(\tau)\,.\,d\tau \\
&= be^{-\lambda t}\int_0^t e^{\lambda t} A(\tau)\,.\,d\tau
\end{aligned} \qquad (8.2.8)
$$

By the same mode of argument it is possible to derive the analogous expression of A, namely

$$A(t) = a\, e^{-\mu t}\int_0^t e^{\mu t} B(\tau)\,.\,d\tau \qquad (8.2.9)$$

Making use of results of Section D in the mathematical appendix we find that

$$dB(t)/dt\,. = bA(t) - \lambda\, B(t) \qquad (8.2.10)$$

and

$$dA(t)/dt\,. = aB(t) - \mu\, A(t) \qquad (8.2.11)$$

These are, of course, the Richardson equations. The stability conditions in this case are

$$\lambda\mu > ab \qquad (8.2.12)$$

λ and μ are the 'forgetting' or discount coefficients whereas the a and b are the direct reaction coefficients (see equations 8.2.6 and 8.2.7). In a very loose sense, this condition affirms that, if the forgetting parameters are high with respect to the direct reaction parameters, then the corresponding Richardson system will be stable.

That it is possible to derive the Richardson equations from some prior set of assumptions about behaviour strengthens our belief that they are an appropriate description of the phenomena in question. It is a further point in which the theory 'touches reality'. It is particularly interesting as it is connected to 'social forgetting' which is a fascinating but poorly understood problem. At times forgetting hardly seems to take place at all, as in Ireland today, expressed as λ being small, or, if no forgetting takes place, equal to zero. At other times it seems to be rapid (λ is large), which can come after a period of low forgetting. Alsace-Lorraine seems now to be a largely forgotten problem between France and Germany despite being the focus of passionate resentment for many years. This model does not add to the understanding of the causes of forgetting, but it does add to our understanding of the consequences of different rates of forgetting. Any theory of forgetting would be a prior theory to this.

While I explained this theory initially in terms of hostilities, it could perfectly well have been related directly to arms. A level of arms is a fairly clear-cut statement of hostile intent, and this can be interpreted as an arms level model without any particular difficulty. Interestingly, and potentially usefully, the reverse also applies. The Richardson equations apply to any sort of hostile interaction system from arms levels to people shouting at each other.

Abelson's derivation of the Richardson equations is not the only attempt to find some prior postulates from which they can be derived. Chase (1969) represents the arms system as a 'closed loop system', which is useful in that it stresses more overtly than the basic model its crucial interactive nature. There is a whole theory of closed loop systems in which deductive arguments are used in order to demonstrate the properties of such systems (see Allen 1959, and the detailed argument in Chase). Chase demonstrates that in a closed loop system, if the rule of 'adjust armaments in proportion to the perceived imbalance' is adopted – which as we have shown is the direct implication of the Richardson rule – then the system reduces to the Richardson model. This is not very surprising, given that the transformation rule in the closed loop system is directly deducible from the Richardson movement assumptions. Indeed it would be extremely disconcerting if this were not the case, and it would be necessary to explore the minutiae of the model to see where some small difference in assumptions made a difference. It would also lead to concern about the model that its behaviour was dependent on small differences in specification and hence be less general than might have earlier been supposed. This model is less appealing than that of Abelson, in which the result is not at all self-evident and it comes as something of a surprise that the Abelson assumptions lead to the Richardson equations. In the case of Chase the reverse is true – it would have come as a surprise (and a nasty one) if the assumptions had *not* led to the Richardson equations through being processed in a different way. The same comment can be made about Simaan and Cruz's formulation of Richardson's model as a differential game (Simaan and Cruz 1975). Within the game a 'target level' of arms is introduced, namely

$$x_i = a\, y_i + v_i \tag{8.2.13}$$

which is something very close to the security line of the simple model. That this results in the Richardson model is not very surprising.

3 Arms races between many states

Clearly a two party arms race is easier to analyse than one with many competing groups. The move from two to more than two actors often brings a great increase in the complexity of a problem – witness the theory of games – and the arms race is no exception. Nevertheless it has to be tackled. While some situations, such as the earlier days of the arms race between the United States and the Soviet Union, can be regarded for many purposes as a two party conflict, this would be inadequate for describing many situations which are found in the real world.

The two party model can be extended and written for n parties as follows

$$dx_1/dt = -\alpha_1 x_1 + k_{12}x_2 + k_{13}x_3 + \ldots + k_{1n}x_n + g_1 \tag{8.3.1a}$$
$$dx_2/dt = k_{21}x_1 - \alpha_2 x_2 + k_{23}x_3 + \ldots + k_{2n}x_n + g_2 \tag{8.3.1b}$$
$$\vdots$$
$$dx_n/dt = k_{n1}x_1 + k_{n2}x_2 + k_{n3}x_3 + \ldots - \alpha_n x_n + g_n \tag{8.3.1n}$$

Each x_i now represents the arms level of state i. The k's are the coefficients giving the degree of stimulus of one country to the rate of increase of another's arms. The αs are the damping effects of the level of a country's own levels of arms on its own rate of increase.

If i is an opponent of j then both k_{ij} and k_{ji} would be presumed to be positive. Thus, if this system represented hostility of all against all, all the k_{ij} would be positive. However, in the real world some are states hostile to each other and some friendly. If a friendly state increases its arms level, then the ally can expect to feel the need for less armaments (see Chapter 6: Sections 4 and 5). If i and j are allies then $k_{ij} < 0$ and k_{ji}

< 0. Shrodt (1981) details the conditions which would indicate various sign patterns for k_{ij} and k_{ji}. We should note that it is possible for $k_{ij} = 0$, indicating that i is indifferent to the arms levels of j. In particular, if i is a large country and j is a small country, it is quite possible for $k_{ij} = 0$ and $k_{ji} > 0$ if i is a potential enemy, and $k_{ji} < 0$ if it is an ally. A version of the first of these is discussed in Section 3.

While the n-party Richardson model is comparatively easy to specify, it is not very easy to analyse. Fortunately, the principal conceptual issues are contained in the three-party case, so I shall discuss this. The important issue is whether the model is stable or unstable, that is, whether the path of the system moves away from an equilibrium if disturbed, or towards it. In what follows I endeavour to give the general flavour of Richardson's analysis and draw attention to one or two points which seem to me to have significance in applying it to real world problems. The analysis is both difficult and in its present stage of development is only intermittently applicable to real n-person arms races. For more thorough analysis the reader is referred to Richardson's work itself (Richardson 1960a) and Schrodt's extensions.

Consistent with equations (8.3.1), the three-party Richardson model can be written as

$$dx_1/dt = -\alpha_1 x_1 + k_{12} x_2 + k_{13} x_3 + g_1 \tag{8.3.2a}$$
$$dx_2/dt = k_{21} x_1 - \alpha_2 x_2 + k_{23} x_3 + g_2 \tag{8.3.2b}$$
$$dx_3/dt = k_{31} x_1 + k_{32} x_2 - \alpha_3 x_3 + g_3 \tag{8.3.2c}$$

The equilibrium point of the system is given by the solution of the above three linear equations when $dx_i/dt = 0$. Let us denote this solution by $(x_1^0\ x_2^0\ x_3^0)$. Suppose $(x_1^1\ x_2^1\ x_3^1)$ is some other point in the system. By putting $x_1^1 - x_1^0 = X_1$, $x_2^1 - x_2^0 = X_2$ and $x_3^1 - x_3^0 = X_3$ we express the problem in terms of deviations from the equilibrium, i.e. we have made the equilibrium the origin. This is convenient in that we want to analyse whether the system magnifies or diminishes these deviations from equilibrium. Equations (8.3.2) can now be simplified to

$$dX_1/dt = -\alpha_1 X_1 + k_{12} X_2 + k_{13} X_3 \tag{8.3.3a}$$
$$dX_2/dt = k_{21} X_1 - \alpha_2 X_2 + k_{23} X_3 \tag{8.3.3b}$$
$$dX_3/dt = k_{31} X_1 + k_{32} X_2 - \alpha_3 X_3 \tag{8.3.3c}$$

Let us take a simplified version of this where all the ks are equal to each other and all the αs are likewise equal. The equations are thus

$$dX_1/dt = -\alpha X_1 + k X_2 + k X_3 \tag{8.3.4a}$$
$$dX_2/dt = k X_1 - \alpha X_2 + k X_3 \tag{8.3.4b}$$
$$dX_3/dt = k X_1 + k X_2 - \alpha X_3 \tag{8.3.4c}$$

By addition and subtraction we therefore get

$$d(X_1 + X_2 + X_3)/dt = (2k - \alpha)(X_1 + X_2 + X_3) \qquad (8.3.5a)$$
$$d(X_1 - X_2)/dt = (-k - \alpha)(X_1 - X_2) \qquad (8.3.5b)$$
$$d(X_2 - X_3)/dt = (-k - \alpha)(X_2 - X_3) \qquad (8.3.5c)$$

which by integration, to get the time path, this comes to

$$X_1 + X_2 + X_3 = Ae^{(2k-\alpha)t} \qquad (8.3.6a)$$
$$X_1 - X_2 = Be^{(-k-\alpha)t} \qquad (8.3.6b)$$
$$X_2 - X_3 = Ce^{-(-k-\alpha)t} \qquad (8.3.6c)$$

A, B, and C are arbitrary constants. As $(-k - \alpha)$ is by definition negative $(X - Y)$ and $(Y - Z)$ will tend to zero as t increases so the interesting term is 8.3.6a. If $2k > \alpha$ then $Ae^{(2k-\alpha)t}$ will tend to infinity as t increases. In other words, the equilibrium is unstable. Whether it is plus infinity or minus infinity depends on the sign of A, which is determined by the starting point. The interpretation of this is that from some points the system goes into an explosive arms race, whereas from other positions it goes into a disarmament system given this relationship between k and α. If $2k < \alpha$, then $Ae^{(2k-\alpha)t}$ tends to zero as t increases. Thus the system goes to the now stable equilibrium. Hence, in this simple case, we have a relatively clear cut condition for stability or instability which is intuitively plausible. If the sum of the stimulating elements is greater than the damping elements it will be unstable and vice versa.

Unfortunately when we move from this very simple case, interpretations in real world terms become difficult. The stability or otherwise of the system depends on terms of the form of $Ae^{\lambda t}$, the behaviour being determined by whether λ is positive or negative. The general results in themselves are of only formal interest, and I cannot see any interpretable extension of the stability rule for the two person case. However, nor can I see any presumption that a system will be either stable or unstable. The negative result of the two-party case remains – that there may be instabilities in any system which are not possible to detect without analysis.

Richardson does demonstrate two interesting theorems within this analysis which have direct interpretation. I assert them without the proofs which can be found in Richardson (1960a). First, if there are three nations each of which in their bilateral relationships with each other are unstable according to the criteria of Section 3, then the triple taken together is always unstable. Bilateral instabilities never result in group stabilities. While this is intuitively plausible, the analysis of this chapter, if it does nothing else, suggests that intuitive plausibility is a poor guide to what happens in dynamic systems.

The second theorem is that if there are three states which are all bilaterally stable with each other by the criteria of Section 3, this does *not* guarantee that the group will be stable. This is both counter-intuitive and important. It is common in looking at interactions in a system with many members to look at them on a pairwise basis, usually starting off with the most conspicuous pair. However, this would be inadequate in this particular case, as it would give us the wrong qualitative behaviour. Richardson refers to this as an abstract theorem in that pairs cannot be observed in isolation. I think, however, that he underestimates the significance of the interpretation of his result. While we cannot observe the pairs directly, it is quite possible that in the estimates of the parameters we would have used measures derived from bilateral considerations. This theorem makes it clear that the deductions from the bilateral to the multilateral must be done with care.

Schrodt has used the n-party Richardson model to analyse arms distributions and arms races. He is particularly concerned to analyse the conditions under which certain categories of power are preserved, where the 'categories' in question are such groupings as 'deterrence', 'equality', 'preponderance' and so on. He derives a number of interesting results. I mention three of particular interest. First, the formal conditions under which the two categories of arms control and deterrence are preserved are very similar (which is consoling). Secondly, arms control preservation requires no alliances (which is both counter-intuitive and not at all consoling). In fact it can be modified to argue that while arms control in a world with alliances is quite possible, it might involve higher arms levels. Finally, the conditions for collective security are much easier to meet when the system has a small number of members (which is neither consoling nor otherwise). Intuition gives us little guide in this last case and has led different theorists in opposite directions. Elsewhere (Schrodt 1978) has shown the intriguing result that, when all states react to each other either positively or negatively, any single state can set its reaction coefficients such that the whole system is stable in the sense of there being a stable equilibrium. That is, any state can be a 'balancer'. Unfortunately, while the nature of the equilibrium can be determined, the level of the equilibrium cannot be set, which diminishes the usefulness of this result somewhat, though not its interest as a non-intuitive comment on the behaviour of the system.

Schrodt's work is a significant development of the Richardson n-party model. It shows the ways in which the model can be applied to improve our understanding of reality and even of policy. Further, it

161

does this in ways which would be impossible without the analysis. However, it is not a manual for arms controllers. It is a stage in the development of theory which might, in due course, result in rather better manuals being written.

It will be noted that, while I have laid out the problem of the n-party arms race, I have only asserted the various theorems and proved none of them. That this is a legitimate way of saving space follows from the fact that the proofs of the theorems cited all use standard mathematical techniques and *given the premisses* cannot seriously be doubted. This emphasises that the controversies over the theories reside in the relationship of the terms of the theory to the world they purport to describe. Once one set of propositions has been shown to imply another, the precise details of the argument become relatively uninteresting for the scholar who wishes to exploit the result as a description of the world.

4   The meaning and measurement of armaments

The theories discussed above express relationships between different variables and between them and time. To say anything precise about these variables, it is necessary to have some measures. To what extent precision is required to say anything at all is deferred to the end of the section. First, I shall discuss the measurement of arms levels; secondly, I shall discuss the meaning and measure of hostility as a characteristic of an individual actor in a directly interactive system.

Armaments cost money which suggests one line of approach; they also cause damage, which suggests another. Thus arms can be measured according to the inputs required, or according to the outputs (actual or threatened). While there is a presumption that there would be some loose relationship between the two classes of measure, there is no presumption that it would be particularly close. There is an analogy between the measurement of armaments and the measurement of capital equipment in economics, which can likewise be looked at as something which has required inputs to make it or as something from which a flow of outputs can be derived (Robinson 1956).

As far as the dampening factor in a Richardson model is concerned, it is clearly the input measure which is of relevance. Inasmuch as the underlying feature we are concerned with is something like 'strain on the economy' the proportion of the Gross National Product would seem appropriate. It captures the nature of the problem and has the fortuitous statistical advantage that a proportion is less sensitive than a sum to purely arbitary statistical convention. For example, a comparison between the USA and USSR depends on finding some appropriate rate of exchange between the rouble and the dollar which involves many arbitrary judgements. To some extent these are ironed out in a comparison between the two ratios. In the Richardson model as such, however, a comparison between two countries is not necessary. The cost factor is an internal strain factor, and does not as such depend on comparisons. While not wishing to be too sanguine, the problem of measuring arms as a cost on an economy is no more acute than the problems faced in measuring anything else as a cost on the economy or, indeed, those raised with respect to most economic measures.

However, this cannot be said about the output measure. Arms cannot be regarded as having a certain degree of destructive potential in the abstract. It depends not just on the quantity of arms of a rival but also the nature of the arms. A very destructive missile which is also very vulnerable to defensive measures is not very useful. Further, the crucial issue in deterrent situations is the threat involved. An arms race is what happens prior to a war which may not even happen. Thus, the 'output' of a set of weapons is the damage that a putative victim or aggressor thinks they will do, not the damage that in fact would be done if there were a war. The basic factor is therefore perceptual. What are the perceptions of the people who are in a position to order a change in arms levels? It is obvious that this is a very awkward question with no very satisfactory answers. The simplest assumption is to assume that the input measures are related to the threat and will stand in as a measure of this. This has some justification in that decision makers sometimes also appear to regard this as appropriate, however inappropriate it might really be. Inasmuch as the purpose here is to explain behaviour, we must explain mistakes and all. This particular assumption, fortuitously and uncharacteristically, makes things easier for the social scientist. It is not a very satisfactory assumption, but it is not grossly misleading, provided we always remember that arms as threats and arms as costs have different effects, and that the assumption is precarious and may break down.

The discussion of the Richardson model, was largely confined to the positive quadrant which, in the interpretation of the variable as arms, was quite appropriate. The equations were defined only for $x \geq 0$ and $y \geq 0$. However, in some statements of the Richardson system, including at least one interpretation of Richardson's own, the arms levels themselves are interpreted as measures of hostility which is viewed as a more fundamental factor. While the model is usually interpreted in terms of arms races, it can be applied to any hostile interacting system. This makes the definition of the variables to positive values very restrictive. There is nothing conceptually more problematic about degrees of friendliness than about degrees of hostility, though there may be a less obvious measure. Nothing stands out as a commanding measure of 'negative armaments'. Trade was suggested by Richardson, but it has its weaknesses, not least that trading partners frequently fight each other. Measures of communication such as volume of mail (Deutsch 1957 uses this for similar purposes) are possible measures. The absence of a measure does not mean that the concept is necessarily meaningless, though it does mean that it awaits more precise definition. It would be helpful to analyse some more general concepts of hostility and its obverse, friendliness. However, we must be very careful to be clear what we are talking about.

'Hostility', 'friendliness' and so on are used about individuals to describe their feelings. What do they mean when applied to groups such as governments or states? 'George feels hostile towards Harry' describes a mental state of George. Implicit measurement is admitted when the verb is qualified. It is perfectly legitimate to say that George feels strongly, weakly or whatever. At the very least this ranks the intensity of George's feelings. When we make comments about George's feelings and their intensity we must specify various of George's acts or things that he has said which we deem to indicate the strength of his feelings. Even a sceptic should admit the possibilities of an ordinal ranking of the intensity of George's feelings, and for the sake of pursuing the present argument we shall hope that he is willing to allow a cardinal ranking. If so, we can have a Richardson model which describes an interacting hostility system between George and Harry where the variables are direct indicators of hostility. Suppose now that the actors are groups, not individuals. We can cautiously extend this analysis. If we say 'The United States is hostile to the Soviet Union', we mean that the individual people who are in a position to actually initiate some act, which could be described as indicating hostility or friendship (i.e. inducing parallel feelings in some relevant individuals in the Soviet Union), feel hostility in at least an analogous way to the way in which they feel it in a purely individual interaction. I think this is perfectly meaningful, but it is an extension of the concept. Thus there are two things to be borne in mind. First, hostility is an attitude of mind of individuals which cannot be directly observed. Various forms of behaviour are used to indicate a level of hostility, but there is no direct way of observing it as such. It is perhaps more accurate to say that certain forms of behaviour are *interpreted* as hostile acts in that we cannot even in principle ultimately establish it. The second point is that, while it is a useful shorthand to speak of groups feeling hostility, this is only meaningful, at least in the sense in which it has been used so far, inasmuch as there are individuals who feel in this way.

It is obvious that the measures which are applied to the variables dealt with in this chapter are severely deficient in both precision of definition and accuracy. In this they are not notably worse than many other measures in the social sciences. However, one might raise the issue of whether there is any point in going to any great trouble to develop measures which have such obvious weaknesses. There are three important responses.

First, a variable is defined by the principles which define the manner of its measure. I have considered this earlier in the discussions of utility where the issue is particularly vivid. If it is *impossible*, as opposed to inconvenient, to derive a measure, then we are deluding ourselves in thinking we have meaningful variables at all. This is an issue to which many writers out of the formal tradition address themselves inadequately in the use of concepts such as 'power'.

The second issue is that, in carrying out formal analyses, we see where there is a need for the definition of variables in a measurable way. While there is a lot of important statistical work in international relations which has gone far ahead of any theoretical development, the converse is also true: there is a lot of theoretical development which is at the moment essentially untestable due to the lack of appropriate observational techniques or to the inappropriate definition of variables. This is not an inherently disturbing situation. It has been a commonplace in the natural sciences for some aspects of theory to grow up initially in a largely speculative manner due to the technical impossibility of a test in the current state of knowledge. Tests subsequently became practicable and the theory or some derivative of it became testable. It would be unduly restrictive to be concerned only with variables which could be immediately tested with the current techniques.

The final point is very important and appears again in the next chapter. When does a small error or imprecision in the measurement of a variable matter in the sense of predicting different behaviour in the system under review? To explore this question let us consider the stable version of the Richardson model. Confidence in whether it is in fact stable depends on whether the slopes of the two security lines are

165

sufficiently different for them to be insensitive to variations in the measurements. The condition for the stable model to hold is that

$$\alpha/k > l/\beta \tag{8.4.1}$$

We want to be confident that this condition holds by a sufficiently large margin for it to be impervious to any measurement problems. If we have this confidence, then modest deficiencies in the armaments data (whether of definition or accuracy) are not particularly troubling; the qualitative behaviour of the model will be the same. This is also true of the unstable model, when the reverse of (8.4.1) holds sufficiently securely for the direction to be beyond doubt. The qualitative behaviour of the model remains robust for most values of the arms levels. The exception is in the neighbourhood of the counter diagonal in Diagram 8.3. This divides the system on the basis of those points which move on up to infinity and those which go down to zero. Around here a slight mis-specification of the variables can have a major effect on the prediction of the subsequent behaviour of the system.

This leads to an obvious classification of models and various areas within models. There are values both of the parameters and the variables where small changes can have large consequences. In these areas predictability is low. There are other areas where qualitative predictability is high, and the model can be said to be robust. Clearly if the social scientist can identify those values and characteristics within a real world referent system which are robust and distinguish them from those which are not, this is an important form of predictability in itself. This analysis identifies those situations where poor quality measures are adequate.

9 CONTINUITY AND DISCONTINUITY: CATASTROPHE THEORY

1 Introduction

Catastrophe theory is a relatively recently developed branch of mathematics which has become remarkably widely known in a short period of time. Like the theory of games, its name is catchy rather than accurate. Indeed, it is positively misleading. Except fortuitously, the theory has nothing to do with catastrophes in the conventionally understood sense of disaster and abrupt destruction. It deals with sudden changes in the patterns of behaviour, whether benign, malign or neutral, in systems which for the most part exhibit continuous, smoothly moving forms of behaviour. It is a theory of 'jumps' in normally smooth systems.

The significance of sudden changes in a system, particularly in systems where measures are poor as they are in the international system, was discussed in Chapter 8. A theory which purports to explain such jumps is inevitably going to attract the international relations theorist. Normally, one day's behaviour in the international system is much like that of its predecessor. Often the unwary reader could read last month's newspaper in mistake for today's without it being noticed for some time. Many of the crucial changes which affect the international system such as economic growth go on slowly, and in ways which in the short period are undetectable. However, from time to time there are big changes in behaviour. Crises appear apparently out of the blue, and patterns of behaviour alter dramatically within hours. Such international crises are understandably a point of consuming interest for both student and practitioner of international affairs. It is not just amongst government leaders that these changes occur. In mid July 1914 most Europeans were doing very much what they had been doing in mid July 1913. By mid August of 1914 the behaviour of many was spectacularly different, and their attitudes more so. The system had 'jumped', and in this particular case in a manner which would warrant the word 'catastrophe' in its ordinary sense as well as in its technical sense. Few would deny that such discontinuities exist in the international system, though they might deny that they were problematic and hence in need of theoretical examination. My response, as ever, is that all things are potentially problematic.

Catastrophe theory was developed by the French mathematician René Thom, the basic work being *Stabilité Structurelle et Morphogénès* (1972: translated as *Structural Stability and Morphogenesis* 1975). The first applications were first made to biology (Thom 1972), which is interesting as another instance of the parallelism, with a lag, in the development of theoretical and formal ideas in the biological and social sciences. Subsequently applications have been made to a whole variety of systems, biological, physical and social, in which such phenomena occur, examples ranging from the stability of ships (Poston and Stewart 1978) to prison riots (Zeeman, Hall, Harrison, Marriage and Shapland 1976). Much of this work is associated directly or indirectly with the British mathematician Christopher Zeeman who has been prominent in both popularising and applying the theory. The claims are that catastrophe theory is a general theory with extremely wide application to systems of all sorts. This claim is regarded sceptically by some (Sussman and Zahler 1978). Uncharitable whispers can be heard that some theorists, in an understandable eagerness to apply the method, have been more hopeful than analytical in their specification of problems in catastrophe theory form. However, even on the narrower interpretation of catastrophe theory, namely that there exist systems to which it has application, it would seem appropriate to examine its potentialities for the international system. In this chapter I shall describe the theory in one of its simpler forms, and discuss the applications which have been made in the analysis of international behaviour.

2 A basic outline of catastrophe theory

In this section I shall describe the 'cusp catastrophe' which is the simplest form of a catastrophe which exhibits the power of the theory. For simplicity, I shall interpret this in terms of a physical model and leave the applications to international relations to later sections.

Suppose we have a ball which rests on a track which has two troughs in it. This is illustrated in Diagram 9.1.

The ball would be in equilibrium at either of the two lower turning points x_1 and x_3. At any other point in the system it will move on a downward path towards the equilibrium directly below it. As illus-

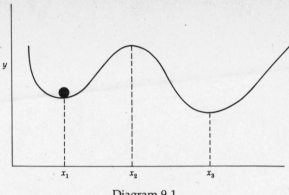

Diagram 9.1

trated, the equilibrium occupied by the ball need not be the lowest, or global minimum. If precisely on the upper turning point x_2 the ball will be in equilibrium but unstably so in that any movement will send the ball away from that point. This unstable equilibrium plays no major role in this analysis.

We can express this problem mathematically. The function, $y = f(x)$, which describes the graph in Diagram 9.1 is called the 'potential function'. We can say that the ball seeks to achieve a minimum point on this potential function.

The equation to the path is

$$y = a_4x^4 - a_3x^3 - a_2x^2 - a_1x - a_o \qquad (9.2.1)$$

As we are interested in the qualitative pattern of the behaviour of the system and not its precise metrical properties we can find out all we need by using the simpler function

$$y = x^4 - \alpha_2x^2 - \alpha_1x \qquad (9.2.2)$$

which has only two parameters (for the justification of this, see Section F of the mathematical appendix). The turning points on function (9.2.2) are given by the roots of its first derivatives, namely the solution of

$$dy/dx = 4x^3 - 2\alpha_2x - \alpha_1 = 0 \qquad (9.2.3)$$

These roots will be denoted by x_1, x_2, and x_3. In the case illustrated two of these will be minima and the other a maximum. It is the two minima we are interested in at the moment. As there are three turning points and hence equation (9.2.3) will have three real roots whose values are completely determined by the values of α_1 and α_2. The question we

169

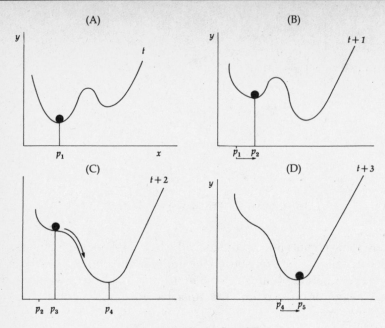

Diagram 9.2A, B, C and D

shall now ask is what happens to the ball which is situated at a minimum point when these parameters are changed in a continuous manner. This is illustrated in Diagram 9.2.

The movements we are interested in are shifts of the ball along the x axis, where it is assumed that the ball moves instantly to achieve an equilibrium if it is found to be out of it. Now as α_1 and α_2 move continuously from the position which generates the shape illustrated in (A) to that illustrated in (B), the ball will also move continuously over the x axis from p_1 to p_2. Notice that at p_2 it is no longer at the global minimum. However, there is no pressure in the system for it to go to the global minimum. An interesting feature appears when we move to shape (C) which is a point of inflexion, that is a point which is neither a maximum nor a minimum but a halting point on the descent of the function. When the parameters have shifted just beyond this point, the ball comes out of equilibrium. Its old equilibrium point has disappeared, and the move to the new equilibrium involves a jump along the x axis from p_3 to p_4. This is the crux of the jump phenomenon. Prior to this point, the continuous moves in the two α's have moved x but in a similar continuous manner. However, at this stage in the proceedings, the only way to maintain an equilibrium was to make the discontinuous jump, or, in the terminology of the theory, make a

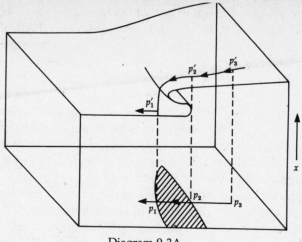

Diagram 9.3A

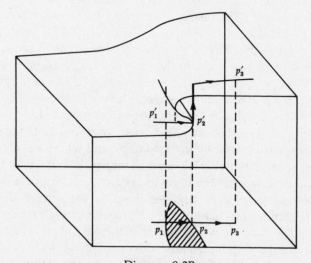

Diagram 9.3B

catastrophe jump. This is the first significant characteristic of the theory.

Let us now continue the story of the ball's movements. Assume the alphas now alter such that there is a simple minimum as illustrated in Diagram 9.2D. At this point let us suppose that the parameters go into reverse and go back to the position illustrated in Diagram 9.2B. The ball still remains at its new minimum point. Further, if the parameters shift such that we achieve Diagram 9.2A again, the ball still remains at

171

the second of the equilibria, and there is no pressure for it to shift back. Thus, for exactly the same set of parameters, the ball, and its associated value of x, is in a different position. Which of the two possible positions it is in depends, therefore, not just on the values of the parameters as such, but on the previous history of the ball in its progress. The parameters on their own are sufficient only to determine the two possibilities. Which of the two is determined by its history. The ball will slide back to its original equilibrium when it has reached the mirror situation of that shown in Diagram 9.2C. The dependence of the position of the ball on the history of the system – that is, the past values of the parameters – and not only on their current values is the second significant characteristic of the theory.

This process can now be represented on a three dimensional diagram in which x, the position of the ball when it is in equilibrium is put on the vertical axis, and the two alphas are put on the horizontal plane. From now on we shall adopt the catastrophe theory terminology and refer to the alphas as 'control variables' and the x as the 'behaviour variable'. The resulting diagrams are shown with a rather curiously folded sheet on the top (see Diagram 9.3A and 9.3B).

The part where the sheet is folded, which casts the shadow on the base, represents those values of the function for which there are two minima. This is known as the 'bifurcation set'. The rest of the surface, covered by just one layer of the sheet, represents those areas where there is just one minimum. When the system moves along the path from p_3 to p_2 along the bottom sheet, this is mirrored on the top slope where x moves continuously from p_3' to p_2' and where x is measured up the vertical axis. If the alphas were to return along the path from p_2 to p_3, x would likewise return along its original path. Suppose now the system moves from p_2 to p_1. x moves along the top surface, declining slowly with continuous changes in the alphas. It moves over the shaded area and finally 'falls off' when it reaches the edge at p_1'. Thus, as the alphas move out of the shaded area, the x exhibits a catastrophe jump. This illustrates the first of the features of catastrophe theory – that discontinuities come about despite the other changes being continuous. Now suppose that the alphas reverse and the system comes back along the same track. This time, the x remains on the lower sheet underneath the fold during the journey of the alphas through the shaded area. It is only when x reaches the end of the lower sheet, directly above p_2, that it makes its catastrophe jump upwards. This illustrates this second and less expected feature of catastrophe theory – that where these discontinuities occur they vary according to where the system has come from, or in other words its immediate past history.

172

There are two further characteristics of catastrophe theory which cause the social scientist to feel hopeful. The cusp catastrophe described above has two control variables. If this were the limit of the model's development it would seem somewhat restricted. However it is not so. The number of catastrophe patterns is relatively limited. With up to five control variables there are only seven 'elementary' catastrophes, which is a small number. Given that a social scientist's life is a constant battle against complexity, such a moderation of patterns is not to be despised. The second point is that the model is 'structurally stable', which roughly means that small errors in the structure lead to small errors in the results.

The cusp catastrophe with a three pointed bifurcation set represents the area in which the minimum, or in our example the position of the balls, can be at one of two positions depending on the direction from which the system has entered the set. This is illustrated in diagrams 9.3A and 9.3B. When the potential function relating to a catastrophe problem involves more terms, this bifurcation set gets more complex and can involve more jumps, which is not surprising. The simple set is sufficient for our immediate purposes.

3   A simple arms procurement model

In this section I develop a model of arms procurement under rather specific conditions. While the details of the sort of situation discussed below are likely to be unusual, the problem is not chosen out of perversity. It illustrates two important principles of modelling. First, the underlying formal model can be applied to all sorts of situations including unusual ones. Given a minimum degree of facility in handling such models, the technique can be applied to any class of problem of interest, even if instances of them are comparatively rare. The second issue is methodological. In the earlier sections, I discussed the issue of models which proceeded in sequence and with minimum feedback between different sets of variables. The same is true of this model. Only a part of the process involves the application of catastrophe theory as such. Earlier parts of the process are the subject of other theories which we can appropriately call 'prior theories' as they are prior to the current centre of interest. In this case, such prior theories concern two issues. One tells us why it is appropriate to formulate the problem in terms of a potential function; the second is an account of why the control variables move around in the way they do; that is, a theory of the movement within the control space. It might be adequate merely to observe that certain movements do in fact take

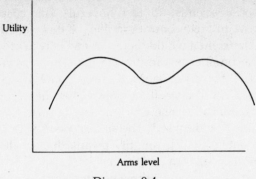

Utility

Arms level

Diagram 9.4

place in the control space without offering any explanation of why one path rather than another is followed. However, a more comprehensive theory of the process is clearly preferable if obtainable.

Let us hypothesise the following situation. There is a small country which believes, as do almost all countries, that it needs armaments for self defence. The level of its arms depends on the arms levels of potential rivals and on the competing demands for resources in the country. However, because of the small size of our country, none of the rivals feels threatened by it, and variations in its arms are viewed by these rivals as trivial and they make no response. During the periods which we are interested in, we also assume that the rivals do not increase their arms. Thus, any variations are due to changes in internal preferences. There are two defensive policies which have appeal, but which require different quantities of arms. The first is a 'High Cost of Entry' strategy which postulates that invaders cannot be kept out of the country but that the costs of invasion could be made so high that it would simply not be worth it. This is a form of deterrent strategy. This sort of policy is followed by a number of small countries such as Switzerland. The second form of strategy is Defence Proper; the invader will be resisted and literally stopped – or at least that is the principle. This policy will obviously require more arms than the first. Assuming that there is a trade-off between civilian and military needs, there will be a governmental utility function with two maximum points as illustrated in Diagram 9.4.

This can be represented by a function

$$U = w^4 + \alpha_2 w^2 + \alpha_1 w + \alpha_0 \tag{9.3.1}$$

The interpretation of this is that, if the level of arms is increased a little above the level required for 'High Cost of Entry', this is a waste of money. It would involve taking resources from the civilian sector without significantly improving the capacity for Defence Proper. This will continue until after the minimum point when sufficient resources are being devoted to the strategy to make it seem serious if not ideal. In principle there is the possibility of adding another strategy into the system – a level of arms suitable for an offensive. Indeed, there might be several of these depending on who was the putative victim. However, this would make nonsense of the earlier assumption that there would be no feed-back mechanism involved. Such an offensive capacity would affect the rivals' arms levels, an assumption which for simplicity I am anxious to avoid.

The problem is posed as a maximising one, whereas for representing the system in the catastrophe theory sense it is more convenient to interpret it as a minimising problem. This is done quite simply by defining a sufficiently large value A and putting $y = A - U$. This can be interpreted as a discomfort measure (to be minimised) as distinct from utility measure (to be maximised). Standardising again to get rid of the constant term, we can carry out our whole qualitative analysis with the function

$$y = x^4 - \alpha_2 x^2 - \alpha_1 x \tag{9.3.2}$$

This will be recognised as the function which gives the cusp catastrophe.

This is a utility function and there is no conceptual problem involved in thinking of it as having an optimum value, nor in it having multiple optima. Such assumptions are not novel. The utility function meets the requirements of a potential function and we have not been involved in any curious contortions in order to thrust it into such a form. Nevertheless, it would not be very interesting if α_2 and α_1 were stable through time, representing a single point in the catastrophe system. Thus we come to the second aspect of a prior theory which is how the utility function changes. In terms of the equations this involves exploring the behaviour of the two alphas; in terms of the referent system it means exploring the shifting preferences between civilian and military expenditures.

There are two approaches to the problem. First, we can simply suppose that they move around in an unstructured way. The second is that we have a prior theory from which we derive the path of their movement. A simple theory is that shifts between a desire for high military expenditure as against high civilian expenditure come in a recurring pattern. As the second approach adds to the battery of unestablished assumptions, at least at this point in the development of theory, I shall confine myself to unexplained paths.

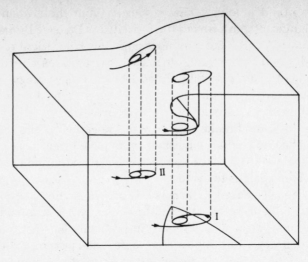

Diagram 9.5

First consider path I on the ground sheet in Diagram 9.5. This path represents the shifting values of the control variables. It moves into the bifurcation set from the left, and thereafter moves around within the area in what for convenience I have drawn as a circle. The 'reflection' of this movement on the upper sheets representing the desired level of arms, initially remains on the lower sheet of these upper sheets and hence the x value (i.e. the vertical value) moves around relatively little. However, suppose that there is a rather larger switch in preferences than usual such that the path of the parameters swings out of the bifurcation set. There will be a catastrophe jump as it crosses the boundary and the arms level, the x value, jumps to the upper sheet. However, when the values of the alphas move back into the bifurcation set, the arms level does not fall back to its old levels. The path remains on the top-most sheet. For exactly the same values of the alphas as before, the arms will move around slightly but always at a higher level. This will continue unless there is some swing out of the left hand side of the bifurcation set (a swing out on the right hand side will not do). Notice that this would explain two possible phenomena – the catastrophe jump, and the different levels of arms which are apparently consistent with the same utility function for the arms levels. Both could be puzzling, but is there a set of real world problems which in fact either do or should puzzle observers of the international system? I shall return to some issues of interpretation in terms of actual problems later.

176

Consider the second of the paths, B, on the control surface at the back. If this stays out of the bifurcation set, then there will be no catastrophe jumps, and the arms levels will move gently up and down in response to changes in preferences. In other words, nothing would appear problematic. Despite coming from the same system, the overt pattern of behaviour would look very different. The interpretation in terms of the utility function which was the basis of the potential function is relatively simple. In this area the splitting factor is relatively small so there is only a single minimum point. Thus the catastrophes which come from shifting between different minima cannot arise.

I deal in some detail later with the problems of interpretation. There are weaknesses and strengths in this particular model. At least it should be accepted as a *possible* system, though whether it is a significant system is a problem I wish to defer.

The methodological point is clear, however. We can look at the problem in terms of catastrophe theory if there is a prior theory which enables us to pose the problem in terms of a potential function. This we have done. There is also an ancilliary theory dealing with the movements of the control variables, though this may be an 'a-theoretical theory' in the sense that all we do is comment that there is movement in certain areas without trying to explain it. We are concerned only with its consequences.

4 The classification of movement

A central feature of catastrophe theory is that there are two types of movement or dynamic. There is the 'fast dynamic' of the behaviour variable x which moves rapidly to restore an equilibrium and there is the 'slow dynamic' of the control variables. The factors which move the control variables are exogenous to the system, whereas the behaviour variable moves as a consequence of the control variables' movements. At the core of catastrophe theory, as it is explained, is that these two different sorts of movement can be distinguished by the rapidity of the movement of the behaviour variable at a catastrophe jump point. It manifests itself to an observer by the rate of change with relation to time. Indeed the observed rapidity of movement of some variable is what alerts observers to the possibility of a catastrophe process in the first place.

However, this reliance on speed of movement as the distinguishing characteristic can provide problems and even conceal some processes which are in fact catastrophe processes. Consider the arms procurement model presented in Section 3 and in particular the point where

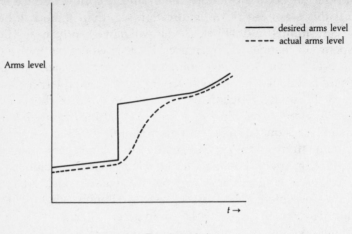

Diagram 9.6

the level of arms jumped from the lower sheet to the upper. Tacitly it was assumed that arms levels could jump instantaneously, or at least quickly. This, however, is not typically the case. It takes time to build up arms levels, particularly in the modern world where they rely on very capital intensive equipment which can take a long time to build. The *desired* level of arms can jump instantaneously, and this could readily be presented as a catastrophe process. However the *actual* level of arms cannot do so. A time series of armaments levels and desired level of armaments around the point where the system leaves the bifurcation set might well look like the paths in Diagram 9.6. The continuous line represents the desired arms level and the broken line represents the actual arms level.

The underlying process here is catastrophic in the sense of catastrophe theory, but the manifest behavioural process is a rather more leisurely affair. There may be other indicators of the underlying behavioural variable, such as expressed attitudes and so on, which might lead us to the underlying process, but the primary observational variable would not help us very much. For example, it is arguable that British attitudes to armaments went through a catastrophe jump in 1938, but, while the rate of re-armament went up, it stretches language to call it a jump, simply because the processes involved took time to put into operation.

A process such as that described above can be looked at in terms of the first expository model illustrated by a ball running down a track to the nearest equilibrium. If an equilibrium disappeared (the system moved out of a bifurcation set), then the ball ran rapidly to the next equilibrium. However, suppose the path had been covered in honey; the ball would have moved slowly and its speed would not necessarily have been different from that of anything else which had been moving in the system. There is nothing in principle to prevent it moving down its honeyed path *more slowly* than the movement of other variables in the system, but we shall shy away from this complication. It is sufficient to say that in this case speed of movement is not necessarily the distinguishing characteristic of the catastrophe process. I shall call such slow processes 'sticky catastrophes'. I suspect that these are common in social life. The assumption of quick adjustments to equilibrium is simply inapplicable to many aspects of social systems, of which the level of arms is an obvious example.

At first sight this might seem to be a severe criticism of catastrophe theory. Superficially it alleges that catastrophes cannot be identified even when they appear. This is not true, though it is a criticism of almost all expositions of the subject. Catastrophe theory still identifies two *types* of change or movement in systems which are different. They are the movement of the parameters of the system which will normally make any equilibrium points move, and the movements within the system as the system adjusts itself to equilibrium. An appropriate analysis of a system obviously needs to distinguish between the two, particularly if there are plans to intervene in a system. My concern is that a behavioural observation will not necessarily distinguish between the two sorts of movements, particularly if the feature of the observation involved is rate of change with respect to time, as is usually assumed. There may be some other characteristics of the movements which distinguish them, but it is not clear what. Thus, there is a problem about how one observes the theory, not about the theory as such. I return to this issue in the last section of the chapter.

5 Pseudo-catastrophes and violence

The interest of the analyst of the international system in catastrophe theory derives from a general interest in discontinuities in generally continuous systems. However, there is a danger of becoming so mesmerised by the charm of catastrophe theory that we attribute all forms of discontinuity to one of its manifestations. This can be seriously misleading and lead us into misunderstanding various processes. I shall illustrate this with three examples.

First, consider a utility function with two maxima. There is no particular conceptual problem in considering a utility function as a potential function. Suppose that war or peace are regarded as prefer-

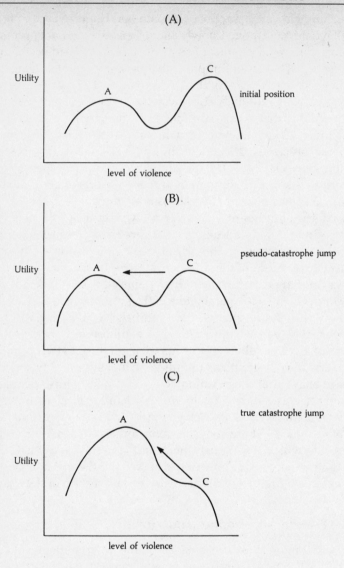

Diagram 9.7

able to some half-way position, that is, they are double attractors. Diagram 9.7A, represents the case where the second peak, C, at a high level of violence, is the global maximum. Let us assume that the system is initially at that point. Now suppose that the control parameters move, as described in the earlier discussion, such that peak C subsides to the same level as peak A as illustrated in Diagram 9.7B.

Suppose then that the system shifts further such that C is no longer the global maximum. In a catastrophe theory model, it is assumed that the system stays at this local but no longer global maximum, for all movement must take place along the potential function. However, if the potential function is interpreted as a utility function, this is not always plausible. Indeed, if full information is assumed, then it is more natural to assume that the system will always move to the global, not the local equilibrium, and jump across to the new maximum as soon as it appears, as illustrated in Diagram 9.7B. In such a system there will still be a pseudo-catastrophe jump when one maximum takes over from the other as the global maximum. The true catastrophe situation is illustrated in Diagram 9.7C where the jump takes place only when the maximum C disappears altogether.

However, such a pseudo-catastrophe jump will reverse itself at the same point in which ever direction it moves, and there is no analogy to the bifurcation set. It is this, however, which adds richness to the whole concept of pseudo-catastrophe. It is important to remember that many systems change their qualitative behaviour at some critical values of the parameters. The jumps to global equilibria can be analysed without resort to catastrophe theory at all. Further, it is also a jump of the sort commonly regarded as a catastrophe jump in the sense of being an equilibriating move within the system, and not some movement of the system itself. This is not to say that behaviour with respect to all utility functions will occur in this way. It may be that movement along the utility function will be local and not global. The decision maker may proceed by making local moves in the immediate neighbourhood of the present point. He does not search for global optima. This is very plausible when there is considerable uncertainty in the system, uncertainty which typically increases the further are the points contemplated from the current level. However, a utility function for which movement is not restricted to local moves is quite plausible and looks very much like a potential function. In the application of catastrophe theory, we have to be clear which movement rules apply, to see whether systems are true or pseudo-catastrophe systems. Very similar problems can be either catastrophes or not. The difficulties of the practising social scientist as distinct from the mathematician are compounded in that both rules will lead to jumps which will be behaviourally similar, except that they come at different points in the system's behaviour. However, this point need not be regarded purely negatively. The search for global as opposed to local optima leads to different behaviour in the system. A system which seeks global optima will be more subject to jumps and in that sense less stable. Further, the position on the behaviour variable will be completely determined by the values of the control parameters and not by its previous history. Hence, by allowing in this sort of pseudo-catastrophe, we have enriched the explanatory tools, not enfeebled them. The only worry is that the conceptual diet may be already too rich for the crudely defined systems it is called upon to deal with.

A second process sometimes mistaken for a catastrophe process is the Richardson model (Feraro 1978). One of the crucial characteristics of the Richardson model is that the qualitative behaviour of the model changes as the parameters reach certain critical levels. It is tempting to interpret this in catastrophe terms, a temptation to which some have succumbed. However, there are two points, one minor and the other major. The minor one is that in the standard model at least, the behaviour variable (the level of arms) does not go through a catastrophe jump as the parameters change for *any* moves of the parameters. The behaviour variables move on to different paths, but these paths are always continuous in time and there is no 'jumping' for any sets of movements of the parameters. The more fundamental point is that what occurs is a change in the pattern of movement throughout the whole system when the parameters reach the critical points of $\alpha.\beta = l.k$. Suppose that the model has moved from the stable version where $\alpha.\beta > l.k$. to the point where this inequality is reversed. In general, the lines of potential movement in the system will simply reverse direction. The level of the system will begin to move away from the equilibrium whereas before it was moving towards it. However, it will not jump to some different point in the system in order to do this, as it would in a true catastrophe model. There is no real parallel to the bifurcation set which gives catastrophe theory its intriguing properties, and the fact that the first derivatives have discontinuous breaks in them which might have raised the hopes of the optimistic catastrophe theorist is no real help. If the parameters were themselves to revert to the original stable relationship then the pattern of movement would again reverse, but it would do so at the same critical point of $\alpha.\beta = l.k$. and not at some different position as would be normal in the catastrophe model. In the case of the Richardson system we are talking about a change in pattern, not a change in variable, and thus really about a totally different phenomenon.

A third process which might be mistaken for a catastrophe process is the jump in the behaviour variable as a consequence of a discontinuous jump in some control parameters themselves. Consider the pattern of violence in Northern Ireland (see Table 9.1). This would

Table 9.1. *Deaths in Northern Ireland by month. 1971 (Military and Civilian)*

Jan	Feb	Mar	Apr	May	Jun	Jul	Aug	Sep	Oct	Nov	Dec	Total
1	12	6	0	4	0	4	35	19	32	21	39	173

delight any catastrophe theorist as an instance of the phenomenon, though as humane scholars the delight would be restricted to their professional roles.

There have been sporadic bursts of political violence in Northern Ireland ever since partition, and of course before. Violence is not a characteristic just of the post 1968 period. However, the Civil Rights movement and its rebuff in 1968 did bring a qualitative change into the picture. For a brief period it appeared that there was some possibility of the political mobilisation of the Catholics in Northern Ireland and, despite the tensions, some possibility of a political solution. This did not happen. However, this was not followed immediately by a great deal of violence. However, 1971 was a critical year. The pattern changed abruptly between July and August. This cannot be dismissed as a brief aberration, as the new pattern has persisted ever since. Clearly something changed. Now this is a time series which immediately suggests a catastrophe. However, it is nothing so sophisticated. In early August, internment without trial was introduced. This measure altered the whole style of the conflict, including the unplanned one from the point of view of the British of a sharp increase in the level of violence. That this discontinuous cause produced a discontinuous effect is not in itself too problematic. Of course it is possible to go back a stage to see if the discontinuous cause of the increase in violence was itself a consequence of a catastrophe process. There are two possible sources for a catastrophe jump in this case. First, in explaining the government's decision to introduce internment, and, secondly, the switch in legitimacy in the way in which violent acts were perceived in both Protestant and Catholic communities. I make a speculative comment on each of them.

In the case of the first problem, the security forces were getting more and more frustrated with what appeared to be an intractable situation. Hence there was an increase in pressure for a big policy change. This can be interpreted as a shift in preferences (that is, a change in the shape of the utility function). The shift in preferences may have been going on more or less continuously, moving in favour of a more hard line policy. An alternative is that it was a change in the actors' probabilities of the consequences of particular policies. These continuous shifts built up to a point where a jump to a more hard line policy was indicated, and in the context of Northern Ireland at that time such an act was clearly internment. Whether the consequences of this were predicted is open to doubt, and perhaps a frustration-aggression hypothesis can as easily explain the moves as any rational, goal-achieving model. This is clearly a possible catastrophe model which would explain the discontinuity which in its turn provoked the increase in violence. However, while it is a possible model, there is clearly a difficult problem in obtaining a sufficient number of relevant observations to confirm this particular interpretation of the strategy of the British government. Undoubtedly a discontinuity exists. But this does not *logically* entail that a catastrophe in Thom's sense exists somewhere down the line. It may or it may not.

The second source of a potential catastrophe process is even more speculative. The situation as described in Northern Ireland has always been one of latent violence, but for a lot of the time it appears that overt violence would not have been acceptable within the community. Such attitudes appear to have changed after 1968. The events of 1968 made a political solution to the problems seem remote to the Catholic community, which meant that political violence acquired a legitimacy that it had previously lacked, at least for many years. Whether the legitimacy of violence had grown up gradually or moved up sharply as a result of the events of 1968 is hard to say. The definition and measurement of a variable as amorphous as the 'legitimacy of political violence' is not easy. However, it may be possible, either directly or by implication, and to do so might yield some insight into the conflict processes in Northern Ireland. Again a smooth increase over time or a sudden jump can both be incorporated into the catastrophe theory programme. The worry returns – is there anything which cannot?

My apparent concern with whether some process is 'really' a catastrophe process or not might appear obsessive pedantry. It may be pedantic, but if so it is a necessary pedantry. If we were simply interested in making a collection of *ad hoc* statements, then categorisations into 'fast' and 'slow' and similar directly observable categories would be quite adequate. However, as we are interested in a deductive theory it is necessary to be able to classify movements correctly. This is equally true if we are concerned with policy. The interesting thing about a catastrophe process is that a discontinuity does not typically occur for the same value of the variables when these variables are moving in one direction as opposed to another. Thus, if there are tensions between two states, some overtly hostile act such as an increase in armaments might be taken at some particular point when tension is increasing, but not be reversed at the same level when (or if) tension is decreasing. Instead it might occur at some very much lower level of tension. The failure of the discontinuity to occur in the overt process should not then be taken as evidence that the values in the underlying tension function have not reversed to their previous level. Instinctively we tend to assume that, if a process is reversible at all, it is a simple reversibility which occurs at the same point in the system as the initial jump. However, such simple reversibilities are not universal and may even be rare. Catastrophe theory conceptualises these more sophisticated reversibilities. Confusions between simple and catastrophic reversibilities can mean we might totally misunderstand some system we are dealing with. Thus, in a hostility system we might misread the significance of the absence of a discontinuity at some point.

10 THE INTERNATIONAL SYSTEM AS A WHOLE

1 Introduction

The analysis so far has mainly concerned the behaviour of individual actors in their separate interactions. We now want to look at some more general characteristics of the system as a whole, and the various patterns which are formed from the behaviour of the individual elements. Clearly there is an intimate relationship between the behaviour of the individual units and the aggregate, the latter being built up from the former. However, in many complex systems, it is not always easy to trace out these relationships, so at a given point of time (such as in our present understanding of the international system) they may not be known. Nevertheless, we are still interested in aggregative behaviour even if the linkage from the components to the aggregate is currently unclear. Consequently we analyse aggregative behaviour without tying it too closely to the behaviour of individual actors. We have done this already to a degree in the Richardson models where the links between behaviour and any decision models was dealt with rather casually. It is a common scientific device to make propositions about one level of a system, without immediately worrying too much about its relationships with other levels, though this is not a final position with which we are content. The relations between systemic analysis (macro-analysis) and the analysis of units (micro-analysis) must ultimately be traced.

I discuss some models in Sections 2 and 3 of this chapter, in which the aggregative features of the systems are the basic variables. Given the nature of variables considered, the prime, though not exclusive actors in these sections are states.

2 The beginning of wars: some puzzling patterns

Let us consider a particular rather curious problem about violent behaviour in the international system during the course of the

186

twentieth century. The way in which the level of violence increased at the beginning of the First World War was quite markedly different from that in the Second. Once war was declared in August 1914, the participants started fighting with a will and the level of violence became very high within days. Any constraints were not political but technical or strategic (for example, the fleets could technically have sailed into battle immediately, but for sensible strategic reasons did not). The start of the First World War can be identified to within days whether one uses political criteria such as declarations of war or behavioural criteria such as the level of battle deaths.

The same is not true of the Second World War. There was a steady increase in violence in the international system throughout the nineteen thirties. The actual declaration of war by Britain and France in September 1939 did not increase the level of violence notably, particularly after the brief Polish campaign. The large increase in violence came after the German invasion of the Soviet Union in 1941. Earlier violence increased steadily over the years. Though there were local jumps both up and down, the basic pattern did not show the sudden jump in violence in the international system experienced in August 1914. In neither political nor behavioural terms is there a clear cut answer to the question 'When did the Second World War start?' Many dates could be proffered with equal plausibility.

Differences between apparently comparable events excite a theorist as much as similarities between apparently disparate ones. On the face of it, these differences seem odd. However, if the underlying structure of the international system is described as a catastrophe system, such differences in behaviour would fit quite naturally under a *common* classification. Holt, Job and Markus (1978) provided such a common classification. I shall now describe their approach to the problem.

The Prior Theory:[1]

The behaviour investigated is something we can loosely conceptualise as 'war/peace' behaviour. The obvious indicator of 'degrees of war' is battle deaths which is in any case the form of behaviour we wanted to analyse in the first place. It is not so obvious how we designate degrees of peace as was discussed in connection with friendliness in Chapter 8. We shall concentrate on hostile behaviour and use battle deaths, denoted by x, as the behaviour variable in the potential function. Notice that the degrees of war are the degrees of war of the system as a whole, that is, battle deaths

[1] See Chapter 8 Section 4.

summed over the actors. The distribution between different actors is not of concern in this model. It is systemic properties we are concerned with. Four control variables are postulated. These are similarly systemic characteristics.

Unsatisfiable systemic demand: α_1
Coalition opportunities: α_2
Violence Potential: α_3
Relative Response Time: α_4

'Unsatisfiable systemic demand' is the aspirations of the international actors which under the present system cannot be satisfied. Notice again that this is a systemic property. A demand, such as the control of the West Bank, might be felt by one actor but there is nothing it can do about it. It is unsatisfiable for the individual actor and for the system. If something happens such that the actor is able to do something about it, then it can only be at the expense of some other member of the system who was not previously dissatisfied. From the point of view of the system as a whole and its proclivities for violence, nothing has changed. This can almost be regarded as a measure of how far the international system is zero sum.

'Coalition Opportunities' are the opportunities for making military alliances. The fewer opportunities are these, the higher is this factor, indicating the degree of rigidity in the system at least as far as alliancies are concerned.

'Violence Potential' is the ability to wage war, indicated by the level of armaments.

'Relative Response Time' is the final factor and indicates the speed with which decision makers respond to each others' messages or actions. It combines the speed with which information flows, with the speed with which it is comprehended, and with the speed with which it is acted upon.

These four factors interact with each other and the behaviour variable. The assertion (which is plausible given these interpretations of the elements in the equation) is that, for any given set of the control variables, it is the behaviour variable which adjusts relatively quickly to bring the system into some sort of equilibrium if the system is disturbed. These factors are then related by the potential function and the theory is expressed as

$$y = x^6 - \alpha_4 x^4 - \alpha_3 x^3 - \alpha_2 x^2 - \alpha_1 x \qquad (10.2.1)$$

The aim of the analysis is to see what the consequences of making these assumptions are. These factors were not selected in a totally

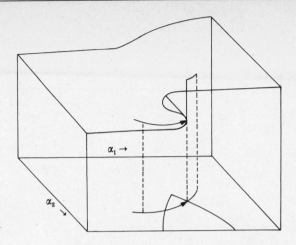

Diagram 10.1

casual manner. They all have some claim to being regarded as significant in the light of research in the behaviour of the international system. However, we have gone further than asserting relevance. We have proposed a particular functional form, specifying the precise nature of their inter-relationships. The purpose of this is to see what conclusions can be derived. Naturally if these correspond with observations of reality we are delighted, and regard this as reason for accepting these premises as in fact descriptive of reality. The delight is increased if we can find no other set of premises which correspond with reality as successfully. However, it would be rash to pretend that this was the case at this stage. The assertions about the significance of these variables, and the later claims about their rough values are highly contentious, to put it in the mildest possible way. For the moment it is ambition enough to get a plausible model, and hope that in the future we might reach closer to the goal of tested theory.

The catastrophe model

Let us suppose then that equation (10.2.1) describes behaviour in the international system. It will produce one of the elementary catastrophes, mentioned in Chapter 9, known as the butterfly catastrophe. Because of this, we already know that the different forms of behavioural change, sometimes coming in a major jump and sometimes in a smooth flow, can be generated from the same system. We have at least reached the point where we can say that such a system is

189

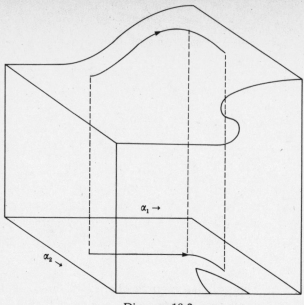

Diagram 10.2

possible. In this case we can go a little further (Job, Holt and Markus) and at least speculate how some of the control variables have altered during the appropriate periods.

First consider the case of the period immediately prior to the First World War. This is illustrated in Diagram 10.1.

The high value of the violence potential during the years immediately prior to the war and the low value of the reaction times (that is, they were fast) reduces the bifurcation set to something more like a cusp shape – the distinctive butterfly extras have essentially disappeared. Unsatisfiable systemic demand; α_1 relatively low in the late part of the nineteenth century when there was still a supply of possible colonial territories, had increased, not least because of the alteration in Germany's aspirations, in a way which could only be satisfied if the other European powers were to become dissatisfied.

In the period immediately prior to the war, we see the system move such that the path now moves into the bifurcation set as unsatisfiable demand, and the increase in rigidity, in the sense of a reduction in the alliance opportunities α_2, becomes progressively more significant. When the control parameters move out of the bifurcation set, the behaviour variable jumps radically from the more or less constant and essentially zero level of before the war to the high levels which characterised August 1914.

The years prior to the Second World War are illustrated in Diagram 10.2 which involves a simplification. The bifurcation set is drawn without the butterfly elements which were arguably present for part of the time, but equally, with the rather loose form of assumption we are making here, were almost certainly not present for other parts of the time. However, that is not the critical issue at this level of analysis. What is more important is the path of the system in relation to the bifurcation set, and in particular whether it passes through the set or not (see Diagram 10.2).

The hypothesis illustrated is that the relatively high values of the coalition opportunities variable, α_2 indicating a lack of alliance rigidity at this time as compared with 1914, keeps the path of the system towards the back of the bottom surface, and away from the bifurcation set. This means that the equivalent path on the upper surface does not go through one of the catastrophe jumps, but moves around on the smooth portion of the upper surface.

This provides us then with some tentative explanation – or, perhaps better, some tentative classification of the relevant issues – of the different behaviour of the international system between the two periods in relation to the other characteristics of the system. Clearly it would be rash to conclude from this limited success that the structure of the international system is in fact one which can be described by this sort of catastrophe model. It is undeniably a highly speculative application. Many other models might well generate the same result. What is significant is that from a common basic model we can generate the rather different patterns of behaviour in these two significant cases. This suggests that this is a structure which is worth a lot more investigation to see what further explanatory successes it can come up with.

3   A general hostility model of the international system

Another attempt to examine the behaviour of the system as a whole has been carried out by Muncaster and Zinnes. This is overtly a very speculative analysis; it is a model which is used to develop a conceptual framework, rather than anything which is likely to lead quickly to practical application. They use 'hostility' as a basic attribute of the international system. They make various assumptions about the factors which generate or dampen the hostility and its rate of change (the prior theories), then examine the consequences of these assumptions. However, this is done in a conceptually very different way from the Richardson model, even in the version of that model which interprets arms as a surrogate for hostility. The Richardson model is an interactive model. By this I mean that a hostile act by A provokes a hostile act by B which provokes a further hostile act by A and so on. Hostility is always regarded as the attribute of an identified actor. However, this other approach is to look at the system without regard to which actor experiences the hostility. Thus we would talk of the hostility in a system increasing or decreasing, which would cover interactive processes but also a number of other processes as well – such as imitative processes by allies. In other words, the problem is posed at another level of analysis. Zinnes and Muncaster (1983 and 1984) have discussed various models in this class at increasing levels of complexity. I present a slightly modified version of one of their models. Like the more complex 'classic' versions of the Richardson model, this is a dynamic model in that it explicitly brings time into the formulation. It is posed in terms of differential equations, which provides a rich body of mathematics readily available for the analysis. For the purposes of exposition, I regard the issue of the measurement (or even meaning) of the concept of hostility as unproblematic. This obvious absurdity I correct in Section 4.

The basic model

The basic element of analysis is $H(t)$, which is the hostility in the system of time t.

Next there is the *motion* in the system which is defined as proportional to the rate of change of hostility. Thus

$$m(t) = C \cdot dH(t)/dt \qquad (10.3.1)$$

The rate of change of this motion is determined by factors outside the system, that is, exogenous forces. Grouped together as $f(t)$ they give

$$dm(t)/dt = f(t) \qquad (10.3.2)$$

From this it follows that

$$C \cdot d^2H(t)/dt^2 = f(t) \qquad (10.3.3)$$

In this model we shall assume that $f(t)$ is comprised of four separate forces, to be analysed shortly, and that their effects are simply additive. They are illustrated in Diagram 10.3 and expressed as

$$f(t) = f_1(t) + f_2(t) + f_3(t) + f_4(t) \qquad (10.3.4)$$

It is this system we now want to investigate. The first step in this is to look at the exogenous forces in detail. Four are specified, but clearly a model of the same class could have either more or less. There is no theoretical reason which suggests any particular number. I shall simply deal with those suggested by Muncaster and Zinnes. The procedure is to specify a hypothesis, and formulate the appropriate expression in terms of the differential equations used in the model.

Hypothesis (1) for the Richardson force: $f_1(t)$. 'The rate of change of hostility is proportional to the level of hostility in the system.' This can be formulated in terms of the equation

$$dH(t)/dt = ah(t) \qquad (10.3.5)$$

Differentiating both sides this gives

$$d^2H(t)/dt^2 = a \cdot dH(t)/dt. \qquad (10.3.6)$$

From (10.3.4) this then gives

$$f_1(t) = C \cdot a \cdot dH(t)/dt \qquad (10.3.7)$$

We note an important feature of this. If $a > 0$ this provides an impetus to the system, whereas if $a < 0$ it provides a dampener to the system. We explore the significance of this later on.

Hypothesis (2) for the grievance force: $f_2(t)$. 'Grievance is inversely related to the current level of hostility.'

The representation of this is relatively straightforward, namely

$$f_2(t) = b/H(t) \qquad (10.3.8)$$

Hypothesis (3) for the fear of war force: $f_3(t)$. 'It is hypothesised that there exists some level of hostility H^* at which the fear of war is at a maximum. This point acts as a repellent in the system.'

At this point a new concept is introduced, though one which seems entirely plausible. The representation of it in terms of the system requires some slight but harmless mathematical trickery. We shall express the hypothesis as

$$f_3(t) = c/[\varepsilon + (H^* - H(t))^2] \qquad (10.3.9)$$

This asserts that the closer $H(t)$ approaches H^*, the greater is the repellent force. The expression $(H^* - H(t))^2$ is squared as a device to make sure that it is always positive, as this force is meant to be a repellent at both sides of H^*. The mysterious ε is a small positive constant which has no interpretation. If it were not there then, when $H^* = H(t)$, $f_3(t)$ would go to infinity and the system become non-sensical. This may seem a totally arbitrary inclusion in the equation which, of course, it is. I do not intend justifying it beyond saying that

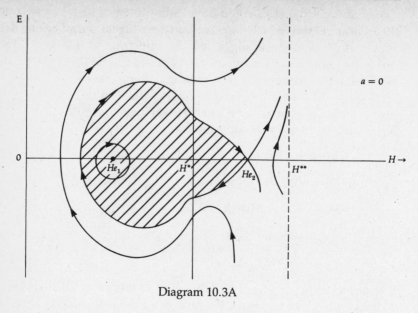

Diagram 10.3A

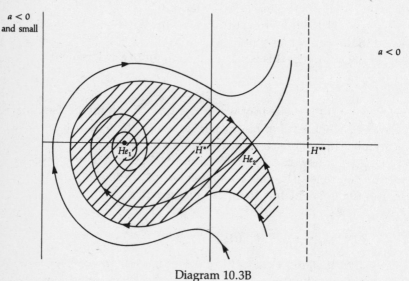

Diagram 10.3B

the introduction of such devices into many mathematical systems such as this appears to work and not to make the systems nonsense. Hypothesis (4) The inevitability of war factor: $f_4(t)$. 'It is hypothesised that there exists a level of hostility H^{**}, where war in the system is inevitable. This is an attractor.'

194

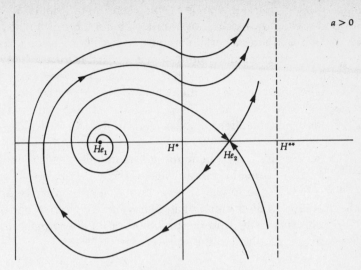

Diagram 10.3C

Unless H^* is redundant, it will be the case that $H^* < H^{**}$. The expression for this hypothesis is

$$f_4(t) = p/H^{**} - H(t) \tag{10.3.10}$$

If we bring these hypotheses together, we get the over-all input of the exogenous variables in the following differential equation

$$Cd^2H(t)/dt^2 = Ca \cdot dH(t)/dt + b/H(t) - c/[\varepsilon + (H^* - H(t)^2)]$$
$$+ p/(H^* - H(t)) \tag{10.3.11}$$

This is now the equation of the main model which has emerged from making the assumptions of the prior model. The problem is now to solve it in the sense of deriving a variety of time paths which follow from different assumptions about the parameters. The parameter to be particularly examined is a, which is found in the specification of the first of the factors or prior theories. The three cases for $a = 0$, $a < 0$, and $a > 0$ are considered. These are illustrated in the three phase Diagrams 10.3A, 10.3B and 10.3C which give a general idea of the sort of behaviour to be expected in this sort of system.

In all cases there are two equilibrium points He_1 and He_2. The lines which emerge from, or move to He_1 and He_2 are the important lines which separate out the different forms of behaviour. In the case of $a = 0$, the system is stable in the shaded area. It oscillates regularly around the equilibrium point He_1. Outside that area, the system is unstable and moves off to H^{**}, the level of hostility which makes war inevitable. In $a < 0$, the system is in some sense more stable. Within the shaded area, the system moves in to the equilibrium point He_1, which it will reach after a certain amount of oscillation. Not surprisingly, given its interpretation, the system is less stable for $a > 0$. Apart from points on the trajectories which go into He_2, from any other position in the system any movement is off to the H^{**} level of hostility. Even He_2 is only partially stable. In all cases trajectories move out of it to H^{**}, meaning that a slight displacement in that direction leads to war.

Two characteristics stand out about this model. First, it is now very unstable, and, even in the more stable versions, there are a lot of possibilities which lead to war. The second is that it is very complex and the problems of discriminating its behaviour from other models is very difficult. This issue, and the problems of its interpretation, are discussed in greater detail in the next section.

4 Measurement and operationalisation

It would be absurd to present these approaches as substantiated theories of the macro-behaviour of the international system. At best they are tentative stabs at the problem. The weaknesses come primarily in the prior models. They are two-fold, involving both the models as such and the definition and measurement of the variables. Both models pick out four central variables, though the number four as such is of no significance. In the catastrophe model they are factors which determine the level of violence, and in the hostility model they determine the level of hostility. While these factors were not selected at random, nor was their selection the result of rigorous procedures. It is possible that fewer variables are relevant – the cusp catastrophe involves only two control variables and would still generate the requisite pattern as was demonstrated in Chapter 9. With less enthusiasm we have to acknowledge the possibility that more control variables will be required, providing us with a more complex catastrophe. It might be that the existing variables are the appropriate ones, but inter-acting in different ways. Thus, while our initial model is undeniably a possibility, it is one of many and not compelling as the only possible option.

Many of the problems of measurement are likewise horrendous. This is not true of the level of violence which is the behaviour variable in the catastrophe model. The concept is adequately operationalised, and the measurements based on this operationalisation are reasonably complete (Singer 1968). Both attributes, and particularly the first, are to be cherished in any analysis of the international system. However, this cannot be said of any of the four control variables. Even assertions about whether they are increasing between one period and another are contentious, much less any assertions about their level. This is not to say that some operationalisation and measurement of these variables is not possible, and in other contexts this has been done. However, as far as this model is concerned, it is clear that it has not been done at this point. Thus, even if the model is accepted as appropriate, it would be perfectly appropriate to challenge its conclusions by objecting to the crudity of the measurements.

However, one consoling feature for the would-be tester of the catastrophe model is that the variables are all attributes of the individual members and the systemic values are simply the individual attributes summed. For example, the 'violence potential' of the system can be simply interpreted as the violence potential of each of its members taken individually and then added together. The same is true of the Richardson model and its close relatives. However, it is not true of the aggregate hostility model. The hostility is a characteristic of the system as a whole and is not simply some addition of the hostility of the individual members. This is clearly a conceptual issue of importance, but it is surmountable. Further, in surmounting it, we can show that such measures significantly broaden the scope of possible analyses of this type of model.

Once again the conceptual point is more easily appreciated in terms of a system where the actors are individual people. Consider a soccer crowd consisting of fans from clubs which are bitter rivals. It is said (often) that 'There is a high degree of tension in the crowd.' 'Tension' is an analogous concept to 'hostility'. The evidence for such an assertion would be shouting, muttering and things of that sort. The critical issue would be whether any violence was likely to occur. One definition of the level of tension would be the probability of some act of violence occurring within some specified short period such as a minute. If we assume that any act of violence would quickly escalate to major violence, it would not much matter what the act was. Now in this situation it is not relevant which individual in the crowd actually initiates the violence. This probability can most conveniently be seen as an attribute of the crowd as a single collectivity.

The same sort of argument can be made in the case of the international system or some subsystem within it. The measure of hostility (or tension) in the system can similarly be defined as the probability that a violent act will be carried out in some period of time (though now more than a minute) no matter which actor in the system carries it

197

out. In this case it is regarded as a property of the system rather than of any individual actor. For much the same reason this is not only legitimate but in some circumstances more appropriate. The problem with the measure, both for the soccer crowd and the international system, is that it is not specified who makes this probability judgement – an issue discussed in greater detail in Chapter 4. This objection can be to a degree surmounted by supposing that there is some probability generating rule, inductively arrived at from the observations of similar situations, which depends on such factors as the degree of violence previously observed in the system. This avoids the difficulties raised in the definition of a probability as an attribute of the observer.

We can go further than this. Let us hypothesise an entity called 'hostility' which can be present in varying degrees. In itself it is not observable. However, its nature is such that if some observable events occur then there will be observable consequences – in this case the outbreak of violence. In some sense the hostility is there irrespective of whether there is the violent manifestation. This is an analogous concept to 'gravitational attraction'. The gravitational attraction manifests itself if there is an unsupported stone which falls. However, we can think of the attraction being there all the time, whether or not there is anything which is affected by it. In the same way there is hostility in the system which is shown in violence if the extra conditions for this show themselves. However, the hostility is there even if those conditions do not show themselves. Thus the probability of violence is derived from the probability of the additional conditions being the case. This sort of attribute is common in the natural sciences. There are many concepts, such as gravity, known as 'theoretical concepts' which cannot be observed directly, even in principle, but play a crucial role in deductive models. This is argued persuasively by Braithwaite (1955a), and I have applied the argument to social behaviour elsewhere (Nicholson 1983). Hostility expressed as a characteristic of a system can be conceived of as a concept of this nature. Clearly it is so far a much less refined concept than those used in physics, and its use in these models is largely speculative. My point however is that it is a perfectly proper concept and, whatever its other weaknesses, the model does not fail because one of its central concepts is meaningless.

The difficulties of quantification and operationalisation will be obvious to all but the most starry-eyed of admirers of formal approaches, and much more so to the legions of detractors. However, there is a powerful case for the defence. Let us pose two questions about the two models discussed. 'Suppose we knew that the world was in fact like this, would it be significant?' The answer is surely unambiguously positive. If we had these or any other macro-theories of the international system, both from the view of scholarly observations and from the more critical view of adjusting the behaviour of the system to make it more benign, these results would be revolutionary. This leads to the second question: 'Suppose the world is like this, how would we know?' The answer is that in the present state of the testers' art we clearly would not know. We are unable to discriminate between one theory and another of the international system at this sort of level. Thus the objection to this sort of analysis is not that the questions are trivial but that they are currently unanswerable. Clearly the world may in fact be as described by Zinnes and Muncaster, and even if we (and presumably they) agree that it is unlikely that they got it exactly right, the world does behave in some sort of way and it is a worthy endeavour to find out which way. The crucial problem is whether the questions posed are inherently unanswerable, or whether our inability to answer them is because we pose them badly, or currently lack the techniques to answer them. If the social world is random, jumping lawlessly and without rhyme or reason from one position to another, then the questions posed are meaningless and we shall never find answers. However, if there are structures which are constant or only move slowly then there is in principle the possibility of finding out what those structures are. Formally this is a metaphysical question. A repeated but fruitless search for structure would not refute the possibility of a structure. More to the point, in our local social lives we firmly believe in structure, otherwise life would be impossible. Further, any analysis or 'explanation' of events in the international system would be completely vacuous as either would be merely comments on the paths taken by a complex set of random variables and would be like 'explaining' the successive results in tosses of a coin. I think there are few people who hold this point of view. Those who do not hold the random theory should then hold that the search for structure is a meaningful one, even if such a search is likely to be speculative for a long time to come.

Even at the present level of analysis, there are two points of importance. I shall discuss them in terms of the catastrophe theory model as it is more directly interpreted in terms of the international system. First, though the discriminatory power of the model is poor, it is not completely absent. It would be easy to derive a battery of models which would be able to account for the observed phenomena just as well as this one, but a number of possible models are excluded, such as, for example, a model relating the incidence of violence to the sunspot cycle – a theory which is dismissed for its failure to correspond with the facts. More significantly, the model shows that the different forms of behaviour observed can result from the same underlying structure. Hence, if one believes, as Singer's results seem to suggest (Singer 1968) that the international system does not change its underlying structure of behaviour and its constraints on behaviour very quickly, then one has to select theories of this structure in which the very different patterns of behaviour discussed by Holt, Job and Markus are permitted. It is possible that the structure of the system did undergo one of its rare fundamental changes in this period, but one must then be explicit in asserting this, and be willing to offer evidence in its justification. If one asserts the constancy of structure, then a catastrophe theory model, though not necessarily the particular one discussed, becomes a good candidate. That is, we have already excluded a large class of models which is what I have earlier asserted is the crux of testability. The second point is that by developing the model we show just where the limitations in currently available testing techniques are. Clearly, we would like to know whether the theory outlined is the case or not. At the moment we cannot tell. What sorts of developments in the techniques of testing do we need in order to be able to discriminate between this particular model, and others which resemble it either closely or not at all? This model is clearly very speculative in the sense that we are unable to tell whether the system resembles this description or not, but it is not thereby useless. It may not answer many questions but it certainly raises insightful ones about both the nature of the international system and the way in which we know what happens within it.

5   Graphs and dominance relationships

The earlier two models of the system as a whole looked at the system through complex relationships; in this section we examine a system which contains only simple relationships. The structures or patterns in which the members of a social system are linked facilitate certain sorts of behaviour and perhaps, thereby, determine the character of the system.

Let us consider a very simple system of five actors called A, B, C, D, and E. We can regard these actors as states, and initially deal in terms of a state-centric model of the international system. Suppose there are various sorts of transactions between them. These may be transactions such as trade, transport, communications: or affective transactions such as hostility and friendliness. Suppose that all parties inter-act with each other directly, then we can represent this in Diagram 10.4A where each point represents an actor and every line a transaction or set of transactions (which can go both ways and would normally be presumed to do so). Such a representation is known as a *graph*, a term which has nothing to do with the more usual connotation of the word where points and lines are related to two axes. The points on the graph are known as *nodes* and the connecting lines are known as *arcs*, though other terminologies are also in common use.

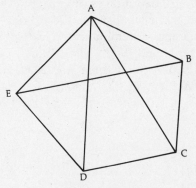

Diagram 10.4A

Suppose now that, while all the parties have transactions directly with A, the remaining members of the group do not relate directly with each other. Any transaction of, say, C with F goes through A. In this case it will be represented by Diagram 10.4B.

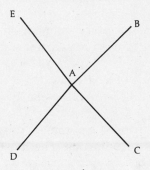

Diagram 10.4B

For obvious reasons, I shall refer to the first pattern as the 'cobweb pattern' and the second as the 'star pattern'.

Now there is an obvious sense in which the star pattern is more centralised than the cobweb pattern. The star pattern, however, has a number of drawbacks, particularly from the point of view of the peripheral members. Even if the central member A is merely an intermediary who passes things on, the transactions are more subject to error. If an interaction involves feed-back processes, these become more elaborate, and also more prone to error. If A is more than an intermediary but an actor on his own account within the system, then his focal position gives him great advantages in manipulating the system to his own advantage. Indeed if the central actor encourages the star pattern and discourages interactions between the outer members, it becomes the familiar 'divide and rule' pattern which is a classic principle of imperial dominance. An extension of this argument is familiar in the structural theory of a 'Feudal' international system due to Galtung (1971). Assume there are two central nodes, F and M, each of which have their satellite nodes, $f_1 f_2 \ldots f_n$ and $m_1 m_2 \ldots m_n$ arranged as shown in Diagram 10.4C.

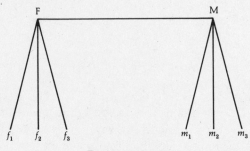

Diagram 10.4C

Messages from any of the peripheral nodes have to go through their relevant centre. Thus the two central actors can effectively control the system between them, by censoring or prohibiting relationships between other members of which they disapprove. This is a model of a bipolar world which at least roughly obtained during the early post 1945 era.

However, the star pattern has some characteristics, which under certain situations are advantagous. The most significant of these is simplicity. By simple observation it is clear that there are more arcs in the cobweb pattern. More formally in a system of n members with cobweb interactions, the number of arcs is

$$K = (n - 1) + (n - 2) + \ldots + 1 = n(n - 1)/2 \qquad (10.5.1)$$

In the case of the star model it is simply

$$L = (n - 1) \tag{10.5.2}$$

Clearly $K > L$ for $n > 2$, and the discrepancy gets larger for higher values of n. Notice that $(n - 1)$ is the minimum number of arcs which can connect n nodes, though they can be arranged in different ways. For example a *linear graph* looks as shown in Diagram 10.5.

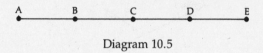

Diagram 10.5

However K represents the maximum number of arcs possible without repetition and hence is unique.

The significance of this cannot readily be seen in the abstract, but only in terms of applications to a particular system. Consider two different forms of transport, railway and air. In the case of the rail system the arcs (the railway lines) are expensive and rigid, but the nodes (the stations) are not so rigid in relation to the system as a whole. However, in the case of air transport, the nodes (airports) are expensive and the cost of providing a given number of arcs (aircraft which can provide so many passenger miles per unit of time) are also expensive, but the pattern itself is extremely flexible. Thus, a system with a large number of arcs cannot necessarily be presumed to be more costly, though in the case of a large system with a large number of nodes, there is a presumption that the most economical system will turn out to be the star or predominantly so.

This argument has obvious implications for the structural theory of dominance. It is pointed out, quite correctly, that a lot of transactions, such as aircraft routes, communications routes, and so on, form a star pattern around a few central nodes. In particular these centre round places such as New York, a few places in Europe, and Moscow. It is easy to conclude from this that the central nodes are occupying a hierarchic role in this and are in some sense in control, as undoubtedly they often are. However, such patterns are likely to grow up innocently as part of a process of running things economically. For example, public transport in cities commonly has a strong star-like tendency which, though it might attract criticism, rarely attracts the accusation of colonialism. There can often be a straightforward conflict of goals in situations of this sort. The occupier of a central node in such a system is subject to constant temptation to manipulate a system to his own advantage, and peripheral members are likely to be constantly and uncomfortably aware of this. However, it can often be the most

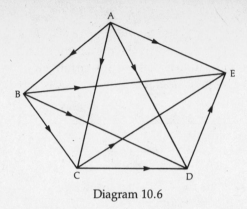

Diagram 10.6

economical principle for systems where the arcs are costly. This is just another case where efficiency in an economic sense conflicts with other desired objectives.

There are other systems of interest to the international relations theorist which can be similarly analysed such as an international language system. Suppose there are n linguistic groups A, B, C, ... whose members wish to communicate with each other. If no one speaks the language of A other than its native speakers, then they must learn $(n - 1)$ languages besides their own. If only speakers of A speak B's language, then B language speakers must learn $(n - 2)$ languages, and so on down to N who is fortunate in that everyone addresses him in his native tongue. We can represent this in terms of the cobweb graphs with a difference. Each line has a direction to it which is read as 'A learns the language of B' but the reverse does not apply. Such graphs with directions to them are known as *digraphs* (see Diagram 10.6).

However, languages are costly to learn in terms of time. Hence, it is much more economical to adopt the system whereby everyone uses a single common language. This may be an external language such as Latin or Esperanto, or a language which has already a large number of native speakers such as English today. Thus, if C and D only learn the language of N, they can communicate with each other in that language, and save the effort of learning a lot of languages. This is now represented by a star pattern with N as its central node (see Diagram 10.7).

This illustrates both the benefits and the drawbacks of the different patterns as they occur in the structural theories of transactions. Undoubtedly the star pattern is more economical, and for this reason

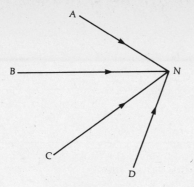

Diagram 10.7

often is adopted in multilingual systems. The Indian sub-continent is a good case in point, where English is a widely used common language, stemming from its earlier imposition in the days of the Raj. The costs are that cultural dominance often goes with linguistic dominance. This is not necessarily the result of a deliberate desire for dominance, but it is real and resented nonetheless, as is frequently witnessed in Western Europe with the acceptance of the English language as a near-universal second language.

11 THE PROCESS OF DECISION

1 Introduction: satisficing

The decision making analysis used so far has been a straight-forward form of maximising analysis. This supposes that a decision maker surveys the whole range of alternatives available and selects the most preferred, where his preferences can be described by some reasonably simple form of utility function. As a simplified model this is very useful and leads to powerful analyses. Nevertheless, it is an implausible theory of decision processes as a whole range of analyses suggests, from the psychological discussions of international decision making such as those of Janis (1982) or Jervis (1976), to the consider-ations of organisational behaviour (March 1958) or the analysis of the informational requirements of such a process in any but the most artificial environments (Simon 1982). This last is a particularly impor-tant development in that Simon has attempted to redress some of the objections to maximising with his concept of *satisficing*. Not all aspects of the analysis of the processes of decision making have been analysed in formal terms, but I shall consider two which have – the analysis of games where perceptions differ, and the analysis of decision makers' conceptual frameworks or cognitive maps.

First let us clarify the objections to a simple maximising model which, superficially, looks the most promising approach to the deci-sion problem. The major objection to it even as a model of individual, much less group, decision processes is that in any realistic situation it implies that the decision maker can cope with enormous quantities of information and be able to process it. Not only has the information about the alternative courses of action and their possible consequences to be understood, but also the preferences have to be formed between these consequences. If these alternatives number hundreds in an environment which is uncertain, it is clear that the problem is much more complex than can be understood in terms of the simple models which are discussed in much of classical decision theory. It seems clear that a decision maker does not consider all possible alternatives in any practical situation. According to Simon the process involves the following. A decision maker knows what he would regard as a satisfactory outcome. He explores the set of alternatives in sequence until he finds an alternative which yields this satisfactory outcome and accepts that. He does not pursue the search further to see if there is an alternative which is even better, which is what the optimiser would do. Clearly this leaves a lot of problems open. How is a satisfaction level determined? To what extent is it determined by the search? If the first alternative examined by the decision maker is satisfactory this might encourage the decision maker to think that his perception of the available alternatives was overly pessimistic and thus put up his minimum satisfaction level. Nevertheless the satisficing hypothesis does get round a number of problems which make the maximisation assumption seem implausible in a situation of any great complexity.

We should note one significant point about satisficing. There may be several alternatives in a choice set which exceed the satisfaction level for some decision maker. The one which is selected depends then on the order in which they are presented to the decision maker; it is not uniquely determined by the consideration of the decision maker's preferences and the set of alternatives itself, which is the case with a maximising hypothesis. This is not in itself an objection to satisficing. There is an understandable prejudice in favour of unique solutions, but if these are achieved only at the expense of distorting reality, we must live with the alternative that we can define subsets from which a solution will be determined but not be able to define some single point within it as a unique solution.

2 Hypergames: perceptions of conflicts

The satisficing approach to decision problems has nothing as such to do with misperceptions. However, there are ways in which the issues can become inter-linked. There have been some efforts to interpret issues of failed perception in terms of concepts related to game theory by Bennett (1979), Bennett and Dando (1977) and various other writers under the title of *hypergames*. I shall argue that this analysis can be interpreted as a natural consequence of the satisficing hypothesis.

In hypergame analysis it is suggested that the full nature of a conflict situation may not be understood. There may be three areas of error. An actor A may be mistaken about the set of strategies of a rival, about the rival's preferences over the outcomes, and finally about who the other players in the game are. I shall confine myself to perceptions of a rival's strategy set, as this adequately illustrates the problems involved.

I shall first illustrate it with one of the first, and still one of the most convincing applications of the hypergame analysis by Bennett and Dando, an analysis of the Fall of France in 1940. The allies attributed two broad strategies to the Germans – whether they would invade by attacking the Maginot line or through Belgium. Thus the problem facing the allies was of distributing their forces such that they could cope with either attack. In the event the Germans chose a third strategy which was to attack through the Ardennes for which the allies were not at all prepared having excluded it from the set of possible strategy options available to the Germans. In effect then the Germans were playing a broader game than the allies, and, because of this, won. It could be argued that military strategy is often the search for a broader game than the rival thinks. Nelson's successes could perhaps be described as resulting from a sound grasp of the concept of a hypergame.

To a degree this might just be regarded as saying that people sometimes make mistakes, and this is partially true. However, given that making mistakes is a constant human activity, any social scientific analysis of events has to have a theory of mistakes as well. First, let us define the n-person hypergame, where each of the actors is aware that the other $(n-1)$ are in the game. Each player i has a strategy set $S_i = (s_1^i\ s_2^i \ldots s_n^i)$. For each player j, i has a perception of his strategy set $S_{ij} = (s_1^{ij}\ s_2^{ij} \ldots s_n^{ij})$. There is no presumption that $S_{ij} = S_{ji}$ though it may do. Nor is there a presumption that either S_{ij} is contained in S_{jj} or vice versa. It is even possible for $S_{ij} \cap S_{ji} = 0$ though one might suppose that in practical situations it is unlikely. The game, as far as i is concerned, consists of $G_{ij} = S_{ii} * S_{i2} * \ldots * S_{in}$ For each $s\ \varepsilon\ S_i$ and $s\ \varepsilon\ S_j$ there is an outcome $M_i\ (s_1\ s_2 \ldots s_n)$ which is a vector representing the pay-offs to each actor. Each actor has a utility function over the set of pay-offs. As far as i is concerned the game is represented as any other n-person game. However, in this representation an n-person game as ordinarily understood is the special case where $G_{ij} = G_{jj}$ for all i and j.

This can be illustrated by the Falklands War of 1982. Prior to the war, the Argentine Government's options could be simplified to three: (a) do nothing, (b) increase diplomatic pressure on the United Kingdom, (c) invade the Falklands. The British strategies before the war can likewise be simplified to three: (i) do nothing, (ii) increase the seriousness of negotiation, (iii) build up deterrent defences in the islands. Clearly one can make a pay-off matrix which results from these joint possibilities. In fact the British appeared to play strategy (i) and Argentina strategy (c). The question is why Britain did not play strategy (iii) – which was not inconsistent with playing one of the other two as well. This would have made (c) unattractive to Argentina and would certainly have been less expensive to Britain than fighting the war which in fact resulted.

Putting it in a hypergame framework, the game from Britain's point of view was $S_{BB} = $ (i, ii, iii) and $S_{BA} = $ (a,b). The game from the Argentinian point of view was $S_{AA} = $ (a,b,c) and $S_{AB} = $ (i,ii).

On the face of it there are two hypotheses. First, that the above formulation appropriately describes the situation and the British did not consider the possibility of invasion at all, in much the same way as the allies did not consider the Ardennes as a possible invasion route in 1940. Secondly, that it was considered, but was regarded as having a low probability such that the expected value of building deterrent defences was too small to make it worth while. These are analytically somewhat separate approaches. In the second case we have a pay-off matrix consisting of the expected values but with the full range of options. In the first we have a column (or row) missing from the matrix itself.

A true optimiser would adhere to the second of these interpretations. The uncertainty about the availability of a strategy to an opponent might come from doubts about the feasibility of the strategy at all, or because it was assumed that the preferences of the opponent, taking into account the costs of activating the strategy, would mean that it would not be considered. That is, there is uncertainty about the utility function of the opponent.

However, this assumption that individuals or organisations make a complete analysis of all possible alternatives is a difficult position to hold. It seems to be the case that an individual can only hold a limited number of alternatives in any degree of salience at a time. Hence, whatever the range of options an opponent may have, he will only be perceived as having a small number, and unfortunately these may not be the ones the opponent sees. Clearly an organisation which is capable of ranging over a larger group and of considering novel alternatives has an advantage, but as a matter of fact, a lot of groups do not do this. Thus, as a descriptive, though not prescriptive model of a decision making process, the hypergame perspective may be better, at least in some instances, than the low probability perspective.

While this does not logically follow from the satisficing hypothesis, it is consistent with it. One way of simplifying a problem is to exclude very low probability events. It can be rationally done providing the

209

expected value of the alternative is lower than the expected value of other alternatives. However, even when this condition does not hold one suspects that such low probability events are excluded in people's reasoning. Thus people rarely dwell on the low probability that they will be killed in a traffic accident today for the perfectly simple reason that any day's range of possibilities would rapidly become impossibly complicated to comprehend. Thus the hypergame analysis can be related to the satisficing analysis in that both are consequences of the need to simplify very complex problems. A problem now arises. Suppose that evidence comes up which suggests that the probability of the event should be increased to some level above the threshold level. If the decision procedure is such that once an option is excluded from the range of possibilities it stays excluded, then the option will remain unconsidered. This would seem an inefficient rule, but if it does not apply, then we are back dealing with horrendously complicated problems. This is a possible interpretation of the British policy towards Argentina in the period before the Falklands War. For many years, the event had such a low probability that it was appropriate to exclude it from a salient position on the decision making agenda. When the probability in some experts' eyes increased it remained excluded from the agenda. An efficient decision procedure would find some way of reintroducing items to the agenda which had been properly excluded under earlier information assumptions.

Hypergames, as described here, have proved useful tools for the ex-post analyses of some interesting problems. They are mathematical pictures, but have not gone further in answering the rather crucial questions they raise. They do make clear that it becomes necessary to probe into the whole decision making structure of an organisation if one is to analyse its behaviour in a complex environment.

3 Cognitive maps: belief and value systems of decision makers

In general in the development of decision theory, the value and belief systems of the actors are regarded as externally given. This is clearly inadequate and recognised as such. Models have been developed representing the belief systems of various decision makers in international situations using the theory of graphs, introduced in Section 5 of the last chapter. Some significant studies, and an analysis of the theory, have been gathered together by Axelrod (1976). The data amongst which inter-relationships were sought were the verbal statements of the actors. These were deemed to be causal and of the form,

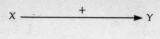

Diagram 11.1

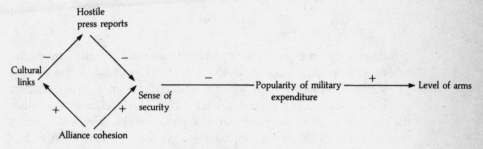

Diagram 11.2

'If more countries acquire nuclear weapons, there will be an increase in the probability of nuclear war.' This is an assertion of belief by the actor. It is a characteristic of the actor and its truth or otherwise is a separate issue. The statement can be regarded as an assertion of a relationship between two variables. X is the number of countries with nuclear weapons; Y is the probability of nuclear war. The relationship is that as X increases, so does Y, though the details of the relationship beyond this (the functional form) is not specified. It is an asymmetric relationship in that it is asserted that it is the shift in X which affects Y and not vice versa. This can therefore be expressed by an arrow with a direction to it. There is a positive sign beside the arrow to indicate that the direction of change of the second is the same as the first. This means if X increases, so does Y, and if X decreases so does Y. This is illustrated in Diagram 11.1

On its own, this is a relatively trivial translation of the basic statements. It becomes more interesting if a string of assertions are involved. Consider the group of six statements which are strung out in a causal path in a signed digraph (see Diagram 11.2).

Starting on the left hand end and taking the top two arcs, this says that if there are increased cultural links this will decrease hostile press reports, and that the decrease in hostile press reports will increase the sense of security. The net effect is that the increase in cultural affinity will increase a sense of security (two minus paths lead to a positive effect). On the bottom pair of arcs, increased cultural affinity makes for stronger alliance which makes for a greater sense of security. The two positive paths lead to an overall positive effect which is in the same

211

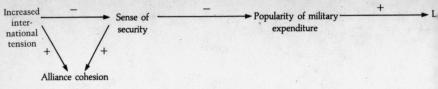

Diagram 11.3

direction as the top path. Moving rightwards in the path, comes the assertion that an increase in the sense of security decreases the popularity of military expenditure, and vice versa, so the variables move in the opposite direction to each other. The final assertion is that the popularity of military expenditure moves in the same direction as the level of arms. Thus the conjunction of a positive and a negative link gives an over-all negative link. In this outline, we can say unambiguously that an assertion that there has been a change in cultural affinity should lead to an assertion that there should be a change in the opposite direction of the level of arms of a country. This 'should' is used to imply that this will be the case if the statements a person asserts are to be mutually consistent. It is certainly a recommendation for rational thought, though the degree to which it is empirically correct is another matter.

However, consider the following model, illustrated in Diagram 11.3.

The last (i.e. right-hand) three variables are the same, as in Diagram 11.2, but we modify the earlier stages. The starting variable is 'increased international tension'. This has a positive effect on the strength of the alliance which, as in the earlier model, affects the strength of security positively, and thus there is an over-all positive effect. However, there is a direct negative affect from the first variable to 'sense of security'. As there are two pressures in opposite directions, the effect on the 'sense of security' variable is ambiguous. Notice what this means in terms of the interpretation of the model. From the evidence of the statements alone, the actor could consistently make either assertion about whether the sense of security went up or down with the increase in international tension. It does not mean, however, that he makes one or the other on a random basis. Implicit in his statements there may be a functional relationship which will determine whether one or the other variable predominates for a given increase in international tension. Thus, he may have a perfectly coherent picture, which could be found out by delving deeper into his cognitive map. It requires more evidence than just the simple state-

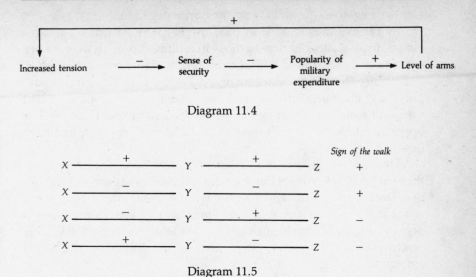

Diagram 11.4

Diagram 11.5

ments to derive this. Unfortunately we can say nothing more of the later part of a graph in relation to the earlier once we have reached such an ambiguous point.

Finally, let us consider another possible cognitive framework. Suppose that if there is an increase in international tension the 'stronger alliance' variable is deemed unimportant. However, we add in another link from the level of arms to the level of international tension, with a positive sign to it. (see Diagram 11.4)
A path which leaves a node and ultimately returns to it is known as a *cycle*.

There are one or two general points about graphs which come out of this and which can be asserted intuitively. If we move along the arcs from node to node within a graph, this is known as a *walk*. Consider a walk in a graph of three nodes with two arcs. If both arcs are positive, the net effect from X to Z is positive; if both arcs are negative, the link from X to Z is still positive; if they are of opposite signs, then the link from X to Z is negative, irrespective of the order of these signs. This is illustrated in Diagram 11.5
More generally, the over-all sign of a walk is positive if the number of negative arcs along the walk is even in number, and negative if the number of arcs is odd. The order in which they are arranged is irrelevant. A special case of note is when all the arcs are positive. The sign of the walk is of course positive (there are 0 negative arcs where 0 is regarded as an even number). A warning is necessary when all the

arcs are negative, the walk is not nessarily negative, but is only so if the number of arcs is odd. In this, the negative and positive signs behave in an analogous way to those in multiplication. In the case of a cycle, such as illustrated in Diagram 11.4, the same principle applies. In that case there are two negative arcs, so the over-all sign of a path out of any node is positive, and if the variable increases it means that the input which results from this will provoke a further increase. The opposite would have been the case if the sign of the path had been negative.

As far as inputs into a node are concerned, if there is more than one then they have all to be of the same sign if one is to say anything about the effect on the node, and hence anything about later stages of the walk. If they are all negative, the effect is the same as for a single negative input. Similarly, if all are positive, the effects are for a single positive input. However, any mixture at all makes the effect ambiguous.

The signed digraphs are effectively mathematical pictures, with a few consistency requirements. In the fictitious examples given, they clarify the situation, but do not open vast new vistas. The strength of the technique is that the models can be complicated almost indefinitely to represent very complex cognitive maps, and thus it makes it possible to see problems of a degree of complexity which would be impossible to grasp otherwise. For example, Bonham and Shapiro (1976), in a model of the cognitive map of an American Middle East expert in the State Department identify 51 variables (nodes). This degree of complexity in these sorts of models is often exceeded.

It is important to be careful just what these cognitive maps are supposed to be. They are derived from statements made by the actors. For them to be maps of the actors' actual belief structure, the statements have to be made in good faith, which of course is often not the case. Nevertheless as an attempt to get at a belief structure, such techniques are useful. Clearly such a cognitive map can be made about a group as well as an individual on the basis of statements made on behalf of the group. This can only be called cognitive by analogy, though, for the individual, the word can properly be applied. Cognitive maps are simply pictures of belief patterns. They are not a theory of them. It is reassuring if they are consistent belief patterns, but they may not be. If they are not, they can still be represented in this form though with the priviso that the map is inconsistent.

Clearly it is in general useful to have a cognitive map of a significant individual's thought processes. If we believe that individuals can make a difference to the behaviour of the international system, then

214

they are invaluable. One of the most interesting features of such a map is whether it exhibits the consistencies they are supposed to with regard to negative and positive paths. The empirical analyses reported by various scholars show a gratifyingly high level of internal consistency in individuals' cognitive structures. Axelrod's analysis of the British Middle Eastern Committee in 1922 is a particularly fascinating interpretation of belief structures in this context which strongly supports the internal consistency view. Maps also have a normative interest in being possible devices in helping people to improve their cognitive consistency. Consistency of belief can be a difficult thing to achieve, and such visual aids can be very helpful.

The representation of cognitive systems in graph theory form is particularly helpful in that it is visually appealing. Less visually appealing, but capable of much greater complexity, are computer models of decision processes, and a number have been developed. Anderson and Thorson (1982), for example, consider two separate problems under the general heading of Artificial Intelligence. The first is a computer model of the cognitive system of President Kennedy at the time of the Cuban Missiles Crisis. This is cognitive in the sense in which the above models are cognitive, namely a model of various psychological processes. The second is a computer model of the Saudi Arabian decision making process, in which various arms procurement processes were considered. This is a model of various interacting systems within the Saudi Arabian decision making procedure consisting of the different interests and elements which were involved in the choice. It is not, as such, a model of cognitive processes, and is thus only tenuously an artificial intelligence model. There is controversy over whether 'artificial intelligence' is in any case an appropriate way of describing simulations even of cognitive processes (Searle 1984). 'Intelligence', it is argued, implies consciousness. However, as we are only interested in whether the computer simulates correctly, this, for us, is not an important issue.

12 CONCLUSIONS

The basic question to be asked about the use of formal methods of analysis in the study of international relations is whether, by applying them, we know anything more about the substantive issues within the discipline or not. Failing that, is there good reason for assuming that in due course we will know more, even though at the current state of development we do not? It will be no surprise to the reader to know that I interpret the results of this book as giving support for both present understanding and future possibilities. Formal methods have had a lot of success in clarifying problems – discussions involving simple game theory models such as the prisoners' dilemma and probability models being conspicuous. They have had a limited success so far in providing testable theories which provide clearer criteria for belief; they have had a modest success but great potential in asking significant questions which could not even be posed without the use of formal methods, such as was found in the discussion of arms race systems. Clearly these categories over-lap.

1 Types of theory

The problems discussed in this book are clearly problems of international relations, though they have obvious interpretation in any social system characterised by conflict and cooperation. However, beyond this, the problems and approaches were often rather different and might appear to be linked only by the rather tenuous association that they are discussed by formal methods. They can be categorised under two broad headings. First, there are the decision making approaches which consider the consequences of people making decisions where they actively seek to pursue certain goals; secondly, are the systemic theories which consider the consequences of certain variables moving according to some given rules of behaviour. These approaches are not mutually inconsistent. The systemic can be viewed as defining the background in which particular decisions are made,

216

the background itself being determined by a mass of previous and current decisions.

In fact the decision making approaches form the core of most of the book. The crucial issues of cooperation and conflict are analysed on the assumption that the actors are concerned with maximising their own well-being however they define it. Often known as the 'rational actor' tradition, this originates in micro-economic analysis, adapted in many cases to the problems of the international system, and is most conspicuous in the theory of games and its derivatives. It is supposed that an actor wishes to achieve some specifiable set of goals, has limited resources, and is subject to a variety of specifiable constraints. The problems are then posed as optimisation problems, where the relevant entities are utility, expected utility, power, or whatever variable is appropriate to the problem. Our later analysis of conflict, cooperation, uncertainty, and coalitions is in this mode. The term 'rational actor models' is unfortunate as it carries connotations of approval for the activities involved. 'Optimising models' would be a better term. Adopting the classic methods of simplification, these issues were examined over a number of chapters in the context of a world of just two actors. Other complications were however brought in, notably the crucial problem of uncertainty. This was extended to include a world of many actors with a corresponding increase in complexity, but an increase we were still able to cope with. The decision making process was still simple, much simpler than that of any real life decision maker, but this simplicity led to clarity and an ability to see the essences of problems which otherwise would have been obscured behind the complexities of real life. However, towards the end, some concessions were made towards a wider view of decision making which was still simple enough to have explanatory power. Much useful work in this sort of area has been done by the psychologists and in particular in the area of computer simulation.

At the other extreme we examined the behaviour of the system as a whole, its macro-behaviour, in which the nature of the decision making processes was not considered. The international system became a collection of complex interactions in which even the identity of the actors was unclear. There were no overt decision makers maximising, satisficing, or doing any of the other things decision makers in decision making theories are supposed to do. There were simply interacting forces which impelled the system in various directions.

Awkwardly ambiguous, and falling neatly into neither category, are the arms race models. Goals from which behaviour was deduced were absent, and simple reactive behaviour rules were posited. From these, powerful conclusions were deduced. In methodology they are closer to the macro-systemic models, though in the problems they attacked they were more like the decision models. As the classification is by methodology rather than by problems it is better to classify these as systemic models but to identify the class of problems they involve by referring to them as micro-systemic models as distinct from the macro-systemic models which address the problems of the system as a whole.

The two sorts of model are not inconsistent. One could set up an optimising model from which the Richardson equations could be derived and, with greater difficulty, set up optimising models from which the macro-systemic models could be derived. Indeed at some point this would be necessary as the micro- and macro-models cannot be mutually contradictory. The micro-theories are logically prior to the macro-theories. In formulating the assumptions of a macro-theory, it is tacitly implied that there is some appropriate micro-theory which could back it up. However, finding the link might take a long time.

While in this book the models are mainly used descriptively, the decision making models also can be used prescriptively. Despite the superficial similarity, this in fact is a rather different type of model and activity. If an actor wants to achieve the goals assumed by the analysis, and approaches the analyst for advice, then the descriptive and prescriptive model would be identical in formal terms. Sometimes the nature of the prescription is very clear – people ought to reason according to the rules of the probability calculus and it is dangerous if they do not. The formal analyst can help a lot in providing the means of consistent thought. The types of models should be kept separate, however. There is always the danger of mistaking an 'ought' for an 'is' or an 'is' for an 'ought'.

Classifications are arbitrary, but these seem convenient to me (Intriligator, 1982, has nine categories). My categories relate closely to Rapoport's categorisations of philosophies of war in his introduction to Von Clausewitz's classic book *On War*. Rapoport classifies philosophies of war into three, the political, the cataclysmic and the eschatological. The first views war as the consequence of rational decision making; the second views war as a consequence of underlying patterns in the system, which from time to time burst out in the form of war in much the same way as epidemics burst out; the final view sees war as the consequence of the battle of good and evil. While war and its avoidance does not form the whole of international relations, it forms a lot of it, and philosophies of war correspond closely with philosophies of international relations. These in their turn colour the various approaches to its study. The political and the cataclysmic are the underlying philosophies behind the decision making and the systemic approaches respectively. Eschatology – the science of the four last things, death, judgement, heaven and hell – is somewhat beyond the scope of this book.

2 Models as clarificatory devices

Some of the most significant achievements, as distinct from hopes, in the applications of formal methods to international relations are as clarificatory devices. This is particularly true of clarification in the sense of inducing a greater awareness of definitions and of providing appropriate pictures to see the essences of certain types of conflict. The prisoners' dilemma, chicken, assurance and kindred games, in their very simplicity, have clarified the essential nature of different sorts of conflict, and have provided classifications which lead to a greater understanding of the features of the international system. These are mathematical pictures in the sense in which the term was used earlier. No deductive reasoning is involved. The pictures are simply different ways of expressing things and are ultimately psychological tools. This is not to disparage their significance. They have direct application to the international system.

The more complex clarificatory devices, such as the analysis of options, which involve sequences of operations, go beyond the point of psychological clarification. They can be used as methods for presenting the data of a problem so that solutions can be seen which would otherwise have been obscure. They are not merely explanatory devices but also devices which can actually be used to illuminate problems in a way which improves decision making. This sort of technique is applied more in industrial than international contexts though there is no inherent reason why it should not be used in the latter. Though less widely applied than the simple game models, their usefulness is clear and they can be and are recommended as practical tools for the investigation of conflict problems.

The genuinely deductive models have been shown to be important both in the sense that the issues under discussion are of manifest importance and in the sense that these sorts of analyses could not be done without the use of formal methods. It is often the case that the implications of an argument can only be fully understood by posing a set of propositions in formal terms. A deductive model demonstrates

219

that one set of propositions implies another, so that believing one set involves believing the other, even though the mutual relationship initially may not be obvious. An example of the significance of this sort of analysis was shown in the discussion of the provision of collective goods, such as security, in an alliance of partners of different sizes. This example is particularly useful as it demonstrates an issue of manifest importance in the international system; it comes to a conclusion which is counter-intuitive; and it does so by involving concepts which could not be handled other than by formal methods. The model used is a simplified version of the real world, but it corresponds to reality sufficiently for the conceptual point to be applicable to real situations. The magnitudes involved are sufficiently gross for the simplifications not to be important. It would be inadequate if more precise answers were wanted. Applicability of simplified models requires that the relevant characteristics should be correspondingly crude. This applies to some of the principles involved in discussions, for example, of technological arms races and the problems of the verification of arms agreements.

The analysis of deductive chains also gives us other sorts of information which, though negative in the sense that it alerts us to unexpected possibilities rather than predicts actualities, is significant if we are to understand international behaviour. The prime example of this sort of negative result is in the analysis of the Richardson theory where it is shown that a relatively simple model of the arms race might demonstrate either stability or instability, depending on relatively modest changes in the parameters of the model. Inasmuch as a system is described by this sort of process, then quite careful knowledge of it must be gained before we are able to say whether it is a stable or an unstable system. This is a disturbing result. If very similar systems can demonstrate very different behaviour, such that it is hard to discriminate one system from the other before the behaviour has manifested itself, then this suggests low predictability in the international system. The 'coarser' its behaviour, or, in terms of the earlier discussion of catastrophe theory, the more structurally stable are the models, the greater is the predictability of the system, in that crude data enables us to make qualitative predictions. The unsettling converse is that, if a system is sensitive to small shifts in the data, then our qualitative predictions require precise data. The Richardson model alerts us to this problem. However, the problem is a much more general one. This sensitivity was not at all obvious without the Richardson analysis. Other dynamic systems exist in the international system about which we know little. But this in itself suggests that there may be a lot of other structurally unstable subsystems, which again might lead us to poor predictability. The only way out of this is to examine the dynamic characteristics of the international system with care, but this, as is obvious from the work so far discussed, is likely to take us a long time. There is no reason whatever to assume that the international system has any particularly stabilizing properties – indeed the converse would seem to be the case. It should be emphasised that this is a problem of the world, not a problem of the mathematics which is used to describe it. If the conclusions of the analysis are unpalatable, one should object to that which is analysed, not the analysis.

Discounting is another phenomenon whose significance becomes clearer in the context of formal analysis. People clearly do discount both the future and the past. Whether they ought to or not is another matter (though by interpreting it as a consequence of uncertainty we can give some ethical rationale to the phenomenon). I know of no estimates of a social discount rate parallel to an economic discount rate which can be used in the analysis of decisions which involve pay-offs over time. Still less am I aware of a government explicitly espousing some specific discount rate except in economic matters. It nevertheless makes many forms of behaviour comprehensible which would otherwise not be, and it is appropriate to argue that people act as if they had a discount rate however puzzled they may be to hear it. Any analysis over time must bring in this widespread characteristic of human perceptions, though it appears to be only in formal analyses that there is any explicit recognition of the issue.

Formal methods are commonly helpful, indeed necessary, in order to make our belief system consistent in trying to solve problems – that is, in a normative context. This is particularly clearly shown in the case of analyses of probability. The general proposition concerning the cumulation of probabilities is frequently not fully understood. If there is a 0.1 probability of a system failing during one year, then, if the probability of failure is the same each year, there is a $1 - (0.9)^{(10)} = 0.6513 \simeq 2/3$ of the system failing at some point over a period of ten years. This is an issue of logic, irrespective of whether the system in question is an automobile, a human body, or the international system. If one of the numerical values is held, the other must also be. Given that we live in an uncertain world, it is important to be clear about questions of probability and the emphasis on this in this book is offered unapologetically. In particular, the section on the probability of nuclear war therefore has direct relevance to our beliefs about the international system. It does not provide an answer to the problem, but it does offer a set of principles for the consistency of analysis and the clarification of terms in a way which does not seem to be followed by writers who do not work in this tradition. This is a prescriptive analysis outlining some principles of consistent belief (with the implied recommendation that they should be adopted). It is not claimed that people necessarily hold consistent beliefs. On the contrary it appears that the rules of consistency are often violated in probabilistic matters (Cohen 1972). While the general rules of probability are not difficult to understand, their implications are often unclear without working through the relevant analyses, and intuition is an uncertain guide in many situations, even apparently simple ones. The work on the 'Expert Problem' is one where a surprising, counter-intuitive result is the consequence of mathematical analysis and which is of manifest importance to any normative or descriptive decision making approach to the international system. There are two rather separate functions for this form of analysis. The first, is to provide a basis for theories of how people in fact behave under situations of uncertainty, and the second is to provide a set of rules for consistent belief in situations of uncertainty. The two must not be confused, as I emphasise yet again.

3 Deductive theories and their tests

Formal theory is placed in the classical mode of scientific enquiry, namely the hypothetico-deductive tradition. Some hypotheses are formulated, the logical implications of these hypotheses are worked out and then these implications (and if practicable the initial hypotheses) are tested by means of confronting them with the evidence of the real world. This is a form of scientific analysis which in one form or another is widely accepted, and which is expounded by such writers as Braithwaite (1955), Russell (1948), and Popper (1959). However, it is a procedure which deals in generalisations and makes the assumptions that we can classify different manifestations of arms races, for example, and argues that they have sufficient in common for us to group them together and theorise about them as a group. Older analyses of international relations tended to concentrate on the individual events. Social scientific analyses concentrate on generalisations, and attempt to explain singular events in terms of tested generalisations. Formal methods are appropriate to generalisations, but if generalisations are deemed to be impossible or illusory then analysis based on such assumptions is inherently flawed. The mathematical methods which may have helped in broadening the knowledge of these generalisations have merely broadened the domain of an illusion. If all arms races are held to be *sui generis* there is no point in developing a theory of the arms races. On this view the Richardson model is inadequate, not because it has not as yet been sufficiently developed, but because the underlying supposition that there can be generalisations is misconceived from the beginning. If one holds this view then the scope of formal analysis is limited, though the form of any sort of analysis is likewise limited. There is the weakness that informal explanations give the illusion of understanding by referring events to highly speculative generalisations dressed up as theoretical statements 'known' by intuition rather than by a rigorous analysis of the data. However, if one does not deny that generalisations are in principle possible, even though weakly developed as yet, the range of meaningful questions can be expanded. A 'meaningful question' is one for which an answer is possible if not yet achieved; that is, we know what sorts of things an answer should consist of and would recognise it if we had one. To 'know more' about the international system becomes not just a question of knowing more of the same sorts of things (that is, more about singular events), but being able to 'know more' about different sorts of question about international systems which were impossible or at least difficult to ask without formal analysis. This applies to most of the topics discussed in this book, but applies particularly strongly to the macro-systemic models discussed in Chapter 10. It would be impossible even to express them except in formal terms. As far as the immediate understanding of the international system is concerned these do us little good. They have not yet reached a stage of development where they are applicable either now or in the near future but represent the beginnings of what would be expected to be a long and arduous research programme. However, it is difficult to overestimate the significance of the ultimate results of such a research programme which has broadened the range of askable questions in dramatic directions.

I have not discussed the testing of theory even though this is commonly regarded as the ideal type of scientific investigation for which formalised methods are particularly appropriate. Any model or theory involving significant generalisations and involving deductive reasoning beyond the very basic is likely to be expressed in mathematical form. The ambitions of social scientific international relations theory is to develop such a body of theory. However, its successes are not impressive once we have moved out of the domain of 'coarse' theory described above. There are many hypotheses which have been proposed and which have been tested – indeed there is now a rich body of tested generalisations in international relations (Starr 1976). This aspect of social scientific development is well developed.

However, for the most part, they are not members of theories of any deductive complexity. The hypotheses stand in isolation such that there are no other hypotheses drawn from the same deductive net whose verification increases the degree of belief in the prime hypothesis. They are tests of hypotheses which are interesting in themselves, because of their policy significance, because they seem plausible, or because they seem relevant to some interesting if not strictly specified theory. However, it is not enough for the deductivist to be 'relevant'; propositions have to be directly deduced. This is not to say that there have been no developments on these lines. There have been various attempts to test the Richardson model, some but not all of which have been reasonably encouraging (see Schrodt 1981 for a brief summary of these studies); Bueno de Mesquita (1981) has tested an expected utility theory, though there are some reservations about both the model and the testing (Nicholson 1987). However, the hoped for development of tested deductive theory has not so far appeared to the degree that might have been supposed given the amount of work which has gone into both empirical work and deductive theory. International relations is still at the model building rather than the theory building stage. Hopefully the models will develop into theories, and the gap between the tested, 'atheoretical' generalisations and the deductive body of theory will narrow on a grander scale than is currently the case.

4   Finale

Some of the most useful applications of formal methods considered in this book are methods of clarifying concepts and forms of behaviour and bringing coherence to an understanding of the international system. While the development of deductive, tested theory is still not very far advanced, the formalisation of some of the theory in international relations has both been derived from and has led to theory in other areas of knowledge. Many of the topics in this book were not originally applied particularly to international relations. A lot of the work derived from the theory of games was originally devised with different applications in view. Even the more recent work on the prisoners' dilemma in the form of the computer tournaments of Axelrod (himself an international relations specialist) appears as work on the general theory of conflict and not directed to international relations in particular. This leads to a view of the discipline as being an aspect of the general study of conflict and cooperation which has its own particular and peculiar manifestations in the international sphere. However, the underlying theoretical base is common to all manifestations. This becomes more obvious when this theoretical base is formalised. The generality of the theories of conflict are even more extended when we recognise the relationships with disciplines such as biology. It seems that here we are moving towards general systems theory (GST) which originates from the view that many diverse phenomena can be interpreted in the same systemic structure. The period of high fashion of GST in the nineteen sixties seems to have waned somewhat – this particular revolution in science proved somewhat disappointing. Despite it being unfashionable, there is still a lot we can learn from the underlying view that common structural and systemic patterns exist in diverse phenomena. The attitudes which lie behind formalisation readily extend to generalisation and the search for broad features of behaviour, and away from the unique features of events. In my view this is entirely healthy. While it is absurd to neglect the unique aspects of behaviour, the main trends in international relations have historically been concerned with the particular at the expense of the general. The development of social scientific approaches and in particular the formal approaches have produced some balance in the discipline.

My final point is this. Our knowledge of the behaviour of complex social systems, of which the international system is one, is poor. The consistency of a lot of its behaviour suggests that it is structured but we have very little idea of what the structure is. Given the lethal nature of a lot of the behaviour in the system it is important to find it out. Unless there is some simple issue which has escaped us all, which is improbable, the nature of the complexities of the international system cannot be analysed by natural language alone. Formal techniques and formal languages are not some curious and esoteric optional extra, but are required if we are to make any serious advances in our knowledge of the systems structure and behaviour.

APPENDIX

An Outline of some mathematical methods

Most of this book requires no knowledge of mathematical methods, at least in principle. However, in discussing problems of rates of change, I used some techniques of what is known as differential and integral calculus. In this appendix I briefly outline these methods in relation to the problems discussed. I also justify one or two results used earlier, which require justification, but would have held up the main discussion in the text unduly. This is a sketch over the issues, nothing more, to introduce readers to the terminology. There must be literally thousands of introductions to calculus methods so another introduction would be unnecessary. This brief summary of some issues should be thought of as akin to a phrase book in a foreign language – with its aid you will not be able to indulge in witty repartee with the natives, but you may be able to buy yourself a (metaphorical) beer.

Section A: Differentiation

Calculus deals in rates of change. Here we have been largely concerned with rates of change with respect to time, but any pair or more of variables will do. Consider the following function between y and x

$$y = - x^2 + c \qquad\qquad A1$$

A segment of this is shown in Diagram 1. Consider a specific point on it $(x_1\, y_1)$, and a point very close to it $(x_1 + \delta x, y_1 + \delta y)$, where δx and δy denote a very small increment of x and y respectively. (It is drawn large for clarity.) $\delta y/\delta x$ represents a rough approximation to a measure of the slope of the curve (its tangent) at $(x_1\, y_1)$. The smaller are δy and δx, the closer is the approximation to the tangent at $(x_1\, y_1)$. Now let us consider this analytically.

As $x_1 + \delta x$, and $y_1 + \delta y$ are on the function A1, it follows that

$$y + \delta y = - (x + \delta x)^2 + c \qquad\qquad A2$$

226

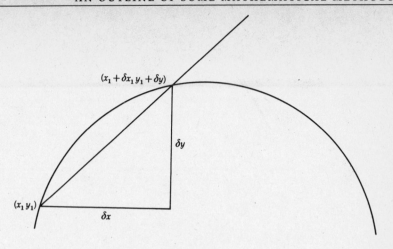

Diagram 1

and thus $y + \delta y = -x^2 - 2\delta x - \delta x^2 + c$ A3

Thus from A1 and A2 and it follows that

$$\delta y = -2\delta x . x - x^2 \qquad \text{A4}$$

Dividing throughout by δx we get

$$\delta y / \delta x = -2x - \delta x \qquad \text{A5}$$

$\delta y / \delta x$ it will be remembered was the slope to the line at x. Now as the two δ terms get smaller and smaller, that is tend to 0, δx becomes negligibly small, and in the limit

$$\text{Lim. } \delta y / \delta x \rightarrow -2x \qquad \text{A6}$$

We represent this limit by $dy/dx = -2x$. This process is known as 'differentiation'. Notice carefully that the letters d do not represent numbers but 'operators', that is, dy denotes 'an infinitesimal increment of y' and not 'd times y' (which would be meaningless).

I have explained this process with a particular function, but it is a very widely applicable technique. A particularly common type of function which is frequently used in the text is the polynomial. Suppose we have a sum of two terms both with a power of x in them such as

$$y = ax^m + bx^n \qquad \text{A7}$$

In this case

$$dy/dx = a(m-1)x^{m-1} + b(n-1)x^{n-1} \qquad \text{A8}$$

227

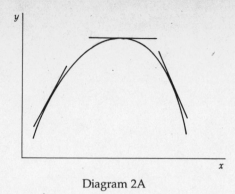

Diagram 2A

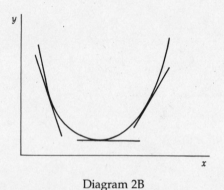

Diagram 2B

The interpretation of the derivative as the slope of the function gives us a powerful technique for finding the turning points of functions. In Diagram 2A and B three examples of slopes are given with the signs of the derivatives at the points of tangency. Specifically at the maximum value the derivative is zero.

We can go further than this and find out the derivative of the derivative, or second derivative. That is the rate of change of the rate of change denoted by d^2y/dx^2. A common application is acceleration which is the rate of change of speed where speed is the rate of change of distance. This has immediate application to the problem of maxima and minima. In Diagram 2A as x increases dy/dx decreases. Thus, a graph of dy/dx plotted against x would give a decreasing curve indicating its derivate (i.e. second derivative of the original function) was negative. If we look at Diagram 2B we find the opposite is happening and the second derivative is therefore positive. We can use this property to find out whether a turning point (which is all $dy/dx = 0$ tells us) is a maximum or a minimum. The second derivative is

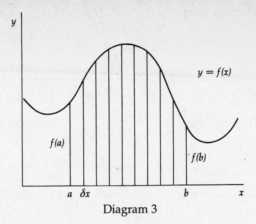

Diagram 3

negative if the turning point is a maximum and positive if it is a minimum. We can go on to derive third derivatives, fourth derivatives, and so on, though in many functions the process stops with a constant whose derivative is zero. (A car moving at a constant speed has zero acceleration and also zero change in the rate of acceleration).

There are many standard forms for differentiating but the following result is important and is used in the text. Suppose we have $f(x)$ which is a function of two functions of x multiplied together, such as $f(x) = \phi(x) \cdot \mu(x)$. Put $\phi(x) = u$ and $\mu(x) = v$ so $f(x) = u \cdot v$. In this case, a standard result is that

$$dy/dx = u \cdot dv/dx + v \cdot du/dx \qquad \text{A9}$$

Section B: Integration

Integration is the reverse process to differentiation, though initially this might not be obvious. Consider Diagram 3 which is of a function $f(x)$. Suppose we want to find the area under the curve between a and b. We can divide it into small rectangles, find each individual area, and add them up. If the base of each rectangle is δx, then this sum will be

$$A = \delta x \, f(x_a) + f(x_2)\delta x + \dots f(x_b)\delta x \qquad \text{B1}$$

or $\quad A = \sum_{a}^{b} f(x_i) \cdot \delta x \qquad \text{B2}$

We can put this more generally and place b equal to any x giving

$$A = \sum_{a}^{x} f(x) \cdot \delta x \qquad \text{B3}$$

229

which clearly varies with x that is, is a function of x. Now write A as $\phi(x)$ and we have

$$\phi(x) = \Sigma f(x) . \delta(x) \qquad\qquad\qquad B4$$

Supposing we are moving rightwards underneath the curve and seeing how the area increases with increases in x, the increase in area

$$\delta\phi(x) = f(b) . \delta(x)$$

or $\qquad \delta\phi(x)/\delta(x) = f(b)$

More generally $\delta\phi(x)/\delta(x) = f(x)$. $\qquad\qquad\qquad B5$

If the deltas are made infinitesimally small and we also denote $\phi(x) \rightarrow F(x)$ we have

$$dF(x)/dx = f(x) \qquad\qquad\qquad B6$$

and by writing the stylised summation sign we can represent the general process of summation or integration as

$$F(x) = \int f(x) . dx \qquad\qquad\qquad B7$$

where $f(x)$ is the derivative of $F(x)$, the area. Notice that $f(x)$ is also the derivative of $F(x) + c$, so in integrating $f(x)$ we get a class of functions and not just a single one as in differentiation. A common notation is $dF(x)/dx = F'(x)$.

If we want to find the area between the two particular points a and b on the Diagram 3 then we find that between b and 0 and a and 0 and take one from another. That is, we denote the area between a and b by

$$\int_a^b f(x) . d(x) = F(b) - F(a) \qquad\qquad\qquad B8$$

That is substitute first b for the value and then a for the value and take one from the other.

Section C: Differential equations

Differential equations involve working back from an equation involving the derivatives of a function to the function itself. The most direct form is when we are given $dF(x)/dx = f(x)$ and we wish to find out what $F(x)$ is. In this case we just integrate (which may not be an easy process). As the differential equations we use in the book are largely concerned with time, the question in fact becomes one of finding the time paths of the various variables. An important pair of differential equations came in the Richardson model where, for country A we had arms changing according to the equation

$$dy/dt = ky - \alpha x + c \qquad \text{C1}$$

In other words the rate of change (the derivative) depended on the level of arms of both the rival and itself. In that analysis we were more concerned with the stability characteristics of the equation than its precise path through time, though, in later parts of the chapter when we dealt with the three party arms race, we did form expressions for the time paths.

In the general hostility model of the international system discussed in Section 3 of Chapter 9, differential equations were used which employed second and third derivatives. Here the task was explicitly to derive time paths, the results of which were illustrated in the diagrams. Such more complex differential equations are common enough in the physical sciences, but less often applied in the social sciences and only rarely as here in international relations.

Section D: Note on Chapter 5, Section 1

The problem posed was how would the over-all probability of war develop if the probability per period of time decreased. We show that the probability of war does not tend to unity under these conditions.

The probability of war in period 1 is p, in period 2 is kp and in period n is $k^{n-1}p$ for $0 < 1$ and $0 < p < 1$. If we define the probability that there has been no war by period n as π this is represented by

$$(1 - p)(1 - kp)(1 - k^2p) \ldots (1 - k^{n-1}p)$$

$$= \overset{n-1}{\underset{0}{\pi}} (1 - k^r p) = \pi \qquad \text{D1}$$

We examine this as $n \to \infty$. The basic result used is the Taylor expansion for $\log(1 + x) = x - x^2/2 + x^3/3 - + (-1)^n x^n/n \ldots$

Taking logarithms in the case of D1 we have

$$\text{Log } \pi = \sum_{0}^{n-1} \log(1 - k^r p) \qquad \text{D2}$$

Now $\log(1 - k^m p) = -kp - k^2p/2 - k^3p/3 \ldots - k^m p/n$

$$= -\sum_{1}^{m} (k^r p)/n \qquad \text{D3}$$

Thus D2 can be written $\log \pi = -\sum_{0}^{n} \sum_{1}^{m} (k^r p)/m \qquad \text{D4}$

$$= -\Sigma p/m . (\Sigma (k^r)) \qquad \text{D5}$$

231

$$\text{As } \sum_{1}^{m} (k^r) = 1/(1 - k) \tag{D6}$$

it follows that $\log \pi = - \sum p/m[1 - k)]$ \hfill D7

From the value of k, $-\frac{1}{m} > - 1/m(1 - k) > - 1/(1 - k)$ \hfill D8

Hence $\quad - \sum p/m > \log \pi > - \sum p(1 - k)$ \hfill D9

Remembering the two terms at the beginning and end of D9 are logarithmic series it follows that

$$\log (1 - p) > \log \pi > [1/(1 - k)] . \log (1 - p) \tag{D10}$$

Hence, $\quad (1 - p) > \pi > (1 - p)^{1/1-k}$

The upper bound on the probability is obvious and trivial, but the lower bound is not so.

Section E: Note on Chapter 8, Section 2

In the discussion of the results of Abelson's work we made use of several of the above results.
In Chapter 8 Equation 8.2.8 we had

$$B(t) = b e^{-\lambda t} \int_0^t e^{\lambda t} A(\tau) . d\tau \tag{E1}$$

This is the sum of two functions of x which we write as

$$u = b e^{-\lambda t} \tag{E2}$$

and $\qquad v = \int_0^t e^{\lambda t} A(\tau) . d(\tau)$ \hfill E3

from which $\quad du/dt = - \lambda b e^{-\lambda t}$ \hfill E4

and $\qquad dv/dt = e^{\lambda t} A(t)$ \hfill E5

Thus $\qquad u . dv/dt = b e^{-\lambda t} e^{\lambda t} A(t) = bA(t)$ \hfill E6

and, $\qquad v du/dt = -\lambda b e^{-\lambda t} \int_0^t e^{\lambda \tau} A(\tau) . dt$ \hfill E7

which, from D1 $= - \lambda B(t)$ \hfill E8

Hence $\qquad dB(t) = bA(t) - \lambda B(t)$ \hfill E9

which was the result asserted in the text.

Section F: Note on Chapter 9 Section 2: the Polynomial

The potential function used in the catastrophe theory analysis was of the form

$$y = x^r + a_{r-2}x^{r-2} + a_{r-3}x^{r-3} + \ldots + a_1 x \qquad \text{F1}$$

which was alleged, without demonstration, to have the same qualitative characteristics as

$$y = \alpha_r x^r + \alpha_{r-1}x^{r-1} + \alpha_{r-2}x^{r-2} + \alpha_1 x + \alpha_0 \qquad \text{F2}$$

I shall now justify this. Both expressions generate the same shapes in the sense of turning points and so on; they merely differ in terms of the measures or dimensions. The legitimacy of substituting the first for the second expression comes directly from the supposition that the variables involved are only unique up to a linear transformation, that is, that x' can be substituted for x where $x' = mx + c$, for $m > 0$ and c without restriction, and similarly for y' for y. No transformation is either a more or a less appropriate statement of the problem (see the discussion of utility in Chapter 4 Section 5 for a further discussion of this level of measure).

1   Clearly α_0 merely defines the whole surface with respect to the ordinate and, given the arbitrary zero relating to y, is also arbitrary. Thus, without loss of generality, it can be set at zero.

2   The scale is likewise arbitrary and hence F2 can be divided throughout by any positive number including α_r. Doing this we replace each coefficient α_i in F2 – which represent the control variables – by $a_i = \alpha_i/\alpha_r$ and specifically α_r by 1.

3   In any polynomial, the sum of the roots equals $-\alpha_{r-1}$. Denote the ith root of the polynomial F2 by x_i. Then

$$x_{r-1} + x_{r-2} + \ldots + x_1 = -\alpha_{r-1} \qquad \text{F3}$$

As $(x' + c)$ can be substituted for x in the polynomial, simply shifting the equation along the abscissa, the sum of the roots can be stated as

$$(x_{r-1} + c) + (x_{r-2} + c) + \ldots + (x_1 + c) = \alpha_{r-1} + (r-1)c \qquad \text{F4}$$

Hence, by setting $c = -\alpha_{r-1}/(r-1)$ we can eliminate the second term of the polynomial which gives us the expression F1.

233

BIBLIOGRAPHY

Allen, R. G. D., 1959. *Mathematical Economics*. London: Macmillan.
1962. *Basic Mathematics*. London: Macmillan.
Anderson, Paul and Stuart Thorson, 'An Artificial Intelligence Based Simulation of Foreign Policy Decision Making Analysis' 1982 (April) *Behavioral Science*. 176–93.
Ashford, Oliver M., 1985. *Prophet – or Professor? The Life and Work of Lewis Fry Richardson*. Bristol and Boston: Adam Hilger Ltd.
Axelrod, Robert, 1970. *Conflict of Interest, A Theory of Divergent Goals with Applications to Politics*. Chicago: Markham.
1976. *Structure of Decision: The Cognitive Maps of Political Elites*. Princeton University Press.
1984. *The Evolution of Cooperation*. New York: Basic Books.
Azar, Edward E. and John W. Burton, 1986. *International Conflict Resolution: Theory and Practice*. Sussex: Wheatsheaf Books.
Banks, Michael, 1986. 'The International Relations Discipline: Asset or Liability for Conflict Resolution' in Azar and Burton (1986).
Bennett, P. G., 1977. 'Toward a Theory of Hypergames' OMEGA 5, 749–51.
Bennett, P. G. and M. Dando, 1979. 'Complex Hypergame Analysis: a hypergame perspective of the fall of France' *Journal of the Operational Research Society*, 30 (1) 23–32.
Bennett, P. G. and C. S. Huxham, 1982. 'Hypergames and what they do' *Journal of the Operational Research Society*. 33, 41–50.
Bentham, Jeremy 1823. *An Introduction to the Principles of Morals and Legislation*. 1st edn 1789, London: Original Publisher, T. Payne.
Bernardo, J. M., De Grout, M. H., D. V. Lindley and A. F. M. Smith (Eds.). 1984. *Bayesian Statistics*. Amsterdam: North Holland.
Black, Duncan, 1958. *The Theory of Committees and Elections*. Cambridge University Press.
Blumberg, A. A., 1971. 'Model for a Two Adversary Arms Race' *Nature* 234: 158.
Bonham, G. Matthew and Michael J. Shapiro, 'Explanation of the Unexpected: The Syrian Intervention in Jordan in 1970' in Axelrod, 1976.
Bracken, Paul, 1983. *The Command and Control of Nuclear Forces*. London and New Haven: Yale University Press.
Braithwaite, R. B., 1955. *Scientific Explanation*. Cambridge University Press.
1955b. *The Theory of Games as a Tool for the Moral Philosopher*. Cambridge University Press.

Brams, Steven J., 1975. *Game Theory and Politics*. New York: Free Press.

1976. *Paradoxes in Politics: An Introduction to the Nonobvious in Political Science*. New York: Free Press.

1977. 'Deception in 2 × 2 Games' *Journal of Peace Science*. 2 (Spring) 171–203.

1985. *Superpower Games: Applying Game Theory to Superpower Conflict*. New Haven: Yale University Press.

Brito, Dagobert and Michael D. Intriligator, 1976. 'Formal Models of Arms Races' *Journal of Peace Studies*. 2, 77–88.

1981. 'Strategic Arms Limitation Treaties and Innovations In Weapons Technology' *Public Choice*. 37, 41–59.

1981. 'Nuclear Proliferation and the Probability of Nuclear War' *Public Choice*. 37, 247–60.

1984. 'Can Arms Races lead to the Outbreak of War?' *Journal of Conflict Resolution*. 28, 63–84.

Bueno de Mesquita, Bruce, 1981. *The War Trap*. New Haven: Yale University Press.

1985. 'Toward a Scientific Understanding of International Conflict: A Personal view' *International Studies Quarterly*. 29, 2, 121–36.

1987. 'Conceptualizing War: A Reply' *Journal of Conflict Resolution*. 31, 2, 370–82.

Burns, Arthur Lee, 1968. *Of Powers and Their Politics: a Critique of Theoretical Approaches*. Englewood Cliffs: Prentice-Hall.

Burton, J. W., 1968. *Systems, States, Diplomacy and Rules*. Cambridge University Press.

Carr, E. H., 1939. *The Twenty Years Crisis: an Introduction to International Relations*. 1st Edn London: Macmillan.

Carter, C. F. and J. L. Ford (Eds.), 1972. *Uncertainty and Expectation in Economics: Essays in honour of G. L. S. Shackle*. Oxford: Basil Blackwell.

Chase, P. E., 1969. 'Feedback Control Theory and Arms Races' *General Systems*. XIV, 139–49.

Cioffi-Revilla, Claudio, 1979. 'Diplomatic Communication Theory: Signals, Channels, Networks' *International Interactions*. VI, 3, 209–65.

Cioffi-Revilla, Claudio, 1983. 'A Probability Model of Credibility: Analyzing Strategic Nuclear Deterrence Systems' *Journal of Conflict Resolution*. 27, 73–108.

Coddington, Alan, 1968. *A Theory of the Bargaining Process*. Chicago: Aldine Press.

Cohen, John, 1972. *Psychological Probability: or the Art of Doubt*. London: George Allen and Unwin.

Cross, John, 1969. *The Economics of Bargaining*. New York: Basic Books.

Deutsch, Karl W, 1957. *Political Community and the North Atlantic Area*. Princeton University Press.

Deutsch, Karl W., 1978. *The Analysis of International Relations*. 2nd Edn, Englewood Cliffs: Prentice-Hall.

Deutsch, Karl W. and J. D. Singer, 1964. 'Multipolar Power Systems and International Stability' *World Politics*. 16 (April), 390–406.

De Vree, Johan, K., 1982. 'The Behavioral Function: an Enquiry into the Relations Between Behavior and Utility' *Theory and Decision*. 15, 231–45.

Dougherty, James E. and Robert L. Pfaltzgraff, 1981. *Contending Theories of International Relations: A Comprehensive Survey*. 2nd Edn, New York: Harper and Row.

Feraro, Thomas J., 1978. 'An Introduction to Catastrophes' *Behavioral Science*. 23, 291–317.

Fiorina, M., 1975. 'Formal Models in Political Science' *American Journal of Political Science*. 19, 133–159.

Fisher, Franklin F. and Albert Ando, 1962. 'Two Theorems on *Ceteris Paribus* in the Analysis of Dynamic Systems' *American Political Science Review*. LVI, 108–13.

Fraser, Niall M. and Keith W. Hipel, 1984. *Conflict Analysis: Models and Resolutions*. New York, Amsterdam: North-Holland.

French, Simon, 1984. 'Group Consensus Probability Distributions: a Critical Survey' in Bernardo *et al.*, 1984.

1986. *Decision Theory: an Introduction to the Mathematics of Rationality*. Chichester: Ellis Horwood.

Friedman, David, 1977. 'A Theory of the Size and Shape of Nations' *Journal of Political Economy*. 85, 1, 59–77.

Galtung, Johan, 1971. 'A Structural Theory of Imperialism' *Journal of Peace Research*. 8, 2, 81–191.

Garden, Timothy, 1985. *Can Deterrence Last? Peace through a Nuclear Strategy*. London: Buchan and Enright.

Garner, Wendell R., 1962. *Uncertainty and Structure as Psychological Concepts*. New York and London: John Wiley.

Gillespie, John V. and Dina Zinnes, 1977. 'Progressions in Mathematical Models of International Relations' *Synthese*. 31, 289–321.

Good, I. J., 1966. 'The Probability of War' *Journal of the Royal Statistical Society*. Series A, 129, Part 2.

Harary, Frank, 1961. 'A Structural Analysis of the Situation in the Middle East' *Journal of Conflict Resolution*. 5, 167–78.

1972. *Graph Theory*. Reading Mass.: Adison-Wesley Publishing Company.

Harris, Richard J., 1969a. 'A Note on Howard's Theory of Metagames' *Psychological Reports*. 25, 825.

1969b. 'Comment on Dr. Rapoport's Comments' *Psychological Reports*. 25, 765–66.

1970. 'Paradox Regained' *Psychological Reports*. 26, 264–6.

Herbst, P. G., 1970. *Behavioral Worlds*. London: Tavistock.

Hollist, W. Ladd. (Ed.), 1978. *Exploring Competitive Arms Processes*. New York and Basel: Marcel Dekker, Inc.

Holloway, David, 1984. *The Soviet Union and the Arms Race*. New Haven and London: Yale University Press.

Holt, Robert T., Brian L. Job and Lawrence Markus, 1978. 'Catastrophe Theory and the Study of War' *Journal of Conflict Resolution*. 22, 2, 171–208.

Howard, Michael, 1983. *The Causes of War and Other Essays*. London: Temple Smith.

Howard, Nigel, 1969. ''Comments on Harris' ''Comment on Rapoport's Comments''' *Psychological Reports*. 25, 826.

1970. 'Note on the Harris-Rapoport Controversy' *Psychological Reports*. 26, 316.

1971. *Paradoxes of Rationality: Theory of Metagames and Political Behavior.* Cambridge, Mass.: and London: MIT Press.

Intriligator, Michael D., 1982. 'Conflict Theory Research: Analytical Approaches and Areas of Application' *Journal of Conflict Resolution.* 26, 2, 315–27.

Intriligator, Michael D. and Dagobert Brito. see Brito and Intriligator.

Janis, Irving, 1982. *Groupthink: A Psychological Study of Foreign Policy Decisions and Fiascos.* 2nd Edn., Boston: Houghton Mifflin.

Jervis, R., 1976. *Perception and Misperception in International Politics.* Princeton University Press.

Kaplan, M. A., 1957. *System and Process in International Politics.* New York: Wiley.

Kemeny, John G. and J. Laurie Snell, 1962. *Mathematical Models in the Social Sciences.* Boston: Ginn and Co.

Körner, S., 1960. *The Philosophy of Mathematics.* London: Hutchinson University Library.

Lotka, Alfred J., 1956. *Elements of Mathematical Biology.* New York: Dover.

Luce, R. Duncan and Howard Raiffa, 1957. *Games and Decisions: Introduction and Critical Survey.* New York and London: Wiley.

Mansbach Richard W. and John A Vasquez, 1981. *In Search of Theory: A New Paradigm for Global Politics.* New York: Columbia University Press.

March, James G., 1958. *Organisations.* New York and London: Wiley.

1950. 'The Bargaining Problem' *Econometrica* XXI, 128–40 (Reprinted in Young, 1975).

Maynard Smith, John, 1982. *Evolution and the Theory of Games.* Cambridge University Press.

McClelland, Charles A., 'Access to Berlin: The Quantity and Variety of Events 1948–1963' in Singer 1968.

Meyer, Stephen M., 1983. *Nuclear Proliferation: Models of Behavior, Choice and Decision.* Chicago University Press.

Morgenthau, Hans J., 1974. *Politics Amongst Nations: the Struggle for Power and Peace.* 5th edn, New York: Knopf.

Nash, John, 1951. 'Non-Cooperative Games' *Annals of Mathematics.* 54, 286–95.

Newman, James R. (Ed.), 1956. *The World of Mathematics.* (Four Vols), New York: Simon and Schuster.

Nicholson, Michael, 1967. 'The Resolution of Conflict' *Journal of the Royal Statistical Society* (Series A) 130, Part 4. 529–40 (Reprinted in Young, 1975).

1971. *Conflict Analysis.* London: English Universities Press.

1972a. *Oligopoly and Conflict: A Dynamic Approach.* Liverpool University Press.

1972b. 'Uncertainty and Crisis Behaviour' in Carter, C. F. and J. L. Ford (Eds.), 1972.

1983. *The Scientific Analysis of Social Behaviour.* London: Frances Pinter.

1987. 'The Conceptual Bases of The War Trap' *Journal of Conflict Resolution.* 31, 2, 346–69.

Olson, Mancur, 1971. *The Logic of Collective Action: Public Goods and the Theory of Groups.* 2nd Edn Cambridge, Mass.: Harvard University Press.

Olson, Mancur and Richard Zeckhauser, 1966. 'An Economic Theory of Alliances' *Review of Economics and Statistics*. XLVII, 266–79.

Ordeshook, P. C., 1986. *Game Theory and Political Theory: An Introduction*. Cambridge University Press.

Owen, Guillermo, 1968. *Game Theory*. Philadelphia: W. B. Saunders and Co.

Pierce, J. R., 1962. *Symbols, Signals and Noise: The Nature and Process of Communication*. London: Hutchinson.

Phillips, Warren and Richard E Hayes, 1978. 'Linking Forecasting to Policy Planning: An Application of the Theory of Noncooperative Games' in Hollist, W. Ladd, 1978.

Phillips, Warren and Richard Rimkunas, 1978. 'The Concept of Crisis in International Politcs' *Journal of Peace Research* 15, 259–72.

Pillar, Paul, 1983. *Negotiating Peace: War Termination as a Bargaining Process* Princeton University Press.

Popper, Karl, 1959. *The Logic of Scientific Discovery*. London: Hutchinson (First published in German in Vienna, 1934).

Poston, Tim and Ian Stewart, 1978. *Catastrophe Theory and its Application*. London: (Pitman).

Press, James, S., 1984. 'Multivariate Group Assessment of Probabilities of Nuclear War' in Bernardo *et al.*, 1984.

Ramsey, F. P., 1928. 'A Mathematical Theory of Saving' *Economic Journal*. 38, 543–51.

Rangarajan, L. N., 1985. *The Limitation of Conflict: A Theory of Bargaining and Negotiation*. London and Sydney: Croom Helm.

Rapoport, Anatol, 1957. 'Lewis Fry Richardson's Mathematical Theory of War' *Journal of Conflict Resolution*. 1, 249–99.

Rapoport, Anatol. 1967. 'Escape from Paradox' *Scientific American*. 217, 1, 50–6.

1969. ''Comment on Dr. Harris' "Note on Howard's Theory of Meta-games"' *Psychological Reports*. 25, 765–6.

1970a. 'Comments on "Paradox Regained"' *Psychological Reports*. 26, 272.

1970b. *N-Person Game Theory*. Ann Arbor: Michigan University Press.

1983. *Mathematical Models in the Social and Behavioral Sciences*. New York and Chichester: Wiley.

1974. *Fights, Games and Debates*. Ann Arbor: Michigan University Press (2nd Edn).

Rapoport, Anatol and Albert Chammah, 1965. *The Prisoners' Dilemma: A Study of Conflict and Cooperation*. Ann Arbor: Michigan University Press.

Rapoport, Anatol, M. J. Guyer and D. G. Gordon, 1976. *The 2 × 2 Game*. Ann Arbor: Michigan University Press.

Rashevsky, Nicolas, 1951. *Mathematical Biology of Social Behavior*. Chicago University Press.

1972. *Looking at History through Mathematics*. Cambridge, Mass.: MIT Press.

Reynolds, P. A., 1970. *An Introduction to International Relations*. London: Longman.

Richardson, Lewis Fry, 1948. 'War Moods' *Psychometrica*. 13, Part 1, 147–74. Part 2, 197–232.

1960a. *Arms and Insecurity*. Pittsburgh: The Boxwood Press.

1960b. *Statistics of Deadly Quarrels*. Pittsburgh: The Boxwood Press.

Riker, William H., 1962. *The Theory of Political Coalitions*. New Haven: Yale University Press.

Robinson, Joan. 1956. *The Accumulation of Capital*. London: Macmillan and Co. Ltd.

Roth, A. (ed.), 1985. *Game Theoretic Approaches to Bargaining Theory*. Cambridge University Press.

Russell, Bertrand, 1938. *Power: a New Social Analysis*. London: George Allen and Unwin.

1948. *Human Knowledge: Its Scope and Limits*. London: George Allen and Unwin.

Russett, Bruce (Ed.), 1968. *Economic Theories of International Politics*. Chicago: Markham.

Saarty, Thomas L., 1968. *Mathematical Models of Arms Control and Disarmament*. Englewood Cliffs: Wiley.

Savage, Leonard J., 1972. *The Foundations of Statistics*. 2nd Edn, New York: Dover.

Schofield, Norman, 1973. 'A Game Theoretic Analysis of Olson's Game of Collective Action' *Journal of Conflict Resolution*. XIX, 3, 441–61.

Schrodt, Philip A., 1978. 'Richardson's n-nation model and the balance of power' *American Journal of Political Science*. 22, 364–90.

1981. *Preserving Arms Distributions in a Multi-Polar World: A Mathematical Study*. Denver: Monograph Series in World Affairs, University of Denver.

Searle, John, 1984. 'The Reith Lectures' *The Listener*. 8th November – 13th December.

Shackle, G. L. S., 1952. *Expectation in Economics*. Cambridge University Press.

1955. *Uncertainty in Economics and other Reflections*. Cambridge University Press.

Shubik, Martin, 1970. 'Game Theory, Behavior and Paradox: Three Solutions' *Journal of Conflict Resolution*. XIV, 2, 181–93.

Shubik, Martin, 1982. *Game Theory in the Social Sciences: Concepts and Solutions*. Cambridge, Mass.: MIT Press.

Simaan, M. and J. B. Cruiz, 1975. 'Formulation of Richardson's Model of the Arms Race from a Differential Game Viewpoint' *Review of Economic Studies*. 42, 67–77.

Simon, H. A., 1969. *Sciences of the Artificial*. Cambridge, Mass.: MIT Press.

1982. *Models of Bounded Rationality*. Cambridge, Mass.: MIT Press.

Singer, J. David (ed.), 1968. *Quantitative International Politics: Insights and Evidence*. New York and London: The Free Press.

Smith, Teresa Clair, 1980. 'Arms Race Instability and War' *Journal of Conflict Resolution*. 24, 2, 253–84.

Smoker, Paul, 1963a. 'A Mathematical Study of the Present Arms Race' *General Systems Yearbook*. 8, 51–60.

1963a 'A Pilot Study of the Present Arms Race' *General Systems Yearbook*, 8, 61–76.

Snidal, Duncan, 1985. 'The game theory of International Politics' *World Politics*. 28, 25–57.

Starr, Harvey, 1976. 'An Appraisal of the Substantive Findings of the Correlations of War Project' in Zinnes and Hoole, 1976.

Sussman, H. and R. Zahler, 1978. 'Catastrophe Theory and the Social and Biological Sciences: a Critique' *Synthese.* 37, 117–216.

Sutton, John, 1986. 'Non-cooperative bargaining theory: introduction' *Review of Economic Studies.* LIII (5), 176, 709–26.

Taylor, Michael. 1976 *Anarchy and Cooperation.* Englewood Cliffs: Wiley.

Taylor, Michael. 1987. *The Possibility of Cooperation: Studies in Rationality and Social Change.* Cambridge University Press.

Taylor, Michael and Hugh Ward, 1982. 'Chickens, Whales and Lumpy Goods' *Political Studies.* 30, 3.

Thom, René, 1975. *Structural Stability and Morphogenesis: an Outline of a General Theory of Models.* Reading, Mass.: W. A. Benjamin, Inc. First published in French in 1972.

Thomas, L. C., 1984. *Games, Theory and Applications.* Chichester: Ellis Horwood.

Thompson, D'Arcy, 1917. *On Growth and Form.* 1st Edn, Cambridge University Press.

Von Neumann, John and Oskar Morgenstern, 1953. *The Theory of Games and Economic Behavior.* 3rd Edn, Princeton University Press (1st Edn, 1944).

Wagner, David L., Ronald T. Perkins and Rein Taagepera, 1975. 'Complete Solution to Richardson's Arms Race Equations' *Journal of Peace Science.* 1, 2, 159–72.

Wagner, R. Harrison, 1982. 'Deterrence and Bargaining' *Journal of Conflict Resolution.* 26, 329–55.

1983. 'The Theory of Games and the Problem of International Cooperation' *American Political Science Review.* 77, 2, 330–46.

Wallace, Michael D., 1979. 'Arms Races and Escalation: Some New Evidence' *Journal of Conflict Resolution.* 23, 1, 3–16.

Wallace Michael D., 1982. 'Armaments and Escalation' *International Studies Quarterly.* 26, 1, 37–56.

Waltz, Kenneth N., 1981. *The Spread of Nuclear Weapons: More May be Better.* London: Adelphi Papers. No. 185. International Institute for Strategic Studies.

Ward, Hugh, 1979. 'A Behavioral Model of Bargaining' *British Journal of Political Science.* 9, 201–18.

1987. 'The Risks of a Reputation for Toughness: Strategy in Public Goods Provision Problems Modelled by Chicken Supergames' *British Journal of Political Science.* 17, 23–52.

West, Mike, 1984. 'Bayesian Aggregation' *Journal of the Royal Statistical Society.* 147, part 4, 600–7.

Wight, Martin, 1977. *Systems of States* Leicester University Press.

1979. *Power Politics.* Harmondsworth: Penguin Books.

Young, Oran R., 1968. *Systems of Political Science.* Englewood Cliffs: Prentice Hall.

Young, Oran R. (Ed.), 1975. *Bargaining: Formal Theories of Negotiation.* Urbana, London: University of Illinois Press.

Zeeman, E. C., 1976. 'Catastrophe Theory', *Scientific American.* 23, 65–83.

Zeeman, E. C., Hall, C. Harrison, P. J., Marriage, H. and Shapland, P., 1976. 'A Model for Institutional Disturbances' *British Journal of Mathematical and Statistical Psychology*. 29, 66–80.

Zinnes, Dina, 1967. 'An Analytical Study of Balance of Power Theories' *Journal of Peace Research*. 4, 270–288.

Zinnes, Dina and Francis W. Hoole (Ed.), 1976. *Quantitative International Politics: an Appraisal*. London and New York: Praeger.

Zinnes, Dina A. and John V. Gillespie, 1976. *Mathematical Models in International Relations*. New York: Praeger.

Zinnes, Dina A., John V. Gillespie, Philip A Schrodt, G. S. Tahim and R. Michael Rubison 'Arms and Aid: A Differential Game Analysis' in Hollist, 1978.

Zinnes, Dina A. and Robert G. Muncaster, 1983. 'A Model of Inter-nation Hostility Dynamics and War' *Conflict Management and Peace Science*. 6, 2.

1984. 'The Dynamics of Hostile Activity and the Prediction of War' *Journal of Conflict Resolution*. 28, 2, 187–229.

INDEX